Family Law
Issues, debates, policy

Family Law

Issues, debates, policy

Edited by
Jonathan Herring

WILLAN
PUBLISHING

Published by

Willan Publishing
Culmcott House
Mill Street, Uffculme
Cullompton, Devon
EX15 3AT, UK
Tel: +44(0)1884 840337
Fax: +44(0)1884 840251
e-mail: info@willanpublishing.co.uk

Published simultaneously in the USA and Canada by

Willan Publishing
c/o ISBS, 5824 N.E. Hassalo St,
Portland, Oregon 97213-3644, USA
Tel: +001(0)503 287 3093
Fax: +001(0)503 280 8832

First published 2001

ISBN 1-903240-20-4 (cased)
ISBN 1-903240-19-0 (paper)

British Library Cataloguing-in-Publication Data

A catalogue record for this book is available from the British Library.

Printed by T.J. International, Padstow, Cornwall

Contents

Table of cases

Cases from other jurisdictions

Table of statutes

Introduction

Recently the European Court of Human Rights heard the case of *X, Y* and *Z v. UK*[1] which involved an applicant who had been born a woman, undergone a 'sex-change' operation, and now lived as a man. He had formed a relationship with a woman and together they had received assisted reproductive treatment, as a result of which a child was born. The issue for the court was whether the applicant had a right under the European Convention for the Protection of Human Rights to be registered as the father of the child. The facts of the case and the legal difficulties it raised would have been virtually unimaginable fifty years ago. Questions such as 'What is a man or woman?'; 'Who are the parents of a child?'; 'What is marriage?' are questions that would not even have been asked then – the answers would have been self-evident. Now such questions can be the topic of books.[2] Some commentators even argue that family law itself is in turmoil: its standard tools (such as parenthood and marriage) have lost their meaning following social, scientific and academic developments. Others reply that throughout history the law has had to respond to changes in the way people conduct their personal relationships, and the present struggle for the law to adapt to developments in practices and beliefs concerning family life is no different from many other occasions in the past.[3]

This book is designed to give readers an overview of some of the theoretical approaches and arguments concerning family law. It assumes that readers are aware of the law itself and aims to introduce them to some of the issues and debates over the way the law interacts with family life.

---

[1] [1987] 2 FLR 892; [1997] 3 FCR 341.
[2] e.g., A. Bainham, S. Day Sclater and M. Richards (eds), *What is a Parent?* (1999, Hart).
[3] See the discussion in L. Fox Harding, *Family State and Social Policy* (1996, Macmillan).

Each chapter outlines some of the topics that the author considers of particular interest in various key areas of family law. The chapters also include suggestions for further reading, enabling the reader to pursue ideas of especial interest discussed in the chapter.

Some of the themes which run throughout this book will now be briefly outlined.

The public – private divide

When analysing family law it is common to refer to the public/private distinction. Many of the limits of family law can be explained by the argument that the law should not (and to some extent, cannot) intervene in private areas of life, unlike public areas of life where legal regulation is appropriate.[4] This analysis has been challenged. Some feminist critics have pointed out the dangers in placing too much weight on the distinction between legal intervention in public areas of life and non-intervention in private life. They have argued that if the state does not intervene in a particular area of life, the status quo is thereby supported by the law. They then go on to argue that the status quo often involves the oppression of women. So what can be described by one person as non-intervention can be seen by another as reinforcement of inequality. Further, the distinction between the public and private areas of life leaves open some difficult issues over the definition of what is public and what is private. For example, is abuse of children a public or private issue?

The complexity of the public/private divide is revealed in Stuart Bridge's chapter on marriage. He notes that marriage is in part public in the sense that it is 'an institution' which politicians seek to promote and support, but that it is also 'the ultimate private arrangement'. He goes on to refer to potentials for the contractualisation of marriage, whereby couples are encouraged to reach their own agreements which then form the basis of the law governing their marriage.[5] Such a move could be regarded as part of a shift in the nature of marriage towards being more of a private than a public matter.

Joanna Miles demonstrates in chapter 3 on domestic violence that the traditional distinction drawn between criminal proceedings, which provide the 'public' response to spousal abuse, and civil proceedings, which represent the 'private' response, is under challenge. For example, under

---

[4] Such an approach can be justified under Article 8, European Convention for the Protection of Human Rights, which protects the 'right to respect for family life'.

[5] But as he points out this is not a one-way process: it is not possible to contract out of the Child Support Acts which govern the law on the private financial support for children.

the Family Law Act 1996 there is the possibility of public bodies pursuing the 'private' remedies on behalf of a victim of domestic violence. This in part reflects an increasing perception that the state has a role in protecting citizens from violence, and that this is a legitimate role for the state, even if it involves the law restricting behaviour in the family home – traditionally seen as the most private of arenas. Joanna Miles suggests it would be more profitable to see a continuum from private to public rather than there being a sharp distinction between the two.[6] The benefit of this may be to produce a more interactive relationship between civil and criminal procedures, rather than seeing them as two independent limbs of the law.

Balancing the interests of family members

It might be thought that the law's approach to balancing the interests of family members is straightforward – the welfare of the child is paramount. However, it is stressed in chapter 4 on parents and children that the welfare principle does not apply to all questions relating to children. Further, the Human Rights Act 1998 requires the court to protect the rights of adults, as well as children. How the courts deal with cases where the protection of an adult's rights will not be in a child's interests remains to be seen. Although it is widely accepted that if there is a clash between the interests of parents and children, the interests of children should be given especial weight. Exactly what sacrifices parents are expected to make in order to promote the interests of children is highly controversial. For example, as chapter 6 reveals, the issue in relation to adoption is complex. There is a need to balance the interests of parents, children and potential adopters.

Chapter 5, on children in the public law arena, reveals the difficulty in balancing the interests of children whom it is feared have been abused, and their parents. The approach of the Human Rights Act requires the state to intervene in family life only so far as it is necessary to do so. This means that the intervention should be proportionate to the threat to the child's welfare and the parent's interests should be protected to as great an extent as is possible in the light of the child's interests. This chapter stresses the importance of involving both parents and children in decisions that are taken, so that the interests of all the parties involved can be taken into account.

---

[6] For a different analysis see Eekelaar (1989) 'What is "Critical" Family Law?' (1989) 105 *Law Quarterly Review* 244.

Moral values or ideals and family law

The recent outcry that greeted the government's proposal to encourage schools to teach the value of marriage indicates the controversy that can surround any attempt by the state to promote values or ideals in the context of family life. This is particularly so given that we live in a religiously and culturally diverse society. It is increasingly hard to say that our society has certain accepted values on the best way to bring up children, for example. The unwillingness to promote exclusive moral values through the law could be said to be revealed in a number of recent developments in family law: the lack of significance attached to conduct in divorce and disputes concerning property and children; the move away from court resolution of family disputes and towards mediation; and the use of a rigid formula in the Child Support Acts.

On the other hand some areas of the law still promote moral values. In chapter 6 Caroline Bridge emphasises the power of the ideal of marriage in adoption law, under which the selection criteria used by local authorities in choosing adoptive parents and the law itself on adoption is based on an assumption that married potential adopters are the ideal candidates. Unmarried heterosexual and homosexual couples are seen to be second-best candidates. Louise Tee, in chapter 2, notes a recent decision of the House of Lords[7] which emphasises the importance of equality in determining how the property of a couple should be divided between them on divorce. This judgment could be regarded as the law promoting the moral value of equality between spouses. Louise Tee also discusses the debates surrounding the issue of whether pre-marriage contracts should deal with any dispute over spouses' property on divorce. Such a proposal could be seen as the law becoming reluctant to tell couples what is a fair distribution of their property and instead leaving that issue to the couple themselves.

Status or contract

Family law used to be based around status: once a person or relationship fell within a relevant definition then certain legal consequences followed, regardless of the intentions of the parties. For example, if a couple have gone through the legal formalities for a marriage, then the couple would have the legal benefits and obligations of marriage, even if in fact they did not live together or did not want those obligations to be imposed upon them. The use of status has come under challenge from critical and feminist analysis, which has suggested that the definition of statuses such

---

[7] *White* v. *White* [2000] 3 FCR 555.

as 'mother', 'father' and 'family' cannot be regarded as 'givens', but rather reflect a particular 'world-view'. Increasingly family law is moving away from placing weight on status and is instead focussing more on the intent of the parties. However, there is much debate over whether family law still has a use for status or whether a contractual approach would be preferable.

One of the difficulties with the use of statuses is that the status may not reflect reality. For example, Caroline Bridge (chapter 6) notes that the status of adoption changes the legal position of a child: an adopted child is treated as a child born to the marriage of the adoptive parents. This, she suggests, is artificial, especially given that many adopted children might know who their birth parents are. A further difficulty is that a status may carry historical baggage. Stuart Bridge (chapter 1) notes the antiquity of some of the incidents of marriage (such as consortium or unity) which may appear outdated. There are, however, benefits in the use of status. Chapter 2 indicates the difficulties that have arisen for land law in providing an appropriate legal regime for those couples who have not accepted the status of marriage, but are (or have been) in a long-term relationship.

Costs and legal systems

The present political climate places a high value on efficiency. The legal system, it is said, should be low-cost and high-quality. Reform proposals of family law nowadays inevitably involve an assessment of the cost implications of reform. The requirement of providing an efficient legal system throws up difficult questions for family law: would efficiency be promoted by more or less court involvement? If we reduce the number of cases coming to court, how do we decide which should not reach court? Are there family questions where the court and lawyers could be replaced by a different kind of forum?

A difficulty with making the system cost-effective is revealed in the public law area where there is tension between the different decision-makers (the parents, the local authorities, the courts and, to a limited extent, the child him or herself). As Lindley, Herring and Wyld note in chapter 5, the relationship between these decision-makers 'may lead at best to an uneasy relationship, and at worst to outright conflict'. The Children Act does not, by any means, give the court complete control over all aspects the care proceedings. Many important decisions are left to the local authority with only limited means of challenging those decisions.

Costs can also be regarded as influencing the debate over the extent to which the courts should be given discretion in family law disputes. Some argue that the less discretion the courts have, the more certain the outcome of any potential court hearing, and therefore the more likely it is that the parties will reach a settlement without going to court, therefore saving costs. The concern over costs has certainly been influential in the development of the law relating to financial disputes, as chapter 2 shows.

Enforcement and family law

All of the chapters reveal difficulties in the enforcement of family law. First, the means of enforcement may defeat the purpose for which an order was made in the first place. For example, in chapter 4 it is noted that the courts have faced great difficulties in enforcing orders for contact. Having made an order that there be contact, with the aim of promoting the welfare of the child, the court may be in the position of only being able to enforce the order effectively by imprisoning the residential parent, which would itself harm the child.

A second difficulty is that family obligations involve the most intimate aspects of a person's life. For a court to compel a person to act in a particular way in one of the most private areas of their life requires the strongest justification. This may explain the reluctance of the court to make occupation orders following domestic violence, as discussed in chapter 3.

Thirdly, most family obligations take place in private. This means that such obligations are difficult to police. For example, the law could not effectively order a resident parent to ensure that a child is in bed by a particular time, because there would be no practical way of ensuring that this was done. Even if there are effective ways of enforcing a court order, it may be that the legal system is not the best way of resolving the underlying issues. Family therapy or mediation could perhaps be more effective in the long term. This leads to the question of what extent family law should consist of enforceable obligations and to what extent statements of aspiration. Alternatively, it may be that although the law sets out legal obligations different means could be used to enforce those obligations. Stuart Bridge notes in chapter 1 the tensions between wanting to remove no fault from divorce, while at the same time not rendering marriage a legal status without any legal obligations. However, whatever the law on divorce is it cannot compel two people to stay together against their wishes. Stuart Bridge also discusses the difficulties the pilot studies have uncovered in the Family Law Act in attempting to require the parties to behave in an ideal way.

As is clear from these chapters, it is hard to predict what family law will look like in twenty years time. The surprisingly strong reaction against treating married and unmarried couples way in an identical way in the context of domestic violence, which led to last-minute reforms of what was to become the Family Law Act 1996, demonstrates that predictions about the future of family law cannot be made confidently. However, this book outlines some of the arguments and debates that will shape the road ahead.

1

Marriage and divorce: the regulation of intimacy

Stuart Bridge

Introduction

It can be forcefully argued that the twentieth century presided over the decline of marriage. As the availability of divorce increased, marriage could no longer be seen as a lifetime union, many people choose not to marry at all, and many others cohabit for some considerable time before deciding to marry. Yet marriage remains popular, particularly so in the United Kingdom, where despite its massive divorce rate it also has the highest marriage rate in the European Union. Marriage has political mileage, being seen as a desirable state for many reasons, the most important (at least to those without religious conviction) being the economic advantages, relationship stability and emotional support, reasons which still make marriage the favoured vehicle for the upbringing of children. It also has legal significance, the entry into marriage effecting a transformation of status as a result of which certain legal consequences will inexorably follow.

While it may no longer be the centrepiece of family law it once was, marriage cannot be ignored. In this chapter, the continuing legal significance of marriage will be explored with particular reference to current and likely future developments. The impact of the new human rights agenda on how the state may control entry to marriage and on the characterisation of the individual's right to marry is first examined. We shall then consider the effect on the legal relationship of the spouses by the imposition of the marital status, and then analyse the extent to which those spouses remain free to regulate their relationship for themselves. We shall consider the termination of marriage by divorce, still very much on the political agenda as the UK government contemplates its future following the demise of Part II of the Family Law Act 1996. Finally, we consider by way of overview a possible vision of marriage to be carried forward into the next century.

Protecting the right to marry

'The freedom to marry has long been recognised as one of the vital personal rights essential to the orderly pursuit of happiness by free men.'[1]

In the famous case of *Loving* v. *Virginia*, decided in 1967, the US Supreme Court held that the state's miscegenation laws not only discriminated on the basis of race in violation of the Equal Protection Clause, but also deprived the interracial couple of the freedom to marry, which was a fundamental liberty protected by the Due Process Clause. In other decisions, the Supreme Court has rigorously asserted that the right to marry is part of the fundamental 'right of privacy' protected by the Fourteenth Amendment.[2] Thus, an attempt by Wisconsin to require those defaulting on maintenance payments for their children to obtain the sanction of the court prior to entering into a marriage was struck down.[3] Although the state might have a legitimate concern with the financial soundness of prospective marriages, this was not sufficient to deny those who wished to exercise their fundamental right to marry from doing so.

As the Human Rights Act comes into force, the English courts must anticipate challenges to such limitations on marriage as are currently imposed by its domestic legislation. The European Convention on Human Rights sets marriage aside for special treatment. It is the only personal relationship within which the right to found a family is specifically guaranteed.[4] By Article 12:

Right to marry

Men and women of marriageable age have the right to marry and to found a family, according to the national laws governing exercise of this right.

Article 12 is notably unspecific. It does not state, for instance, what is meant by marriage, or indeed marriageable age. Not only do the final words appear to give states considerable latitude in the restrictions which are imposed on parties wishing to marry, the definition and status of marriage is also left to the state. Whether a state could unilaterally determine, as Professor Clive has advocated, that marriage should no longer have any legal significance, is a matter of some doubt.[5] Would a

---

[1] *Loving* v. *Virginia* 388 US 1 (1967).

[2] See in particular *Griswold* v. *Connecticut* 381 US 479 (1965).

[3] *Zablocki* v. *Redhail* 434 US 374 (1978).

[4] See Swindells, Neaves, Kushner, Stillbeck, *Family Law and the Human Rights Act 1998* (1999, Jordans), p. 225.

[5] Clive, 'Marriage: an unnecessary legal concept?', in Eekelaar and Katz (eds), *Marriage and Cohabitation in Contemporary Societies* (1980, Butterworth), p. 186.

right to marry be of any meaning if there were no legal consequences which flowed from its exercise?

The limits which English law places on the right to marry are to be found by reference to the law of nullity, specifically the law of voidness of marriage.[6] A marriage will be void where the intended spouses are within 'the prohibited degrees'; the law imposes an age limit of 16 or over (with a requirement for parental consent up to the age of 18); it insists upon certain basic formalities being complied with; the parties to a marriage must be respectively male and female; bigamous marriages, and polygamous marriages entered into outside England and Wales by a party then domiciled within the jurisdiction are also invalid. The European Court of Human Rights has already rejected challenges to the English law based on age and on the bigamy and polygamy restrictions on the ground that they did not comprise a violation of the right under Article 12.[7] More effective were the attempts by serving prisoners to enforce their right to marry, as a result of which, following successful complaint to the ECHR, the domestic legislation was duly amended.[8]

The most active litigation has concerned the question who may marry whom, as gay couples and transsexuals attempt to assert their right to marry the partner of their choice. English law imposes a requirement that the parties to a marriage must be a man and a woman, the Matrimonial Causes Act 1973 providing that where the parties to a marriage are not respectively male and female, the marriage is void.[9] In the celebrated case of *Corbett* v. *Corbett*[10], Ormrod J held that marriage was a union between a man and a woman, and that a person's sex was fixed at birth by a consideration of chromosonal, gonadal and genital factors. Any later surgical intervention could not change the sex of the individual as a matter of law: sex was immutable. Thus where a person born as a man underwent gender-assignment surgery, they could not subsequently contract a valid marriage with a man. Although the person's gender may have changed, their sex had not. In *Cossey* v. *UK*, the European Court of Human Rights agreed with the line of reasoning in *Corbett* that the applicant's inability to

---

[6] Matrimonial Causes Act 1973, section 11.

[7] *Khan* v. *UK* Application No 11579/85 (7 July 1986) 48 DR 253; *Bibi* v. *UK* Application No 19628/92 (29 June 1992) unpublished.

[8] *Hamer* v. *UK* Application No 7114/75 (13 December 1979) 24 DR 5; *Draper* v. *UK* Application No 8186/78 (10 July 1980) 24 DR 72; Marriage Act 1983.

[9] Section 11.

[10] [1971] P 83. The reasoning of Ormrod J was recently applied in finding that a person with male chromosones, male gonadal sex, 'ambiguous' genitalia and female gender orientation was a woman: *W* v. *W* (*Nullity: Gender*) [2001] 1 FLR 324, Charles J. In *B* v. *B*. (*Validity of Marriage*) [2001] 1 FLR 389, Johnson J held that it was up to Parliament to change the law if it thought it appropriate to do so, and that he remained bound by the decision in *Corbett*.

marry a woman 'does not stem from any legal impediment and, in this respect, it cannot be said that the right to marry has been impaired as a consequence of the provisions of domestic law'.[11] By a cruel irony, the person still had the right to marry, but it was a right to marry a woman, a right which they would have no inclination to exercise.

The European Court of Human Rights has withheld challenges to the reasoning of *Corbett* on several occasions,[12] but there has been a gradual move towards greater liberality as other states have legislated to enhance the rights of post-operative transsexuals, recognising that they should be treated as being of their re-assigned gender for the purposes of marriage.[13] Moreover, in other areas affecting transsexuals, the European Court has shown greater readiness to intervene. Thus in *B* v. *France*,[14] the Court found a violation of the right to respect for private life when the French Government refused to rectify the birth certificate of a post-operative transsexual to reflect her new sexual identity. *Rees* v. *UK* was distinguished on the ground that a birth certificate was a more significant document in France than in the UK.[15] And in its most recent, and potentially most important, pronouncement, *Sheffield and Horsham* v. *UK*, the Court criticised the British for not keeping the area under review as there was an increased social acceptance of transsexualism and an increased recognition of the problems encountered by post-operative transsexuals.[16] At least one judge, Judge van Dijk, albeit dissenting, was prepared to go further, stating the conundrum as follows:

> … denying post-operative transsexuals in absolute terms the right to marry a person of their previous sex while marrying a person of their newly acquired sex is no longer an acceptable option would amount to excluding them from any marriage.

Such an absolute denial, argued Judge van Dijk, fell outside the margin of appreciation by virtue of Article 17 as it affected the right 'in its essence'.

---

[11] [1991] 2 FLR 492, p. 504.

[12] *Rees* v. *UK* [1987] 2 FLR 111; *Cossey* v. *UK* [1991] 2 FLR 492; *X Y Z* v. *UK* [1997] 2 FLR 892: *cf B* v. *France* [1992] 2 FLR 249.

[13] See *B* v. *B (Validity of Marriage)* [2001] 1 FLR 389, where Johnson J noted (at p. 402) that 'what I have described as the plight of the transsexual has been recognised not only in judgments around the world but in legislatures too. In Europe at least, the law on this matter in England and Wales is, or is becoming, a minority position.'

[14] [1992] 2 FLR 249.

[15] [1992] 2 FLR 249, p. 265. In particular, it was intended to be updated throughout the life of the individual, thereby defining the person's current identity, whereas in England it did not purport to do more than 'record a historic fact'. English law allows a person to change their name at will, as was noted by the ECHR in *Rees* v. *UK* [1987] 2 FLR 111, p. 120 (para. 40).

[16] [1998] 2 FLR 928, p. 942.

It must be recognised that while, up until now, the ECHR has been reluctant to intervene in promoting recognition of the transsexuals' right to marry, pressure from the Court is likely to increase, and unless legislation reverses *Corbett*, the current entrenched position of the English courts may ultimately be declared contrary to the European Convention.[17]

The traditional view of marriage advanced by the ECHR holds out little hope for those who would like to see the more radical step of sanctioning marriage between individuals of the same sex. Marriage is clearly perceived by the Court to be a legal union between persons of the opposite biological sex.[18] Thus, while the Convention recognises 'the right to marry', marriage to a person of the same sex has been declared not to be within the scope of this right.[19] Several European jurisdictions have now enacted legislation providing a regime for domestic partnerships, which parties (of the same or sometimes of the opposite sex) can contract into, usually by registration, and which thereby imposes rights and obligations which are in certain respects similar to those of married couples.[20] However, they have resisted the temptation of referring to same sex partnerships as marriages, and the conferment of proprietary consequences has generally proved more politically acceptable than the imposition of any rights in relation to children (for instance, the right to adopt).[21] There is no evidence that the United Kingdom, or for that matter many other European jurisdictions, is likely to make any reforms of this nature in the foreseeable future. Nicholas Bamforth, in a compelling recent article,[22] has argued that there is considerable scope in using Article 8 of

---

[17] For the current state of progress in the UK, see *B v. B (Validity of Marriage)* [2001] 1 FLR 389, at pp. 400–402.

[18] *Rees v. UK* [1987] 2 FLR 111, p. 123 (para. 49).

[19] '… in the present state of the law within the Community, stable relationships between two persons of the same sex are not regarded as equivalent to marriages or stable relationships outside marriage between persons of opposite sex.' (*Grant v. South West Trains* [1998] All ER (EC) 192, p. 208)

[20] Denmark (1989), Norway (1993), Sweden (1994), Iceland (1996), Netherlands (1998), Belgium (1998), France (1999). See Bradney, *Family Law and Political Culture* (1996, Sweet & Maxwell); Forder, 'An Undutchable Family Law: Partnership, Parenthood, Social Parenthood, Names and Some Article 8 ECHR Case Law', in Bainham (ed.) *International Survey of Family Law 1997* (1997, Martinus Nijhoff) pp. 260–268; Forder, 'Opening Up Marriage to Same Sex Partners and Providing for Adoption by Same Sex Couples, Managing Information on Sperm Donors, and Lots of Private International Law' in Bainham (ed.) *International Survey of Family Law 2000* (2000, Jordans), pp. 240–253.

[21] For a recent survey of the various approaches, see Probert and Barlow, 'Displacing marriage – diversification and harmonisation within Europe', [2000] *Child and Family Law Quarterly* 153. There is an excellent exposition of the recent reforms in France in Steiner, 'The spirit of the new French registered partnership law – promoting autonomy and pluralism or weakening marriage?' [2000] *Child and Family Law Quarterly* 1.

[22] 'Sexual Orientation Discrimination after *Grant v. South West Trains*', (2000) 63 *Modern Law Review* 694.

the European Convention on Human Rights to protect persons of lesbian, bisexual or gay orientation from discrimination.[23] There has been acceptance, at ECHR level, that differential treatment on the basis of a person's sexual orientation can violate the prohibition on discrimination in relation to enjoyment of other Convention rights under Article 14.[24] But it remains a matter for speculation whether this may ultimately lead to a successful challenge to laws which restrict marriage to persons of opposite sex.

In the United States, as one would expect, there is huge diversity in state practice. The most radical jurisdiction has proved to be Hawaii, where its Supreme Court, invoking *Loving* v. *Virginia*,[25] asserted the right of same sex couples to marry on the basis that homosexuals would otherwise be denied their right to equal protection of the laws, and that the state's ban on same-sex marriages was therefore unconstitutional.[26] Two consequences followed. Hawaii conducted a state referendum as a result of which the constitution was amended, effectively to preclude same-sex marriage.[27] Then Congress enacted the Defense of Marriage Act, denying federal recognition of same-sex marriages and giving each state the right not to recognise such marriages even if validly celebrated in another state.[28] The view of marriage as a legal relationship contracted into by two persons of the opposite sex still holds in the United States as in the United Kingdom, and it is likely that this will remain the position for some considerable time. In most respects, traditionalism prevails.

Marriage as status: when does marriage matter?

Marriage seems such a central part of modern society that it is almost impossible to imagine what life would be like without it. It is a social institution as well as a legal concept. Yet Professor Eric Clive, writing in 1980, considered whether the legal concept of marriage was necessary and whether marriage could be abolished as a legal status altogether.[29] If so, the legal system could ignore marriage, regarding it as an exclusively private

---

[23] Much reliance is placed on *Smith* v. *UK* [2000] 29 EHRR 493.

[24] *Da Silva Mouta* v. *Portugal*, application no. 33290/96; judgment 21 December 1999.

[25] See above, n. 1.

[26] *Baehr* v. *Lewin* (1993) 852 P 2d 44.

[27] This legislative action was upheld following challenge in the Hawaii courts: *Baehr* v. *Miike*, 11 December 1999: see Bamforth, 'Sexual Orientation Discrimination after *Grant* v. *South West Trains*' (2000) 63 *Modern Law Review* 694, at p. 707.

[28] See generally Katz, 'State regulation and personal autonomy in marriage: How can I marry and whom can I marry?', in Bainham (ed.) *International Survey of Family Law 1996*, pp. 487–504; Strasser, *The Challenge of Same-Sex Marriage: Federalist Principles and Constitutional Protections* (1999, Praeger).

[29] 'Marriage: an unnecessary legal concept?' in Eekelaar and Katz (eds), *Marriage and Cohabitation in Contemporary Societies* (1980, Butterworth), pp. 71–82.

matter, 'no more regulated by law than friendship or entry into a religious order.' Professor Clive presents a persuasive argument, proposing for example that support obligations could be more fairly based on existing dependency rather than actual status, and that as obligations to live together and to be sexually faithful are 'manifestly unenforceable' they could be discarded without difficulty. He lists the most important consequences flowing from marriage, and contends that there is no good reason to link them inextricably to the marital state. But, as Clive concedes, it is one thing to say that marriage is unnecessary. Is it, nevertheless, convenient (as a legal concept that is)?

Unity and consortium

Traditionally, the two major incidents of marriage, from which most marital rights and obligations have derived, have been considered to be 'unity' and 'consortium'. The authority for marital unity is biblical, perceiving man and wife to be as one person.[30] This doctrine, favoured by Blackstone[31] and applied intermittently to justify certain restraints on the legal capacity of married women, was never universally accepted as a 'consistently operative principle',[32] and gradually its illiberal traits were dealt with. Thus from the late nineteenth century onwards, wives slowly emerged from the class of 'persons under a disability' which they had occupied together with bankrupts, infants and lunatics and achieved gradual recognition as legal persons in their own right. The Married Women's Property Acts of 1870 and 1882 enabled wives to own property and to sue in the English courts in their own name; the Law Reform (Married Women and Tortfeasors) Act 1935 ended the derivative liability of husbands for the torts of their wives; and the Law Reform (Husband and Wife) Act 1962 enabled spouses to sue each other in tort. Modern courts have not shown any enthusiasm for perpetuating the doctrine of unity, which has been described as a 'fiction', 'eroded by the judges who have created exception after exception to it', and 'cut down by statute after statute until little of it remains ... The severance in all respects is so complete that I would say that the doctrine of unity and its ramifications should be discarded altogether, except in so far as it is retained by judicial decision or by Act of Parliament.'[33] Ironically, Parliament has retained it (or, to be more accurate, one of its 'ramifications') in relation to the crime of

---

[30] 'Therefore shall a man leave his father and his mother, and shall cleave unto his wife: and they shall be one flesh.' *Genesis*, ch.2, v.24.

[31] *Commentaries*, 17th ed., (1830), vol. 1, p. 442.

[32] *Tooth & Co. Ltd.* v. *Tillyer* (1956) 95 CLR 605, p. 616, approved by Oliver J in *Midland Bank Trust Co Ltd* v. *Green (No. 3)* [1979] Ch 496, p. 519.

[33] *Midland Bank Trust Co Ltd* v. *Green (No 3)*, [1982] Ch 529, pp. 538–9, *per* Lord Denning M.R.

conspiracy, which cannot to this day be committed by husband and wife unless there are other parties to the conspiracy.[34] It is, however, difficult to identify any other areas of common law or statute law where rules clearly derived from the doctrine of unity remain. Indeed, the accumulated experience of the last century has been that of spouses coming to be treated as separate and equal individuals within the marriage, itself now to be viewed as a joint enterprise for the maintenance of a home and the upbringing of children.[35]

'Consortium', another abstract notion, and itself akin to 'a symbol of the unity of the married couple',[36] is defined by Bromley as 'living together as husband and wife with all the incidents (insofar as these can be defined) that flow from that relationship.'[37] It 'connotes as far as possible the sharing of a common home and a common domestic life.'[38] Beyond that, as the texts concede, it is difficult to be precise, and even thus far there is vagueness and uncertainty. Consortium is based on an anachronistic and gender-biased vision of marriage, where the husband was entitled not only to the wife's company, but also to her services both domestic and sexual. Deprivation of those services by a third party – whether tortfeasor or adulterer – gave rise to remedies in damages, against the tortfeasor in negligence (or the Fatal Accidents Acts), against the adulterer in 'criminal conversation'.[39] Although it was never realistic to attempt to enforce obligations to cohabit, the legislative abolition of the decree of restitution of conjugal rights did not occur until 1970.[40] The rejection by the Court of Appeal of a husband's argument that he could confine his wife in order to enforce his consortium rights was probably of greater long-term importance.[41]

The duty to cohabit which is central to consortium remains a duty of the most nebulous kind. A court cannot compel spouses to cohabit against their will, and if the duty cannot be specifically enforced, and its breach gives no right to damages, in what sense, if any, is it a duty at all? Under the divorce laws currently applied in England, a spouse who leaves the

---

[34] Criminal Law Act 1977, section 2(2)(a); *R v. Chrastny (No 1)* [1992] 1 All ER 119.

[34] Shultz, 'Contractual Ordering of Marriage: A New Model for State Policy' (1982) 70 *California Law Review* 204, p. 274; Glendon, *The Transformation of Family Law* (1989, The University of Chicago Press), p. 103, citing *Eisenstadt v. Baird* 405 US 438 (1972); *Midland Bank Trust Co Ltd v. Green (No 3)*, C.A., above, *per* Lord Denning M.R. at p. 538. See also the recent decision of the House of Lords in *White v. White*, referred to below at n. 93.

[36] Glendon, *op. cit.* n. 34, p. 95.

[37] Lowe and Douglas, *Bromley's Family Law* 9th ed. (1998, Butterworth), p. 55.

[38] *Ibid.*, p. 56.

[39] For an interesting commentary on whether a third party can be made liable in damages to a 'wronged' spouse, see Pascoe, 'Can English Law Uphold the Sanctity of Marriage?' [1998] *Family Law* 620.

[40] Law Reform (Miscellaneous Provisions) Act 1970.

[41] *R v. Jackson* [1891] 1 QB 671.

matrimonial home permanently, not intending to return and without the consent of the other, commits desertion. This will (after two years) give rise to a fact evidencing irretrievable breakdown of marriage on which the deserted spouse can base a divorce petition – and in the meantime it is a ground on which the deserted spouse can claim an order for financial provision.[42] As a matter of divorce practice, desertion is rarely invoked, as where the spouses agree upon the marriage being terminated, two years' separation will of itself suffice.

One consequence of consortium being a recognisable right was the deeply unsatisfactory and anachronistic rule that a husband could not be guilty of raping his wife, at least while no court intervention qualifying their duty to cohabit had occurred. Following a line of cases which had developed the exceptions to the general principle,[43] the House of Lords finally threw out the rule in 1991, declaring that a husband could not disregard his wife's lack of consent, have sex against her wishes and claim immunity from conviction. A wife had the right to revoke her consent, as marriage was 'in modern times regarded as a partnership of equals, and is no longer one in which the wife must be the subservient chattel of the husband'.[44] This sensible decision brought wives within the protection of the criminal law. But a refusal of sex without good reason, or attempts to place unreasonable limits on its frequency, may still provide the frustrated partner with grounds for a divorce, arguing that the other has behaved in such a way that they cannot reasonably be expected to live with them.[45]

If no-fault divorce is eventually introduced in England, in whatever form, the role and function of consortium will be even less clear. Adultery, desertion and behaviour will cease to be relevant matters for courts to consider, and even less interest than at present will be focussed on the history of the parties' marital relationship. As it is, conduct during the marriage is rarely an issue in the context of the ancillary relief proceedings.[46] For those who seek to reduce state interference in private relationships, this is a development to be encouraged. For those who

---

[42] Matrimonial Causes Act 1973, ss. 1(1), 1(2)(b); Domestic Proceedings and Magistrates Courts Act 1978, s. 1.

[43] Notably *R* v. *Clarke* [1949] 2 All ER 448 (justices' order provided wife no longer bound to cohabit); *R* v. *O'Brien (Edward)* [1974] 3 All ER 663 (offence subsequent to decree nisi); *R v. Steele* (1976) 65 Cr App Rep 22 (defendant living apart from wife had undertaken to the court not to molest her).

[44] *R.* v. *R* [1992] 1 AC 599, p. 616, *per* Lord Keith of Kinkel. For the partnership model of marriage, see further below at text above n. 121.

[45] See *Mason* v. *Mason* (1980) 11 Fam Law 143, C.A., for a case where the court was called upon to adjudicate what refusal of sexual demands was reasonable. In the circumstances of the case, a restriction of sex to once a week was not thought to comprise unreasonable behaviour.

[46] The leading case after the 1969 divorce reforms was *Wachtel* v. *Wachtel* [1973] Fam 72. See for further developments, Matrimonial and Family Proceedings Act 1984, s. 3, amending

support the institution of marriage, and seek to uphold it by making divorce difficult, the removal of any imputation of fault is more controversial. Brenda Hale has summarised their argument with characteristic clarity:

> The old grounds for divorce defined the minimum obligations of the marital contract – to live together, to be faithful to one another, and to behave with reasonable consideration for one another. If there are no rules of marital conduct, or no sanctions for breaking the rules that do exist, what incentive can there be for anyone to behave properly?[47]

The consequences of marriage

The truth is that the doctrines of unity and consortium are both outmoded and unhelpful in our attempts to describe the legal status of marriage. Marriage is a status, meaning, in the words of Lord Simon of Glaisdale, 'the condition of belonging to a class in society to which the law ascribes peculiar rights and duties, capacities and incapacities.'[48] Married couples clearly have particular legal capacities. Certain rules apply only to married persons – to state the obvious, in English law a person who is currently married cannot enter into another valid marriage, while a married person has the right to petition for divorce which an unmarried person does not have. Other sets of rules may apply both to married persons and to other classes of persons as well. Ultimately we will need to ask whether marriage is a status which is capable of variation by the parties to the marriage, and the extent to which the privileges and duties of the married state are inexorably fixed by law. It can be asserted, with some evidence supporting the claim, that the rights and obligations which pertain exclusively to the marital relationship have been gradually eroded, while some have fallen into disuse, and that the currency of marriage has thereby been devalued.

Matrimonial Causes Act 1973, s. 25(2)(g). The Family Law Act 1996, s. 66(1), Sch. 8, para. 9(3)(b) was to have amended s. 25 to require the court to have regard to conduct 'whatever the nature of the conduct and whether it occurred during the marriage or after the separation of the parties or (as the case may be) dissolution or annulment of the marriage'. Other provisions of the Family Law Act 1996 which would have resulted in an analysis of marital conduct were s. 10(2) (orders preventing divorce may be made only if it would be wrong, in all the circumstances including the conduct of the parties, for the marriage to be dissolved) and, less directly, s. 7(12) (length of period for reflection and consideration not to be extended where there is an occupation order or a non-molestation order in force against the other party to the marriage). These provisions will not now be brought into force, and will be repealed at the first opportunity.

[47] 'The Family Law Act 1996 – the death of marriage?' in Caroline Bridge (ed.), *Family Law Towards the Millennium* (1997, Butterworth) at p. 9.

[48] *The Ampthill Peerage* [1977] AC 547, p. 577.

Children

The conferment of status on children, according to whether they have been born inside or outside marriage, has now been rejected as a matter of policy.[49] The legislative assault on illegitimacy being complete, the entirely proper focus in child law is on the child's welfare rather than its status.[50] But marriage remains of significance in imputing status to the parents (both parentage and parental responsibility) in relation to the child. Thus, where a child is conceived during marriage, it is presumed that the husband is the father – even where the mother has received fertility treatment so that there is no genetic link between her husband and the child, the husband will be the father unless he can prove that he did not consent to her being treated.[51] Marriage has the effect of automatically imposing parental responsibility on the husband (provided he is, as a matter of law, the father of the child).[52] At present, an adoption order can only be made in favour of two persons if they are a married couple – the same applies in respect of parental orders following a surrogacy arrangement.[53]

Financial consequences

Spouses are mutually liable to maintain each other. This obligation may have repercussions in both public and private support systems. Thus, the state may pursue a husband for income support payments which have been made to the wife following her application for welfare.[54] Failure to maintain a spouse may lead to proceedings before the family proceedings court for a financial provision order, and there is a parallel jurisdiction available in the High Court or county court, which will also enforce maintenance agreements entered into between the parties.[55] In the event of a decree of judicial separation, nullity or divorce, the High Court and county court have wide powers to redistribute the assets, income and capital, of the spouses as it deems fair just and reasonable.[56] There is no equivalent liability to maintain a partner to whom one is not married, and there is no redistributive jurisdiction approximating to that of Part II of the Matrimonial Causes Act 1973 which is applicable to cohabitants outside

---

[49] See Family Law Reform Act 1987, enacting the recommendations of Law Commission Report No. 118 (1982) and Law Commission Report No. 147 (1986).

[50] Children Act 1989, s. 1(1).

[51] Human Fertilisation and Embryology Act 1990, s. 28(2).

[52] Children Act 1989, s. 2(1). *B* v. *UK* [2000] 1 FLR 1.

[53] Adoption Act 1976, s. 14; Human Fertilisation and Embryology Act 1990, s. 30.

[54] Social Security Administration Act 1992, s. 106.

[55] Domestic Proceedings and Magistrates Courts Act 1978, s. 1; Matrimonial Causes Act 1973, ss. 27, 34.

[56] Matrimonial Causes Act 1973, Part II.

marriage. Thus, the financial consequences of entering into marriage are immense. Indeed, it can be argued that the single most important legal consequence of marriage is that it is the only legal relationship terminable by divorce. The availability of divorce means that the draconian judicial powers to reallocate assets are applicable between the parties. While English law does not have community of property,[57] once marriage has occurred, the financial resources of both parties, whether acquired before during or after the marriage, are vulnerable to judicial redistribution.

On death

The intestacy rules put the surviving spouse in a privileged position, obtaining in most cases the lion's share of the estate where the deceased fails to make a will which disposes of his or her property.[58] The spouse is similarly well placed in family provision proceedings, where the most generous standard of assessment of 'reasonable financial provision' is applied to them.[59] Unmarried cohabitants have no entitlement on intestacy,[60] although they may be able to bring a family provision claim if they have been living with the deceased as their husband or wife for a period of two years, or if they were dependant on the deceased immediately before their death.[61] If the death of a spouse is tortiously caused, the survivor may bring a claim against the tortfeasor under the Fatal Accidents Acts as a dependant, and may claim damages both for loss of pecuniary benefit and for bereavement.[62] The survivor of an unmarried couple can only claim as a dependant for loss of pecuniary benefit if they lived with the deceased as their husband or wife for at least two years immediately before the death, and cannot claim bereavement damages in any circumstances.[63]

---

[57] A community of property regime implies that property owned (or acquired during the marriage) by either spouse is treated as jointly owned.

[59] Administration of Estates Act 1925, s. 46(1)(i).

[59] Inheritance (Provision for Family and Dependants) Act 1975, s. 1(2)(a). Thus a spouse can claim that the deceased's will (or the application of the intestacy rules, or a combination of the will and the intestacy rules) has failed to make reasonable financial provision for them, and that an order should be made in their favour.

[60] Although the Crown may make payments out of the estate if the estate would otherwise pass as *bona vacantia*: Administration of Estates Act 1925, s. 46(1).

[61] No distinction is made, however, between a married couple or an unmarried couple (of opposite sexes) where statutory succession to residential tenancies is concerned.

[62] Fatal Accidents Act 1976, s. 1(3); s. 1A.

[63] The Law Commission has made recommendations for improving the position of cohabitants such that any person who can establish dependency could claim for loss of pecuniary benefit, and that certain cohabitants (including the survivor of a same-sex couple) should be able to claim for bereavement damages: Law Commission Report No. 263 (1999), para. 3.46, para. 6.31.

Criminal law

There remain certain rules of evidence applicable to criminal proceedings which are specific to married couples. A defendant's spouse can only be compelled to give evidence by the prosecution (or in the defence of a person jointly charged with the defendant) in certain restricted circumstances involving assault, injury or threat of injury to the spouse or a person under 16 (or a sexual offence against a person under 16).[64] But even here, there have been incursions on long-standing principle. Since 1984, a spouse has been compellable in all cases to give evidence for the defendant unless the married couple are charged jointly. Since 1968, a spouse has been liable to conviction for stealing the other's property (or, for that matter, jointly owned property), although proceedings for such an offence may only be initiated with the consent of the Director of Public Prosecutions.[65] Wives (but not husbands) may invoke the somewhat antiquated defence of marital coercion in respect of criminal liability (save for treason and murder) by proving, the burden being on her on the balance of probabilities, that the offence was committed in the presence of, and under the coercion of, her husband.[66]

The declining significance of marriage

The above is not by any means a comprehensive list of the legal consequences which flow from the husband–wife relationship. It should be clear, however, that the significance of the marital status is in decline. A parallel trend has been that of marriage ceasing to be the only qualifying criteria for a particular right, but merely one of several, as in recent years Parliament has sought to extend various rights to persons who are not married, with the effect of challenging the exclusivity of the marital status. This policy has been seen by the supporters of marriage, who wish married couples to be preferred over other types of relationship, as an attack on the institution itself. The domestic violence legislation is a good example. Until 1976, the right to claim orders protecting a claimant from domestic violence, at least by ousting the violent party from the property which they shared, was strictly limited. Where a spouse brought divorce proceedings, the court could, in the exercise of its inherent jurisdiction, make orders for the petitioner's protection ordering the respondent to leave the matrimonial home or not to assault or molest the petitioner. The unmarried victim of domestic violence was not able to take advantage of this jurisdiction, and in the search for an adequate civil remedy had to

---

64 Police and Criminal Evidence Act 1984, s. 80.
65 Theft Act 1968, s. 30(1); Theft Act 1978, s. 5(2).
66 Criminal Justice Act 1925, s. 47; *R* v. *Shortland* [1995] Crim LR 893.

make do with the relatively unsophisticated and inflexible laws of tort. The Domestic Violence and Matrimonial Proceedings Act 1976 conferred jurisdiction on the county court to make not only non-molestation orders, but also ouster orders, both as between husband and wife and as between 'a man and woman living with each other in the same household as husband and wife' (but not lawfully married to each other).[67] Early decisions of the Court of Appeal on this legislation adopted the absurdly literal interpretation that jurisdiction to make an order was lost if its exercise would override the property rights of the respondent.[68] This argument, which drove the proverbial coach and horses through the statute, was trenchantly criticised by Lord Denning, who convened a five-member panel of the Court of Appeal in an ambitious attempt to reverse the previous decisions. These decisions were ultimately rejected by the House of Lords, not for the first or last time criticising Lord Denning's methods but following his legal reasoning in the court below.[69] The effect, intended by Parliament and eventually identified by the judges, was that married and unmarried couples had similar legal privileges in the realm of domestic violence, and marriage was no longer in a class of its own.[70]

A similar reluctance to confine, as a matter of policy, privileges and even obligations to married couples has also been demonstrated by members of our judiciary in their application of equitable doctrine. In *Argyll* v. *Argyll*,[71] Ungoed-Thomas J, granted an injunction restraining the Duke of Argyll from breaking the confidence of his relationship with the Duchess by selling his story of their colourful marriage to *The People*. There was an implied obligation of confidence in the marital relationship breach of which the court would protect by injunction if necessary. Ungoed-Thomas J was of the view that 'there could hardly be anything more intimate or confidential than is involved in that relationship, or than in the mutual trust and confidences which are shared between husband and wife.'[72]

But it has been subsequently held that protection of confidence is not exclusive to marriage, at least where such an obligation had been

---

[67] 1976 Act, s. 1(2).

[68] *B v. B* [1978] Fam 26; *Cantliff v. Jenkins* [1978] Fam 47n.

[69] *Davis v. Johnson* [1979] AC 264.

[70] The controversy fomented by the popular press concerning the Family Homes and Domestic Violence Bill of 1995 arose from a misunderstanding of the impact of the Law Commission's proposals enshrined in the Bill which for the most part rationalised existing jurisdictions rather than increased rights of those in relationships outside marriage. The Bill was withdrawn, but in the following Parliamentary session, the Family Law Act 1996 obtained royal assent. Part IV of this statute, which came into force in 1997, contains the essence of the earlier Bill. For a brief account of the controversy, see Cretney, 'The Law Commission: True Dawns and False Dawns', p. 2 *et seq.*, in *Law, Law Reform and the Family* (1998, OUP).

[71] [1967] Ch 302.

[72] *Ibid.*, at p. 322.

expressly agreed. In *Stephens* v. *Avery*,[73] Sir Nicolas Browne-Wilkinson VC enjoined a woman from revealing confidences to *The Mail on Sunday* about the sexual behaviour of a former friend who had confessed to that behaviour in her presence. The information had been received in circumstances of confidence, and the defendant had expressly promised not to let others know. It did not matter that the plaintiff and defendant were not married – while the marital relationship might lead to the readier implication of a duty to preserve confidences, it had no exclusivity in this respect.[74]

A good example of the way in which the courts have taken a more nuanced view of relationships is the proliferation of cases in recent years concerning the liability of sureties. Typically, a borrower seeks a loan from a bank or other lending institution. The bank then requests the borrower to provide security in the form of a charge over their home. If that home is jointly owned the bank will require the legal or beneficial co-owner to be a party to the transaction as a surety and will expect them to waive any priority their own interest might have over the charge of the bank. The borrower and surety may be husband and wife, or they may be an unmarried (heterosexual or homosexual) couple. When the bank seeks to enforce the charge, the surety contends that although they signed the relevant documents, and thereby entered into the transaction, they did not do so voluntarily, their consent being vitiated by the undue influence, fraud, or misrepresentation of the borrower. This would have serious repercussions for the creditor seeking to enforce the debt.

In *Barclays Bank Plc* v. *O'Brien*,[75] the House of Lords held that the creditor would be bound by the borrower's undue influence, fraud or misrepresentation provided that the borrower was acting as agent for the creditor in obtaining the surety's consent to the transaction, or (more likely) that the creditor had 'notice' of the situation and failed to take appropriate steps to ensure that the surety received independent legal advice as to the risks of entering into the agreement. In such circumstances, the creditor would be unable to enforce the charge against the surety. Both the Court of Appeal and the House of Lords discussed at length when the creditor would be deemed to have notice of the borrower's acts. Scott L.J., in the Court of Appeal, placed married couples in a special protected class of sureties, and decided that wives who had given security to support their husband's debts were deserving of a 'more tender' treatment than that which was applied to other third party

---

[73] [1988] 1 Ch 449.
[74] See, for subsequent (and likely future) developments in the law of privacy, Phillipson and Fenwick, 'Breach of Confidence as a Privacy Remedy in the Human Rights Act Era', (2000) 63 *Modern Law Review* 660.
[75] [1994] 1 AC 180, H.L.; [1993] 1 FLR 124, C.A.

sureties.[76] But the House of Lords took a different view. Lord Browne-Wilkinson denied that spouses should obtain favoured treatment in deciding whether undue influence had been exerted – thus no presumption of undue influence arose simply from the existence of the marital status between debtor and surety. To the extent that there was an 'invalidating tendency' in cases where (typically) wives stood surety for their husband's debts, it was at least in part because of the parties' sexual and emotional ties which provided a 'ready weapon' for undue influence: 'a wife's true wishes can easily be overborne because of her fear of destroying or damaging the wider relationship between her and her husband if she opposes his wishes.' But there should be no exclusivity of principle based on the marital status. In a passage of potentially great significance for the future development of principle, Lord Browne-Wilkinson stated:

> … the same principles are applicable to all other cases where there is an emotional relationship between cohabitees. The 'tenderness' shown by the law to married women is not based on the marriage ceremony but reflects the underlying risk of one cohabitee exploiting the emotional involvement and trust of the other. Now that unmarried cohabitation, whether heterosexual or homosexual, is widespread in our society, the law should recognise this. Legal wives are not the only group which are now exposed to the emotional pressure of cohabitation. Therefore if, but only if, the creditor is aware that the surety is cohabiting with the principal debtor, in my judgment the same principles should apply to them as apply to husband and wife.

The decision of the House of Lords in *O'Brien* stands as a classic modern example of judicial reluctance to vest rights in parties by virtue of marital status alone. Instead, courts are ready to look more closely at the realities of the relationship in question, and make decisions on the basis of what they find.[77] While this is an elastic approach, it also has disadvantages in terms of the inevitable uncertainty which would result. One argument for attaching rights to marriage is that it is a readily identifiable status. Whether parties are married at any given time can be relatively easily established. Whether there exists a relationship of cohabitation giving rise to emotional attachment may be much more problematic – indeed whether parties are 'cohabiting' at all can cause difficulty. The difficulty of the line taken in *O'Brien* is the way it places a burden on the bank to discover the true nature of the relationship, such as it is, between the borrower and the surety. If it were simply whether they were married to each other, the bank would have a much easier job. Marriage is a status of

[76] In doing so, he relied particularly on *Turnbull & Co v. Duval* [1902] AC 429 and *Yerkey v. Jones* (1939) 63 CLR 649.

[77] Another good example of this judicial approach is the decision of the House of Lords in *FitzPatrick v. Sterling Housing Association* [2001] AC 27.

convenience. Where consequences flow from circumstances which are not readily identifiable, there is inevitable uncertainty.

If the law followed the view of Professor Clive and removed all consequences of marriage, what then? Intimate personal relationships could not be entirely devoid of regulation. One way would be to expect parties to enter into legally enforceable contracts governing such matters as their respective property rights, their mutual financial support, and perhaps matters such as the upbringing of children and even sexual fidelity. Contract, as we will see, creates problems of its own. The alternative, an imposition of status based on cohabitation, is even more fraught with difficulty in terms of practical operation. Marriage may regulate a declining number of relationships, but its ready identifiability, and popular recognition and respect, may still justify its primacy and its protection. We now turn to consider the extent to which the law can, or should, permit those who do elect to marry to stipulate their own obligations.

Marital contracts and the contract of marriage: marriage private and public

The public/private divide

Few legal relationships present the public/private divide in as stark a contrast as marriage. It is on one level so public as to be an *institution*, a word which resonates with notions of church and state. On another, the individual marriage is the ultimate private arrangement the very intimacy of which is deserving of protection from the public eye. Marriage is more than a status: it is also a contract. We have already seen the terms and obligations which the state imposes, in the sense of the legal consequences which flow from marriage. 'Traditional' marriage has changed. But it remains, for the most part, a contract of the standard form. The extent to which spouses can vary the marital obligations by negotiated agreement is doubtful, although it has become a central item on the current political agenda. Much recent consideration has been given to so-called 'pre-nuptial agreements' and the role they might play in the future regulation of marriage. The UK government has made statements supporting their utility as providing the spouses with a means of articulating their respective rights and obligations, and of enabling them to draw up their own marriage contract to deal with their own particular circumstances. Legislation has been contemplated to achieve this intended objective. The contractarians see the contractualisation of marriage as offering freedom of choice, enabling parties to exercise autonomy in negotiating and settling the terms of their own relationship, and perhaps persuading more to enter marriage by tailoring it to suit their individual needs and by allowing them to reject components which appear inappropriate or unduly onerous. It is not yet clear which way England and Wales will go. Here, we will briefly summarise the current legal position, and then consider the theoretical arguments for and against the advocacy of further contractualisation. Should marriage be made-to-measure, or must it remain, as it has been to date, off-the-peg?

Types of marital contracts

Marriage contracts can take several forms. When a married couple purchase a house, they will agree between themselves that a certain regime will apply to that property. It is usual that it be held by the spouses as joint tenants at law, on trust for themselves as joint tenants in equity.[78] An express declaration of trust to this effect will be binding on the parties. When one spouse dies, the property will pass by virtue of survivorship to the other.[79] There is rarely any possibility of a successful challenge being made to the parties' agreement as contained in the documents of title.[80] This kind of arrangement does not usually cause difficulties, as the operation of the principles of joint tenancy on death is accepted, and they have little impact as between the spouses on divorce.[81]

More controversial is the agreement entered into before marriage (called the pre-nuptial or the pre-marital contract or agreement), which may purport to regulate a whole range of matters of mutual interest to the intending spouses. In the United States, such agreements may concern issues which will arise during the marriage itself, such as the place of residence, the effect of changes of employment, the requirement or waiver of marital fidelity, the frequency of sexual activity, as well as the more conventional issues such as the holding of property and the sharing of child-care. Pre-nuptial agreements are also likely to deal with the consequences of relationship breakdown, stipulating in advance who is to have primary care for the children, what contact would be available for the other spouse, and how the accumulated wealth or debt is to be distributed in the event of divorce. It is this final respect which has attracted the attention of our legislators. Should it be possible for spouses, before or during the marriage, to make a legally binding agreement dictating how the matrimonial property is to be divided up on divorce? The argument in

---

[78] Joint tenancy is not, of course, unique to married couples.

[79] See Harpum *et al* (ed.) *Megarry & Wade: The Law of Real Property*, 6th ed. (2000, Sweet and Maxwell) at 9–13.

[80] The trust may be set aside on the grounds of fraud or mistake or a claim to rectify the title documents (for example on the basis of lack of consent) may be made: see Megarry & Wade, *The Law of Real Property*, 6th ed., 9–26.

[81] If the parties divorce, their joint ownership of the house will not fetter the discretion of the court to make whatever order it thinks fit in the exercise of its statutory powers under Part II of the Matrimonial Causes Act 1973.

favour of pre-nuptial contracts is that they can provide the parties with a freedom to dictate their own terms. On marital breakdown, the contract can be applied. The parties know where they stand. There is certainty, and less scope for dispute between the spouses, in particular about their respective rights to family property. With the destination of the family assets being otherwise determined by resort to a reallocative jurisdiction based on judicial discretion, any certainty is better than none.

The case for marital contracts

A leading proponent of contractarian marriage has been Professor Marjorie Shultz. In her major article, published in 1982, she argues the case for the promotion of marriage contracting.[82] As 'traditional marriage' did not provide the diversity which was being sought by those in intimate relationships, and as the option of total deregulation of intimacy was unrealistic, contract offered an important contribution. While by no means a panacea, in that marital contracting could not be 'all things to all marriages', nevertheless its flexibility allows appropriate variation in accordance with the parties' personalities and predispositions. Moreover, changes in the laws relating to marriage have reduced the level of public control by treating spouses as private individuals capable of separate interests, injuries and remedies and recognising that legal dispute resolution in marriage may be desirable. The developments to which she refers include the articulation of the right to privacy (in the US Supreme Court), the tolerance of diverse sexual behaviour, the growth of no-fault divorce and the retreat from the doctrine of marital unity (the 'unit theory of marriage').

The model she ultimately advocates would involve the state leaving the most substantive marital rights and obligations to be defined privately by the parties, but making the legal system available to resolve disputes arising under the privately created 'legislation'. The diversity of marriage produces compelling pressures toward private rather than public ordering of marital obligations:

> Contract offers a rich and developed tradition whose principal strength is precisely the accommodation of diverse relationships. It is designed to regulate those arenas of human interaction in which the state recognises and defers to divergent values, needs, preferences, and resources. Indeed, the deference to individual choice is strengthened, the pluralistic choices themselves legit-imised, by the state's readiness to enforce private expectations or resolve private disputes at the behest of one of the parties to the relationship.

[82] 'Contractual Ordering of Marriage: A New Model for State Policy' (1982) 70 *California Law Review* 204.

There are limits to Shultz's enthusiasm. She accepts that terms in marital contracts which deal with 'non-economic' personal matters where the invocation of the court would be inappropriate should not necessarily be enforceable. Nevertheless, she does not believe that resort to the legal process should be proscribed merely because the parties are still cohabiting.

Objections to marriage contracts

A serious objection to marriage contracts is that they undermine the institution of marriage. Expressed colloquially, marriage contracts are 'not very romantic' in that they do not accord with a romantic notion of marriage. More fundamentally, by addressing the consequences of termination at the outset, the parties are implicitly accepting that marriage is finite and that their union may well not be life-long.[83] This may give the spouses an unduly commercialist approach to their marital relationship and make them consider the severance of the matrimonial ties somewhat sooner than might otherwise be the case. It is easier to buy into divorce when the price is set in advance. As the English law considers the institution of marriage as in itself deserving of protection and support – the most recent divorce legislation laconically commences with a statement to this effect[84] – it would be overtly hypocritical to enforce contracts entered into before or during the marriage which expressly contemplated its termination by divorce. The public interest in the sustenance of marriage as a worthwhile institution is thereby invoked as a reason for rejecting its private regulation. The counter-argument can be expressed succinctly. In so far as it cannot be denied that marriage is a legal relationship, with legal consequences, it is incongruent and unduly paternalistic for the law to disallow parties to a marriage who wish to do so from addressing those consequences and, possibly with the benefit of legal advice, extend, restrict or modify them.

Another public interest of importance is the ready enforceability of private support obligations – for spouses in particular, but also children of the marriage. To permit the mutual obligation of support, which is central to the concept of marriage, to be abrogated by an express contractual stipulation may result in the financial burden of marital breakdown falling on the public purse rather than the private pocket. A basic principle underlying support of families is that the primary responsibility should lie with the spouse, or parents as the case may be, and that the welfare system is a secondary resort where the private support scheme fails. While this is a powerful objection to allowing parties ultimate freedom of regulation, a

---

[83] Brinig, *From Contract to Covenant* (2000, Harvard UP), p. 39.
[84] Family Law Act 1996, s. 1.

state which wished to endorse and enforce parties' marital contracts in this respect could do so by denying recourse to public support systems for those who had agreed to the restriction or exclusion of their spouse's continuing financial liability. Whether it would be politically acceptable would be another matter, in particular where the welfare of children required the enforcement of personal liability as parent if not as spouse. The central tenet of the United Kingdom's legislation on child support is that the parent should not be able to assign their responsibility for their children onto the taxpayer.

The utility of contract as a fair method of regulating private obligations makes certain presuppositions. Contract may be an acceptable means, provided that the parties to the contract can bargain freely and with full recognition of the rights which they are conferring, restricting, moderating or giving up. The need for full disclosure of each party's income and assets will be essential if the bargain is to be fair. Where a pre-nuptial agreement is being negotiated, typically shortly before the wedding, there may be considerable pressure on one of the spouses to come to a final agreement, as the emotional and financial consequences of postponement of the ceremony and reception would be dire. Somewhat surprisingly, this is a difficulty which Shultz hardly acknowledges. Although she concedes the potential for power disparity within a marital relationship,[85] she does not take full account of the possible consequences. Other contractarians have naively rejected rigorous application of doctrines such as undue influence, non-disclosure and misrepresentation on the basis, for instance, that parties to an intimate contract are more likely to begin with norms of fairness and a genuine concern for the other party's welfare.[86] McLellan rightly sees this as a weakness:

> Although it is only too obvious a point, it cannot be repeated too often that inequality of bargaining power means that the construction and enforcement of contracts are liable to be symptoms of such inequality rather than its remedy.[87]

The promulgation of effective marital contracts will place a considerable burden on the perspicacity and foresight of the parties' lawyers. Circumstances will change, and it will be very difficult for the parties to legislate for all eventualities. Children may be contemplated, but what about intervening incapacity, or redundancy, of one of the partners? How is the law to react to circumstances which the parties did not themselves envisage?

---

[85] *Op. cit.* n. 82, p. 332.
[86] Weitzman, *The Marriage Contract: Spouses, Lovers and the Law* (1981, Free Press), p. 242.
[87] 'Contract Marriage – the Way Forward or Dead End?' (1996) 23 *Journal of Law and Society* 234, p. 239.

It could well be that widespread adoption of marital contracts could lead to more litigation rather than less. In the United States, where they are common-place, a litigation industry surrounds them, and the lawyers win both ways. They charge for advising upon and drafting the agreement at the inception of the relationship, or whenever the parties consider such an agreement useful. They then charge for unpicking it, for challenging it through the courts, following marital breakdown, either on points of construction or by invoking one of the vitiating factors listed above.

The enforceability of marital contracts in English law

The current status of marital contracts in English law is far from clear. Before we consider further how reform might be cautiously advanced, the current law can be summarised as follows. A pre-nuptial agreement which attempts to regulate the parties' rights and obligations on termination of the marriage will be unenforceable on at least two, and possibly four, grounds.

1 The parties to the agreement did not intend to create legal relations.

2 There was no consideration provided for the pre-nuptial agreement.

3 The agreement is contrary to public policy.

4 The agreement purports to oust the jurisdiction of the court.

The first two objections can usually be dealt with by a carefully drawn agreement which asserts that the parties do intend the agreement to regulate their relationship, and which indicates that the vital contractual element of consideration is present, perhaps by the mutual exchange of undertakings. The latter two are more difficult, and it is these which usually stand in the way of enforceability. It is argued that a pre-nuptial agreement contemplating the steps the parties will take in the event of divorce is contrary to public policy as it undermines the concept of marriage as a life-long union.[88] In this, it differs from an ante-nuptial *settlement*, which seeks to regulate the parties' financial affairs on and during their marriage.[89] However, the identification of 'public policy' (an unruly horse at the best of times) is a notoriously hazardous exercise, as its character and personality appear to change with social perceptions and attitudes. If the House of Lords can take account of societal changes in determining the meaning of 'family' at the end of the twentieth century,[90]

---

[88] *N* v. *N (Jurisdiction: Pre-Nuptial Agreement)* [1999] 2 FLR 745, p. 752, *per* Wall J.

[89] *Ibid.*, p. 751.

[90] *Fitzpatrick* v. *Sterling Housing Association* [2001] AC 271. See in particular Lord Slynn at p. 38, Lord Nicholls at p. 45 and Lord Clyde at p. 49.

is it not also open to the courts to recognise that there are strong policy reasons for enforcing, or at least taking account of, attempts by spouses to set out in some detail the legal implications of their relationship? Were the parties to a relationship unmarried, and set out to determine their respective rights and obligations on the termination of the relationship, it is unlikely, possibly even unthinkable, that the courts would now refuse to enforce the contract on the grounds of public policy. Why should marriage make any difference in this respect? If there is a public interest in promoting the expeditious compromise of potentially acrimonious litigation, and if this can be done fairly with reference to the parties' own earlier voluntarily agreed terms, any reticence based on public policy seems churlish.

There is statutory recognition of the relevant public interest in section 1 of the Family Law Act 1996 (in force, albeit somewhat technically), which requires a court to have regard to the principle, where a marriage has irretrievably broken down, that it should be brought to an end with minimum distress to the parties and any children affected, with questions dealt with in a manner designed to promote as good a continuing relationship between the parties and such children, and without un-reasonable incurrence of costs. To reject out of hand a carefully negotiated and drafted pre-nuptial agreement freely entered into by the spouses would be hardly consistent with these principles. Although they can be said to have little statutory bite (in that Parts II and III of the 1996 Act, which they govern, will now never be activated), they can be seen to express public policy as identified by Parliament in the last decade of the twentieth century.[91]

The specific jurisdiction which a pre-nuptial agreement will most usually seek to 'oust' is that vested in the court by Part II of the Matrimonial Causes Act 1973 to make orders for financial provision and property adjustment on divorce, judicial separation or nullity. As long ago as 1929, Lord Hailsham stated:

> ... the power of the court to make provision for a wife on the dissolution of her marriage is a necessary incident of the power to decree such a dissolution, conferred not merely in the interests of the wife, but of the public, and ... the wife cannot by her own covenant preclude herself from invoking the jurisdiction of the court or to preclude the court from the exercise of that jurisdiction.'[92]

---

[91] On the other hand, the same section 1 emphasises that it is the duty of the court to support the institution of marriage. If the 'institution' refers to the traditional concept of marriage as a contract the terms of which are immutably set in stone, in other words a state-imposed standard-form contract which the parties can take or leave in its entirety but which cannot be varied at their behest, then the argument is more difficult to advance.

[92] *Hyman v. Hyman* [1929] AC 601, p. 614.

This causes more difficulty than the public policy argument, and it is anticipated that legislative amendment would be necessary if agreements were to be rendered truly enforceable. At present, even agreements to compromise property proceedings ancillary to divorce ('divorce agreements') require the sanction of the court by way of consent order before true enforceability is achieved. The court, in making such an order, is exercising an active discretion, for which purpose full information of the parties' financial positions must be placed before it. The parties' autonomy to make effective agreements is thus seriously restricted. But it is one thing to say an agreement is not enforceable – it is quite another to say that an agreement is irrelevant. Experience with separation agreements has shown a readiness on the part of the courts to examine the terms of such agreements, together with all surrounding circumstances, and to decide whether an order could or should be made along those lines.[93] This, as we will see, is one possible way in which courts could view pre-nuptial agreements.

The case for reform

The challenge for our marriage laws is to cope with variety and to permit flexibility where possible, yet at the same time to ensure that spouses are not exploited or taken advantage of. In 1998, the Lord Chancellor sought the advice of the Ancillary Relief Advisory Group on applying a presumption of an equal division of property between spouses on divorce[94] and the possibility of making pre-nuptial agreements legally binding. The objective of the Government was pragmatic. The system of ancillary relief on divorce was perceived as being productive of too much uncertainty, and the challenge for the review was to balance greater certainty with fairness and justice to all concerned.

The submission of the judges of the Family Division of the High Court to the Advisory Group is illuminating. They agreed as one to a lack of enthusiasm for pre-nuptial agreements which they considered to be in 'profoundly difficult terrain'. They expressed reservations on the effect of such agreements on the stability of the marriage they were seeking to regulate, in that they might condition the couple to the failure of their marriage and thereby help to precipitate it. They recognised that both pre-nuptial agreements and post-nuptial agreements would be likely to be entered into at a moment of 'extreme emotional susceptibility' (just prior to marriage, soon after final marital breakdown, or possibly at the time of post-marital reconciliation), and therefore identified the need for protection of the parties:

---

[93] *Edgar* v. *Edgar* [1981] FLR 19.
[94] See now *White* v. *White* [2000] 3 WLR 1571.

> We are clear that, if it were to have any effect in law, the nuptial agreement would need to have been preceded by not only full financial disclosure but also separate legal advice on each side; and we presume that state-funded legal advice would in principle be available for this purpose. But [they warned] it is the emotional moment when legal advice is most easily brushed aside. Hard cases would fall through this safety-net. We doubt whether any system of registration would narrow the mesh.

The judges were split on the role marital contracts should play in the process of ancillary relief on divorce. The majority felt that the terms of any agreement reached in contemplation of or subsequent to marriage should be expressed as a matter to which the court, in exercising its powers in the ancillary relief process, should have regard. It is doubtful whether this would significantly alter the existing law, although it would provide useful clarification of the position. The minority was in favour of contract having somewhat greater importance, in that a marital contract which satisfied certain elementary requirements should be enforceable 'unless' there were good reasons to depart from it. These reasons were not listed. It would be safe to assume that material change of circumstances since the date of the agreement would suffice to rebut the presumption of enforceability. The difficulty would then be identifying what was material and what was not.

It is interesting to note that the Bar and the Law Society took opposing views on marital contracts in the consultation exercise. The Bar considered that giving greater emphasis to pre-nuptial agreements would create as many problems as it would solve. The public policy argument against enforceability, that such agreements contemplate separation or divorce at a time when the parties should be thinking about the permanence of their marriage, was a valid one. Amendment of section 25 was unnecessary as if and in so far as an agreement departed dramatically from the likely result of exercise of discretion there would be an inevitable dispute between the parties. Indeed, the pre-nuptial agreement would add a further dimension for the parties to argue over, as challenges on the fullness of consent to the agreement were made. The Law Society supported the enforceability of pre-nuptial agreements in principle, but recognised the problem of time lapse and consequential changed circumstances. One possibility was to provide for an entitlement to either party to demand a review, perhaps on giving notice to the other, or to stipulate that the agreement automatically lapses on the occurrence of certain events such as the birth of a child or intervening mental or physical disability. The Advisory Group reported back to the Lord Chancellor in these somewhat divided terms. Further developments are awaited.

The intended advantage in terms of efficiency of the promotion of marital contracts is that they would in most cases result in less resort to litigation following breakdown of a marriage. A policy that 'stressed individual responsibility and the desirability of ordering the future by agreement rather than by belated litigation' is, in theory at least, sound.[95] However, the danger recognised by those practising in the field is that the acrimony of a matrimonial split would lead spouses to challenge the marital contracts which they had previously entered into as the courts advanced another policy – that of protecting the vulnerable. The experience of the last ten years or so in relation to the employment of the defences of undue influence, duress and misrepresentation to mortgagee possession actions indicates that the potential of such claims is very great indeed.[96] The hope that widespread use of marital contracts will lead to a decrease in contested litigation may be little more than a dream. Nevertheless, the conferment of power on the parties to come to their own agreement is consistent with an approach to marriage advocating autonomy and free will, indeed permitting unilateral termination of the marital relationship when either party so desires. Conceptually, the generous recognition and rigorous enforcement of marital contracts is consistent with a system of no-fault divorce.

Looking further into the future: where next with divorce?

'I think divorce is underrated. It gives you insights into some of the trickier aspects of marriage, the more delicate nuances as it were, that couples who've been happy together for thirty years wouldn't begin to grasp.'

(John Cleese)[97]

Divorce is the termination by the state of the legal relationship of marriage between two individuals. Although the state has limited opportunity to control the conduct of those individuals while they are married, the necessity for its sanction in the grant of divorce results in a retention of significant power over the parties. This power can be utilised to advance interests of the state such as the upbringing of children and in the continuing provision of private support so that the financial burden does not fall by default on the public purse. This power, although not exclusive to married couples, allows the state to intervene in relation to the children and the family property to an extent which is not politically tenable where the partners have not been married. The parties' public acceptance of the legal status of marriage provides the state both with justification to act and with a means of readily identifying the status of the relationship.

A recurring question across all jurisdictions is whether parties should be free to terminate their marriage when they wish to do so, or whether the

---

[95] See Report of Lord Chancellor's Advisory Group, chaired by Thorpe LJ, at p. 27.
[96] See further text by n. 74 above.
[97] Skynner and Cleese, *Families and How to Survive Them* (1993, Arrow), p. 16.

state should exercise control not only over the consequences of marital termination but also over the termination itself. Marriage being the voluntary union of a man and a woman, should consent remain central to the issue of its termination, in the sense that the unilateral wish of one partner to terminate the marriage should be conclusive? Although voluntariness is central to a properly functioning marital relationship, and there is now a proper refusal to impute consent to sexual intercourse from the marriage ceremony, the spouses are also fully aware, in entering into their voluntary union, that terminating the marriage is more complicated and that there will be legal repercussions. There is one very clear limitation on state power in this respect. It cannot require two people to live together. If one decides that they can no longer live with the other, and leaves the matrimonial home, there is little the deserted spouse can do about it. Should the law follow the fact – and termination of the marriage follow as a matter of course from marital breakdown – or should there be some resistance built into the system, so that divorce does not inexorably follow? If divorce is rendered more difficult, one argument goes, there is a greater chance that parties will invest more into the marriage or into the reconciliation process. In deciding whether to adopt a divorce law which is permissive or restrictive a variety of factors will be relevant, predominant among which, it would appear, is the extent to which the state wishes to support marriage.

A permissive divorce law respects the autonomy of the parties to regulate the legal status of their own relationship. Typically, it involves divorce on unilateral demand and there is no requirement (or opportunity) for either party to impute fault to the other. In a 'pure' no-fault system such as California, where one spouse asserts that 'irreconcilable differences have caused the irretrievable breakdown of the marriage', this results in a shift of power from the party who wants continuance of the marriage to the party who wants the divorce.[98] In consequence, the state is giving minimal support to the marriage, and by denying the spouses an opportunity to articulate their views of the proposed termination, or indeed their respective conduct during the marriage, the public interest in marriage as an institution is diminished and devalued. As the leading commentator on no-fault divorce has said:

> When the new law abolished the concept of fault, it also eliminated the framework of guilt, innocence and interpersonal justice that had structured court decisions in divorce cases. With this seemingly simple move, the California legislature not only vanquished the law's moral condemnation of marital misconduct; it also dramatically altered the legal definition of the reciprocal obligations of husbands and wives during marriage.'[99]

[98] Weitzman, *The Divorce Revolution* (1985, Free Press), p. 43.
[99] *Ibid.*, p. 22.

There has been extensive research investigating the effect of permissive divorce laws on the divorce rate. In her recent book,[100] Margaret Brinig, analysing the evidence from a law-and-economics angle, concludes that there is some evidence that no-fault divorce regimes have led to increased levels of divorce. The reduction in transaction costs and alimony penalties consequent upon marital misconduct in such regimes made divorce a more appealing option than elsewhere. Ruth Deech considers that the liberalisation of divorce laws in this country has had a snowball effect. Each time the law is reformed, more individuals see divorce as the solution to their marital problems, more evince a willingness to use it, and the resultant pressure on the court system requires further relaxation of practices and procedures.[101] But others have contended that the meteoric rise in divorce rates in the 1970s and 1980s had commenced before divorce reform was instigated, and that such legislation was at least in part a response to that increase rather than a cause of it.[102]

If the support of marriage is an objective which the state wishes to promote, it will tend to lead to the promulgation of restrictive divorce laws, the denial of the easy exit afforded by a no-fault system, and typically the requirement that there be evidence of a breach of marital obligation. Some claim that such a system is fairer and that it promotes justice between the parties.[102] If marriage is a contract, the obligations of which have been broken, the only truly effective legal recourse is through the divorce court. If the divorce court denies the significance of a breach of a marital obligation, then the marriage contract is itself illusory. It is only just, therefore, that some recognition of fault should take place on divorce. Others would resist such a conclusion. The personal cost of making fault allegations is substantial and significant. While it may be frustrating to an apparently 'faultless' spouse that they have no opportunity to establish their 'innocence' and to make recriminations of their former partner, the court cannot realistically investigate the history of each and every marriage which breaks down, and it is highly undesirable that it should do so.

As Michael Freeman said in 1996 (and it is even more true now than then) divorce in England is at a crossroads.[104] Since the reform of the

---

[100] *From Contract to Covenant* (2000, Harvard) pp. 153–158.

[101] (1994) *Family Law* 121. See also Deech, 'Divorce Law and Empirical Studies', (1990) 106 *Law Quarterly Review* 229.

[102] Richards, 'Divorce Numbers and Divorce Legislation' [1996] *Family Law* 151.

[103] Trainor (1992) 9 *Journal of Applied Philosophy* 135, reproduced in *Family State and Law I*, ed. M. Freeman, p. 259.

[104] See Freeman, 'Divorce: Contemporary Problems and Future Prospects' in Freeman (ed.) *Divorce: Where Next?* (1996, Dartmouth), p. 1: 'Divorce in England today stands at a crossroads although perhaps, like roadsigns in Roman times, all routes point to the same destination.' This opening to this fascinating collection of essays on the future of divorce was written at a time when divorce reform along the lines of what became Part II of the Family Law Act 1996 was a virtual certainty.

divorce laws in 1969, the courts have applied a hybrid system which incorporates both fault and no-fault elements. A person seeking divorce is required to establish that the marriage has irretrievably broken down by proof of one of five 'facts'. Three of these are fault-based, and are derived from the former 'matrimonial offences': the respondent has committed adultery and the petitioner finds it intolerable to live with him or her; the respondent's behaviour is such that the petitioner cannot reasonably be expected to live with him or her; or the respondent has deserted the petitioner for a period of two years. Two are 'no-fault', each being based on the parties' separation: two years' separation with the respondent's consent, or five years if that consent is withheld. The expectation, when these reforms were enacted, was that parties would elect to petition on the basis of separation, and that 'no-fault' divorce would become the norm. Indeed, the divorce reforms of 1969 were seen by the judiciary as signalling the demise of the matrimonial offence and the evaluation of conduct in the matrimonial proceedings. According to Lord Denning, capturing as ever the flavour of the moment, divorce now (in 1972) carried 'no stigma, but only sympathy. It is a misfortune which befalls both. No longer is one guilty and the other innocent.'[105]

But the hope that 'no-fault' divorce would become generally used was not realised. The danger with a hybrid divorce law such as that of 1969 was that parties would use whichever route was the most effective to satisfy their personal needs. The no-fault route based on a period of separation was inevitably slower. The introduction of the 'special procedure' in the late 1970s only served to emphasise the advantages of founding a petition on (in particular) adultery or behaviour. A petitioner no longer had to give oral evidence of the reasons for the failure of their marriage. Affidavits and written particulars now sufficed, and only the decree itself would be delivered in court. By articulating allegations of fault, a petitioner can obtain a divorce expeditiously, but at the same time do untold damage to the continuing relations of the parties following divorce, which, where children are involved, is a particularly invidious aspect of the existing regime.

Criticism of the impact of the special procedure led to a reconsideration of the divorce laws by the Law Commission from 1988 onwards. The system was criticised for being confusing, misleading and unfair. The coincidence of fault and no-fault was thought to be unsatisfactory, as was the encouragement indirectly given to parties to rely on allegations of misconduct. It was particularly inappropriate that the law encouraged one party to blame another but then, as a result of the 'special procedure' and its discouragement of contesting divorce, all but denied that other the opportunity to rebut the allegations. The conflict ensuing from mutual

---

[105] *Wachtel v. Wachtel* [1973] Fam 72, p. 89.

blame and recrimination made reconciliation more difficult than necessary and ran the risk of positively harming the children. The solution was not, however, straightforward. Simple removal of the fault grounds, leading to reliance on a fixed minimum period of separation alone, was problematical and discriminatory, as those in receipt of smaller incomes would find it more difficult to secure alternative housing resources and thereby surmount the necessary threshold.

On a positive note, the reform proposals contained a new vision of a divorce process which expected parties to work out their future arrangements before their marriage terminated (thereby giving them a licence to remarry and to complicate further their affairs). This vision saw a role for mediation as a form of alternative dispute resolution which would make lawyers, seen by some as bearing responsibility for increasing acrimony on divorce, less important and which would encourage communication between the spouses on vital questions such as the welfare of the children and continuing financial support. As long as the divorce proceedings commenced with allegations of fault, they were ill-suited to the expeditious and informed resolution of the parties' respective futures by reference to mediation. If this particular mode of case management was to function effectively, a different kind of divorce process was essential.

Thus, the 1996 divorce reform comprised an ambitious attempt by its proponents to promote a 'pure' no-fault system and concurrently to support the institution of marriage. These seemingly contradictory objectives were to be attained by radical reform of the divorce process. The ground of divorce, that is irretrievable breakdown of marriage, was not to be changed. It was, however, to be proved in a different way. Either or both parties were to make a statement of marital breakdown, following which a period of time (for 'reflection and consideration') would elapse. If the divorce was still desired at the end of the period, and if the parties had made arrangements for the future concerning their children and their property, an application could be made to the court for an appropriate order. This is of course a grotesque over-simplification of divorce by a process (memorably described as a 'convoluted procedural gavotte' by one commentator[106]) which promised to make far more extensive demands of the parties than the current divorce laws. Although the making of allegations was to cease, divorce would not become any easier and in most cases the time from instigating the process to obtaining the divorce order would be considerably longer than at present.

The reform proposals included provision for better quality information for the spouses before the process was initiated by service of a statement of

---

[106] Gwyn Davis, 'Researching Publicly Funded Mediation', p. 44, in Thorpe LJ and E. Clarke (eds) *No Fault or Flaw – the Future of the Family Law Act 1996* (2000, Jordans).

marital breakdown. This raised the intensely political question of what information should be provided, and how it should be communicated, to the parties contemplating divorce. It would be necessary to discover how the procedures operated, how disputes about the children and the property were to be resolved, and the role to be played in that process by mediation. Even more controversial was what the parties were to be told about the emotional consequences of divorce, the extent to which they were to be encouraged to seek marriage guidance before starting the divorce process, and how they were to be routed into use of mediation services. 'Information is seldom value-free',[107] and there was confusion as to whether information was different from persuasion.[108]

How the information was to be provided was another concern for the Government. Proposals ranged from individual interviews to group sessions with video presentations as parties attempted to work out a means which would involve the uniform and objective provision of useful information but which did not involve the giving of advice. Standardisation of the information to be given was inevitable, but no blueprint for the delivery of an individual meeting (the ultimately preferred option) was ever provided by Government. From June 1997 onwards, various schemes for the provision of information were piloted, testing various models, and evaluation reports were presented to the Lord Chancellor's Department. The preliminary results of these reports were instrumental in the decision, announced in June 1999, not to implement Part II of the Family Law Act 1996 for the time being. The Lord Chancellor described the results as 'disappointing, in view of the Government's objectives of saving saveable marriages and encouraging the mediated settlements of disputes.' The Final Evaluation Report was presented to the Lord Chancellor in September 2000. In January 2001, the Lord Chancellor stated:

> The Government is committed to supporting marriage and to supporting families when relationships fail, especially when there are children involved. But this very comprehensive research, together with other recent valuable research in the field, has shown that Part II of the Family Law Act is not the best way of achieving those aims. The Government is not therefore satisfied that it would be right to proceed with the implementation of Part II and proposes to ask Parliament to repeal it once a suitable legislative opportunity occurs.

The divorce reforms of 1996 never received universal support from commentators. The dual object of supporting the institution of marriage and providing a workable regime for divorce was always going to be difficult to achieve, and experience in the information meeting pilots so

---

[107] Walker, 'Information Meetings Revisited' [2000] *Family Law* 330.
[108] Walker, *ibid.*, p. 332.

proved, the evaluation suggesting that 'saving marriages is an objective distinct from securing civilised divorce.'[109] It remains unclear how support of the institution of marriage can be most effectively achieved.[110] The reservations of Dr Stephen Cretney[111] were shared by many. The role of mediation in the divorce process, and how parties were to be 'encouraged' to use such services, was never fully articulated. The idea of a period for 'reflection and consideration' was laudable, but wholly unenforceable. As Dr Cretney wryly remarks, that time might be spent, far more pleasurably, in conceiving further children or in brooding on grievances:

> It is in concealing the reality – that divorce is to be available at the unilateral wish of either party, behind a comforting façade of consideration, reflection, reconciliation and counselling – that the government's proposals are most vulnerable to the charge of perpetuating the tradition of hypocrisy and humbug.[112]

Following the Lord Chancellor's decision in June 1999 to postpone implementation of Part II, an inter-disciplinary conference on family law was held at Dartington Hall, attended by judges, legal practitioners, social scientists, psychiatrists, marriage counsellors and mediators, on the subject of the future of divorce. The papers, published as *No Fault or Flaw: The Future of the Family Law Act 1996*, present a comprehensive survey of the problems encountered in the information pilots, how marriage support can co-exist with divorce reform, the difficulties faced in the promotion of an effective mediation service for divorcing spouses, the protection of children on divorce, and the respective roles of lawyers and judiciary. It is impossible to do justice to the variety of arguments and the richness of debate but resort should be had to the discussion by those who consider the next moves to be taken in the interests of divorce reform. There is an invaluable summary by Lady Justice Hale, entitled *The Way Forward*, setting out the resolutions of the various parties represented at the conference.

There was unanimous support for the speedy introduction of no fault divorce. While many felt that amending legislation was desirable, the general feeling was that it would be better to have the present legislation and to make it work rather than have no change at all. The provision of good quality information, well before any proceedings were brought by anyone, was also felt to be essential, as much for the children as for the

---

[109] Walker, *ibid.*, p. 333.
[110] McCarthy, Walker and Hooper, 'Saving Marriage – A Role for Divorce Law?' [2000] *Family Law* 412.
[111] See in particular Cretney, 'Divorce Reform: Humbug and Hypocrisy or a Smooth Transition?' in Freeman (ed.) *Divorce: Where Next?* (1996, Dartmouth).
[112] At p. 52.

spouses themselves, and the emphasis was on the flexibility of the ways in which information might be provided. There was a broad acceptance that mediation services should be widely available and well publicised, and be properly funded, organised and regulated with a uniform set of standards and code of practice. There was considerably less enthusiasm for the role of the court in relation to the children of divorcing couples, partly as it was difficult for the court to identify, on the basis of the limited information before it, which cases called for intervention using the powers of the Children Act 1989, but partly as there were other agencies which could deal with the problem more effectively. Parenting plans were considered valuable tools for parents to construct the agreements they wished to make for their children. Consideration of legal services saw lawyers defending the value of specialist legal services, but there was also support for accreditation schemes as a requirement of practice in the field.

In her concluding comments, Lady Justice Hale emphasised that any divorce law should be seen as providing a service ('the clearest message to come out of this conference'), and that that service could and should be improved. Information and mediation services are provided to help people, not to preach at them, and children need to be considered as real people and 'active participants rather than passive recipients' of the decisions of adults. She was particularly critical of the diversity of court processes, illustrating how a divorcing couple could go through five separate sets of proceedings in five different venues according to five different timetables, causing confusion, anxiety, distress and expense, and articulated the need for a comprehensive procedure which could be employed by all families to resolve all the problems which they need the court to resolve in a way which suits the needs of the particular family.[113] She concluded:

> The present system allows and even encourages the parties to spend a quite disproportionate amount of their resources (or the resources of the legal aid fund which will usually be recouped from them) upon legal proceedings. Small wonder that many of those who have been through it once are reluctant to risk it again by remarrying. More and more young people are choosing to postpone or even reject marriage altogether. It may already be too late to halt that trend, but they are deluding themselves if they think that living together without marriage carries any less risk of legal proceedings. If anything, their problems are even more complex. The price of keeping the individualised discretionary approach to resolving family problems is that we must make the process as genuinely user friendly and as cost effective as we possibly can. Proportionality should be our watchword here as everywhere else in the civil justice system.

[113] The five issues she was considering were regulating the occupation of the family home, obtaining a decree of divorce or judicial separation, applying for contact residence or other orders about the children's upbringing, applying for financial provision or property adjustment and applying for child support.

Marriage in the twenty-first century

Although English divorce law remains in a state of flux, it is highly likely that within the first decade of this century, legislation will finally introduce a system based on no-fault termination of marriage. Such reform would respect the individuals' right of autonomy by permitting them to withdraw from the marriage whenever they wished to do so. Consistent with this approach would be the enforcement of marital contracts, thereby conferring power on the parties to regulate their own relationship and the various consequences to which it might give rise. This willingness to embrace diversity and to advance individual choice would lead some to question whether marriage as an institution can survive, or at least to advance the argument of Professor Clive to the effect that such a radical dilution of the basic foundations of marriage should inexorably lead to the removal of its automatic legal consequences.[114]

The vision of marriage being thus advanced no longer accords with a life-long mutual commitment to cohabitation and the wider sharing of lives and families. It would recognise that while there might be an initial statement of intent that the relationship be long-lasting, even life-long, marriage would provide a legal bond which either spouse could enter and leave with relative, possibly absolute, freedom, and the terms of which could be dictated by the parties themselves. Opponents would claim that this would do untold damage to the 'institution of marriage'. But despite the statutory acknowledgement of the 'institution of marriage' in the Family Law Act 1996, there is as yet no statutory definition of what this elusive phrase means. One difficulty with marriage as an 'institution' is that it suggests something which is essentially retrospective and reactive rather than forward-looking and pro-active. A requirement that the courts support the institution of marriage is thereby to perpetuate an existing state of affairs rather than to innovate or to move on. Another problem can be identification of what actually comprises support. In *Vervaeke* v. *Smith*[115] a female Belgian national went through a ceremony of marriage in a London Register Office with a male British national, paying him £50 and the price of a one-way ticket to South Africa to which he intended permanently to emigrate. She intended to use the British nationality thus acquired to provide her with immunity from deportation for plying her trade as a prostitute. This 'morally reprehensible' transaction was viewed quite differently by the English and the Belgian courts. In English law, once it was established that the parties were free to marry one another, that they had consented to the marriage, and that they had observed the necessary formalities, the marriage was valid – any mental reservations

---

[114] See text by n. 28.
[115] [1983] 1 AC 145.

were wholly irrelevant.[116] As a matter of Belgian law (in accordance with most analogous civil law jurisdictions), 'the disturbance of public order, the protection of what belongs to the essence of a real marriage and of human dignity, exact that such a sham-marriage be declared invalid.'[117] Both jurisdictions could fairly claim that their reaction to the circumstances amounted to support of the institution of marriage, yet their respective reactions would lead to diametrically opposite conclusions.

The ambivalence of the notion of supporting the institution of marriage may well mean that further development of the concept, if not the institution, of marriage may be more effectively promoted by other means – most likely by invocation of the European Convention on Human Rights. The United Kingdom has not yet ratified Article 5 of the Seventh Protocol of the European Convention on Human Rights,[118] which provides:

> Spouses shall enjoy equality of rights and responsibilities of a private law character between them, and in their relations with their children, as to marriage, and in the event of its dissolution. This Article shall not prevent states from taking such measures as are necessary in the interests of children.

The Protocol was temporarily omitted from the impact of the Human Rights Act 1998, as it was felt that certain provisions of domestic law were not (and could not be interpreted as being) compatible, in particular the common law duty of a husband to maintain his wife where there is no reciprocal duty imposed on the wife and the presumption of advancement (that a husband transferring property to his wife makes a gift, whereas no gift will be presumed in the case of a transfer from the wife to the husband).[119] A further difficulty anticipated was the jurisdiction of the divorce court to reallocate property between the spouses which, at least in England and Wales,[120] does not proceed on the basis of equal division of assets. As a result, the government decided not to implement Article 5 until legislation had removed the various inconsistencies.[121]

---

[116] [1983] 1 AC 145, p. 152, *per* Lord Hailsham of St Marylebone, applying *Brodie* v. *Brodie* [1917] P 271.

[117] [1983] 1 AC 145, p. 153.

[118] See Swindells *et al, op. cit.* n. 4, 241 *et seq.*

[119] Two statutory provisions felt to be incompatible with Article 5 are the Married Women's Property Act 1882 and the Married Women's Property Act 1964 (s. 1, dealing with housekeeping allowances), both of which operate in such a way as to prefer wives over husbands.

[120]   Cf. Scotland: Family Law (Scotland) Act 1985, s. 10 provides that the net value of matrimonial property shall be taken to be shared fairly between the parties to the marriage when it is shared equally or in such other proportions as are justified by special circumstances.

[121] White Paper: *Rights Brought Home*, para. 4.15.

Although the government has yet to introduce Article 5 into the domestic law, the idea of marriage as a partnership of equals has already proved attractive to the courts. In *White* v. *White*[122] Lord Nicholls of Birkenhead, giving the leading speech, advanced the cause of spousal equality, asserting that 'the one principle of universal application which can be stated with confidence' is that in seeking to achieve a fair outcome on divorce:

> ... there is no place for discrimination between husband and wife and their respective roles. Typically, a husband and wife share the activities of earning money, running their home and caring for their children. Traditionally, the husband earned the money, and the wife looked after the home and the children. This traditional division of labour is no longer the order of the day ... If, in their different spheres, each contributed equally to the family, then in principle it matters not which of them earned the money and built up the assets. There should be no bias in favour of the money-earner and against the home-maker and the child-carer.[123]

Lord Nicholls denies that a presumption of equal division can be legitimately applied in ancillary relief hearings, or that equality should comprise a 'starting-point', as such activism would be going beyond the permissible bounds of statutory interpretation and would involve 'an impermissible judicial gloss' on section 25 of the Matrimonial Causes Act 1973. One wonders, though, to what extent this argument is semantic. It will surely matter little to the ultimate outcome whether the principle of equality is a presumption, a starting point, or a yardstick against which the proposed order is to be measured.

Nevertheless, the equality principle is inherently attractive. It promotes a vision of marriage which accords respect to the partners as autonomous individuals neither of whom is subservient to the other. It is perfectly consistent with the enforceability of marriage contracts which recognise the ability of the partners to deal with each other and to make provision for the proper regulation of their future relationship. At the same time, it presents a satisfactory and pragmatic basis upon which division of assets following divorce can take place in those cases where no contract is operative to dictate the destination of the marital property. The question which will continue to be asked in the years to come is the extent to which this new vision of marriage should be restricted to those couples who conform to the legal stereotype – or whether any such restriction is in itself a denial of those human rights which the courts are now pledged to recognise and assert.

---

[122] [2000] 3 WLR 1571.
[123] [2000] 3 WLR 1571, p. 1578.

Further reading

Bamforth, 'Sexual Orientation Discrimination after *Grant* v *South West Trains* (2000) 63 *Modern Law Review* 694.

Brinig, *From Contract to Covenant* (2000, Harvard UP).

Clive, 'Marriage: an unnecessary legal concept?' in Eekelaar and Katz (eds), *Marriage and Cohabitation in Contemporary Societies* (1980, Butterworth).

Deech, 'Divorce Law and Empirical Studies', (1990) 106 *Law Quarterly Review* 229.

Forder, 'Opening Up Marriage to Same Sex Partners and Providing for Adoption by Same Sex Couples, Managing Information on Sperm Donors, and Lots of Private International Law' in Bainham (ed.) *International Survey of Family Law 2000* (2000, Jordans).

Freeman, 'Divorce: Contemporary Problems and Future Prospects' in Freeman (ed.) *Divorce: Where Next?* (1996, Dartmouth).

Hale, 'The Family Law Act 1996 – the death of marriage?' in Caroline Bridge (ed.), *Family Law Towards the Millennium* (1997, Butterworth).

McCarthy, Walker and Hooper, 'Saving Marriage – A Role for Divorce Law?' [2000] *Family Law* 412.

McLellan, 'Contract Marriage – the Way Forward or Dead End?' (1996) 23 *Journal of Law and Society* 234.

Probert and Barlow, 'Displacing marriage – diversification and harmonisation within Europe', (2000) 12 *Child and Family Law Quarterly* 153.

Shultz, 'Contractual Ordering of Marriage: A New Model for State Policy' (1982) 70 *California Law Review* 204.

Thorpe LJ and E. Clarke (eds) *No Fault or Flaw – the Future of the Family Law Act 1996* (2000, Jordans).

Weitzman, *The Divorce Revolution* (1985, Free Press).

2

Division of property upon relationship breakdown

Louise Tee

Introduction

One of the most pressing, and intractable, problems facing family law reformers today is to determine how property should be divided upon relationship breakdown. The difficulties are manifold. The extraordinary rate of social change over the last forty years has resulted in an increasingly diverse range of family and informal living arrangements. This, together with evolving ideas of 'fairness' and 'justice', poses fundamental challenges to a body of property and matrimonial law that was developed in more rigid and certain times. Property division upon divorce and upon the break-up of cohabitants now engenders serious political and theoretical debate as to the appropriate role and extent of the law in this area – what it should be trying to achieve, and how.

It is not, of course, only commentators who are concerned. The injury accompanying the insult of a relationship breakdown is that two households are more expensive to provide and maintain than one. This sad fact means that, for all but the super-rich (and sometimes even for them), the collapse of a relationship generally entails an unwelcome fall in standard of living for at least one, if not both, of the parties.[1] A further problem is that there is often little consensus between the parties themselves as to what constitutes a fair settlement. The result is that whether the couple has been married, and so is able to call upon the court's discretionary powers, or whether the couple has cohabited, and are thus

---

[1] Most empirical research suggests that it is usually the woman who suffers a fall in the standard of living after divorce: Perry *et al, How Parents Cope Financially on Marriage Breakdown* (2000, Family Policy Studies Centre). However, Braver, 'The Gender Gap in Standard of Living After Divorce: Vanishingly Small?' (1999) 33 *Family Law Quarterly* 111, argues that (for the USA) the statistics do not support this supposed gender distinction and that both parties suffer economically.

reliant upon general, sometimes obscure, common law principles, dividing the property upon relationship breakdown is rarely accomplished without distress and anger. The role of the law in such an emotional minefield is inevitably subject to intense scrutiny, and often criticism, by the parties involved, and this only adds further urgency to the academic debate as to the law's appropriate function and purpose.

Commentators have responded to the challenge, and property distribution has become a focus around which different arguments and conceptual models revolve. With so little certainty as to even fundamental issues, and so many different models of reform possible, the result is a rich and lively debate which continues unabated.

The relevance of a marriage certificate

When couples break up, the scope of the law which is available to them to help solve property disputes depends solely upon whether or not they were married. For while a former spouse can apply to the court under the Matrimonial Causes Act 1973 and take advantage of the wide range of redistributive powers that are at a judge's disposal, a former cohabiting partner has no such opportunity. For her, statutory powers are very limited[2] and in effect she is reliant upon the common law to determine questions of ownership. And an immediate question is whether such a fundamental distinction can be justified? Why should the presence or otherwise of a marriage certificate affect the distribution of property upon relationship break up? The question brings into focus the issue of the role of law and the balance between the public and the private. There is a legitimate argument that those couples who have eschewed marriage should be allowed to order their private affairs as they wish, and that the state should respect their autonomy and not interfere by imposing undesired norms of behaviour. According to this argument, it is perfectly appropriate for ordinary principles of property law to govern cohabitants' property entitlement – the fact that the couple may have enjoyed an emotional and personal relationship which has now ended is quite irrelevant and of no public concern. Such an attitude has its roots deep in the liberalism that underlies English legal theory and which values privacy and restraints upon government power.[3]

---

[2] Schedule 1 to the Children Act 1989 allows property adjustment orders for a child's benefit, but the courts have, so far, proved reluctant to exercise their extended powers. Pt. II of Sch. 7 to the Family Law Act 1996 allows the courts to transfer a tenancy of a family home to a heterosexual cohabitant. See Bridge, 'Transferring Tenancies of the Family Home' [1998] *Family Law* 26.

[3] O'Donovan, *Sexual Divisions in Law* (1985, Weidenfeld and Nicolson), 205.

Another viewpoint, which also supports the distinction, is rather less liberal in its credentials, and is certainly espoused more vocally, at least by the tabloid press and certain politicians. This is the idea that the status of marriage should be favoured legally, in order to encourage and support 'family values'. The obverse of this is that cohabitants should not enjoy such favoured status, and so should not, for example, be able to enjoy the fruits of judicial redistribution of property. This defensive and protective attitude towards marriage and concomitant disapproval of cohabitation showed itself most clearly in the furore over the Family Homes and Domestic Violence Bill and the Family Law Bill in 1995 and 1996, when attempts to widen the ambit of judicial discretion to include unmarried couples were condemned as undermining the institution of marriage, and the very stability of society itself. To what extent the outcry really reflected contemporary social attitudes is unclear. The widespread prevalence of cohabitation suggests that the public is not as opposed to its existence as some of the more extreme supporters of family values would have us believe, but politicians are well aware of the political pitfalls in this area, and tread warily.

A contrary view is that it is appropriate for the state to concern itself in the question of property distribution upon relationship breakdown, regardless of whether or not the couple were married. This view can be labelled 'paternalistic' – Bailey-Harris, who espouses this approach, calls herself 'a legal maternalist'.[4] It is no coincidence that Bailey-Harris has also advocated a return to functionalist analysis within family law. A functionalist identifies the purpose of a law, and then evaluates the present law in relation to the purpose which it is trying to fulfil. Of course, there are often many difficulties in identifying a purpose or purposes, and this is where a functionalist approach can be criticised. But if one is to interpret the purpose of the adjustive powers of the court under the Matrimonial Causes Act 1973 as to promote fairness and equity between couples who are going their separate ways after a shared life, then there seems no compelling reason why such fairness should also not apply to couples who have similarly shared a joint life, but without a marriage certificate.

This argument is strengthened by the evidence that many cohabitants view themselves as 'common law wives' or 'husbands'[5] and assume that they are entitled to just the same 'legal rights' of maintenance and property transfer as any married couple upon divorce. They can be shocked to discover that they are not.

---

[4] Bailey-Harris, 'Dividing the Assets on Breakdown of Relationships Outside Marriage', in Bailey-Harris (ed.), *Dividing the Assets on Family Breakdown* (1998, Family Law).

[5] McRae, *Cohabiting Mothers: Changing Marriage and Motherhood* (1993, Policy Studies Institute); Pickford, *Fathers, Marriage and the Law* (1999, Family Policy Studies Centre).

And this shows how the crucial questions about the role of law and the balance between the public and the private can be reformulated to fit within the prevailing 'rights' discourse. In this context, the fundamental question is whether these 'legal rights' should be awarded to couples purely on the basis that they have been in a relationship, or whether such rights should only be accorded to those heterosexual couples who have acquired the special status of marriage. There is an economic dimension to this question – which is especially pressing in view of the attempted retrenchment of the welfare state – because the present lack of any duty for (former) cohabitants to maintain each other (only their children) may result in some additional burden on the public purse. There is also a difficult philosophical aspect. If rights are to be awarded on account of a relationship, what type of relationship qualifies? Is a sexual element – whether heterosexual or homosexual – essential, or do other close emotional relationships count? Where does one draw the line?

For several years now the Law Commission has been promising a consultation paper on home-sharing, and no doubt these issues will be addressed when the paper is finally published. In the meantime, and although commentators are increasingly advocating a less rigid distinction between the married and the unmarried when it comes to property division, the world (well, England and Wales) is still divided into the unmarried and the married when considering property questions upon relationship breakdown.

Property law for cohabitants

Land law

It is, of course, the ownership of the house that is often the most pressing property issue upon a relationship breakdown.[6] The house, as home, also represents a profound emotional investment for a couple, and so the question of who will receive what share can achieve a significance well beyond the strictly financial. Such an attitude towards land, that it is special, indeed 'unique', is not new; and indeed it is precisely because the social and political as well as economic importance of land has been well recognised for centuries that special rules have developed concerning its ownership. Thus an unmarried couple in the process of extricating themselves from a relationship may well find themselves wrestling with arcane principles of land law.[7]

---

[6] Some two-thirds of houses in the UK are owner-occupied: *Social Trends 31* (2001, Stationery Office), Table 10.6, and for many families the house is the most valuable asset: Table 5.25 and accompanying text.

[7] See Gray and Gray, *Elements of Land Law* 3rd ed. (2001, Butterworth) for a coherent explanation of land law.

At its most fundamental level, land law reveals its ancient and fairly brutal roots, because ownership of land (or, to be more precise, of an estate in land) depends ultimately upon possession. This is illustrated by the way in which squatters can claim a legal estate in land if they can show sufficient factual possession, supported by the requisite and relevant intention. In practice, of course, ownership is usually acquired in a more civilized way, by gift or purchase from an existing owner. The purchasers will register at the Land Registry. In due course, they too may decide to move on and to transfer their title to other young hopefuls. And thus legal title is passed on, from owner to owner, with due deliberation and formality.

What understandably confuses people, however, is that the crucial interest to hold is not the legal estate at all, but the equitable or, as it is accurately described, the 'beneficial' interest. This is the interest which gives rights of enjoyment and value. Generally, 'equity follows the law', and so the legal owner(s) will also be entitled beneficially. Sometimes, the legal owner(s) will be distinct from the beneficiaries. In either case, if the title deeds or register expressly spell out how both the legal and beneficial interests are held, then this 'express declaration of trust' will be conclusive with regard to the parties (in the absence of fraud or similar vitiating factor), and ownership of the land, both legal and equitable, will accord with the formal expressed intention. So if cohabitants have formally put their house into both their names beneficially, the expressed intention will prevail[8] and upon break-up the shares will generally be clear, and the only room for dispute will be whether or not the house should be sold.[9] This will be the case even though changes in circumstances since the house purchase may mean that such a division no longer seems fair, and may even leave one or other of the former couple homeless.

There are still many cases, however, where cohabitants have shared a house which was in the express name of only one of them (usually, though not invariably, this will be the male in a heterosexual partnership). And when such a couple breaks up, the other may be distressed to discover that she has no automatic claim on the house, however long she has lived there and called it home. She will have to resort to the law relating to resulting and constructive trusts (or, more rarely, proprietary estoppel)[10] to claim any beneficial share in the property. And as a result, these areas of land law

---

[8] *Goodman* v. *Gallant* [1986] Fam 106.

[9] The only circumstance in which the shares will not be clear will be when the couple has specified that they are to hold the land as tenants in common, but have not quantified their respective shares. This, however, is uncommon.

[10] Although some successful claims by former cohabitants have been made under proprietary estoppel (e.g. *Pascoe* v. *Turner* [1979] 1 WLR 431) by far the more common route is to claim under a constructive trust. Lord Bridge in *Lloyds Bank plc* v. *Rosset* ([1991] 1 AC 107) suggested that the criteria for proprietary estoppel and an express constructive

have been brought to a prominence that could never have been foreseen by previous generations of lawyers.

Resulting and constructive trusts: the struggle between principle and fairness

Many judges have responded by trying to evolve the law concerning resulting and constructive trusts to meet the needs of former cohabitants, and to provide a 'fair' outcome, but inevitably strains and stresses have ensued. For although case law is ideally suited to respond to prevailing assumptions and norms within society, with small incremental steps which reflect generally agreed beneficial outcomes, when society changes very rapidly, then the burden placed upon the common law is just too great. Tensions emerge between those who try to develop the common law in the interests of fairness, and those who prefer to retain doctrinal orthodoxy in the name of certainty and principle. Lord Denning was, of course, the outstanding exemplar of the former camp. One of his most ambitious attempts, in the Court of Appeal of the 1950s and 1960s, was to introduce the idea of 'family assets',[11] but this was thwarted by the more cautious House of Lords in *Pettitt* v. *Pettitt*,[12] with Lord Reid explaining that the issue of 'family assets' directly affected the lives and interests of large sections of the community, and as such was a matter of public policy which should be left for parliament to address.

Since then, the 'reformers'' attempts to develop the common law to provide an appropriate mechanism to determine property disputes have been more circumspect, and occasionally more successful, although uncertainty as to the law has been an unavoidable consequence as boundaries have been optimistically pushed out by one court and then retrenched by the next. It is commonly said that cohabitants and indeed married couples vis-à-vis a third party are forced to rely upon the same common law as applies to strangers to determine property entitlement. This is true, but misleading. In fact, what has happened is that many judges have tried to develop the law concerning resulting and constructive trusts to meet the needs of cohabitants, and, if anything, strangers may prove the lucky beneficiaries of such development.

---

trust were the same. Although this is debatable, I do not propose to enter into that argument here, and for reasons of space and relevance, I am not going to discuss proprietary estoppel separately from constructive trusts.

[11] See *Rimmer* v. *Rimmer* [1953] 1 QB 63, *Fribance* v. *Fribance (No. 2)* [1957] 1 WLR 384, *Hine* v. *Hine* [1962] 1 WLR 1124, *Ulrich* v. *Ulrich* [1968] 1 WLR 180.

[12] [1970] AC 777, 795 Lord Reid, 800-801 Lord Morris, 809-810 Lord Hodson, 817 Lord Upjohn.

The development of resulting trusts

The recent judicial treatment of resulting trusts illustrates this tension, and the attempts, of limited success, to broaden the scope of what was once a well-established and clearly defined legal principle. The classic resulting trust case dates from the eighteenth century. In *Dyer* v. *Dyer*,[13] Eyre CB explained resulting trusts as an attempt by equity to temper the strict formality requirements of the common law. If A contributed towards the purchase of land in B's name, and if there were no evidence or stronger equitable presumption to the contrary, equity would presume an intention on A's part that the shares in the newly purchased land should reflect the monetary contributions, and equity would then give effect to such intention and would recognise a resulting trust. It is important to note that the principle of resulting trust was not a rule but an equitable presumption, which was based upon the presumed intention of the contributor and which ceded to evidence of a different intention – if there were evidence that the money advanced had been intended as a gift or a loan, no resulting trust would arise. Thus, in the early cases, a resulting trust was tied firmly to the acquisition of land, and was justified by the intention of the contributor with regard to ownership. This seems fair enough. In the eighteenth and nineteenth centuries, circumstances were very different and resulting trusts were not used to settle disputes between former cohabitants.

Once the (no longer) happy couple emerged as a social force, however, and women tried to use resulting trusts to claim a share in the home, their restricted scope was frustrating and seemed difficult to justify. Every single aspect of resulting trust orthodoxy – the time of acquisition,[14] the

---

[13] (1788) 2 Cox Eq Cas 92.

[14] Before acquisition mortgages were commonplace, resulting trusts were quite easy to identify, and because they were restricted to the particular circumstances of a purchase, they did not undermine or conflict with the strict Victorian principle that a volunteer expended money or work on property other than his own at his peril, and whatever his intention (*Ramsden* v. *Dyson* [1865] LR 1 HL 129). However, a contribution to the purchase money became a much more difficult beast to identify when instalment or endowment mortgages were involved. Should one take into account payments of mortgage instalments, as part of the purchase price, or should one look only at the contribution to the money paid over at time of transfer? The House of Lords considered these issues in *Pettitt* v. *Pettitt* ([1970] AC 777) and in *Gissing* v. *Gissing* ([1971] AC 886). In *Gissing*, Lord Diplock adopted a robust attitude to the identification of the purchase price, and suggested that payment of mortgage instalments, after the initial acquisition of the property, could still generate a resulting trust. However, such an approach has not been problem free. Resulting trust orthodoxy requires the court to give effect to the parties' intention at the time of acquisition, and Lord Diplock's perspective, that the timing of acquisition lasted as long as the mortgage – which would frequently be some 25 years – seemed rather unreal. The courts have now taken a different tack, and have smartly circumvented the problem by extending the concept of constructive trust, as explained in

type of contribution,[15] whether or not the contribution need be direct,[16] the quantification of share,[17] – has been the subject of judicial consideration during the last forty years, with ensuing ebbs and flows. Some sort of equilibrium has now been reached, largely because constructive trusts have evolved to such an extent that they now seem poised to subsume resulting trusts within their embrace. And so it has become less urgent to try to expand resulting trusts as such. The prevailing judicial attitude seems to be that resulting trusts should only apply when a claimant has made a direct financial contribution at the time of original purchase, and to this extent, orthodoxy has been reimposed. Now, the main exception to orthodoxy is the recent, and controversial, judicial activism with regard to the quantification of the claimant's share. Under the original doctrine, the share awarded would inevitably reflect the generating contribution – it was, after all, the contribution which created the presumption of bargain and reciprocity. This straightforward approach can be seen in *Springette* v. *Defoe*,[18] where the beneficial shares mirrored the original contributions even though both the man and the woman had silently assumed that, because the *legal* title had been placed in both their names, they would equally share the *beneficial* interest. Dillon LJ[19] caustically remarked that 'the court does not as yet sit, as under a palm tree, to exercise a general

Lloyds Bank plc v. *Rosset* ([1991] 1 AC 107) to cover the situation where the claimant has contributed to the mortgage instalments.

[15] For example, the advent of the right-to-buy legislation, when certain council tenants were awarded a discount on the purchase price of their former council house, brought the question of non-monetary contributions to the purchase into stark relief. In *Springette* v. *Defoe* ([1992] 2 FLR 388), the Court of Appeal held that the woman's contribution to the purchase price included both the discount and her half-share of the mortgage. In *Savill* v. *Goodall* ([1993] 25 HLR 588), the Court of Appeal left the question of discount open and in *Evans* v. *Hayward* ([1995] 2 FLR 511), Staughton LJ doubted whether a discount amounted to the equivalent of a cash payment.

[16] In *Gissing*, Lord Reid thought that the distinction between direct and indirect contributions was unworkable, and that indirect contributions should generate a resulting trust. The baton was passed to Fox and May LJJ in *Burns* v. *Burns* ([1984] Ch. 317). They considered that a substantial contribution to family expenses could be referable to the acquisition of the house if it enabled the family to pay the mortgage instalments, and it could therefore generate a resulting trust. However, these attempts to widen the basis of a resulting trust have not been generally accepted. In *Lloyds Bank plc* v. *Rosset* ([1991] 1 AC 107), it is apparent from the tenor of Lord Bridge's remarks that only a direct contribution to the purchase price would generate a trust. He called such a trust 'constructive' but it seems clear that he was also including a classic resulting trust in his summary of the circumstances in which a trust would be implied. The approach accords with that of the orthodox property lawyer, encapsulated in Bryson J's remark that 'what one gets for paying stamp duty is a stamp, not a piece of land' (*Little* v. *Little* (1988) 15 NSWLR 43, 46).

[17] *Midland Bank plc* v. *Cooke* [1995] 4 All ER 562.

[18] [1992] 2 FLR 388 (C.A.).

[19] At 393.

discretion to do what the man in the street, on a general overview of the case, might regard as fair'. Maybe not, but the court moved towards the palm grove in *McHardy and Sons [a firm]* v. *Warren*[20] when the same Dillon LJ, in a rather short (and *ex tempore*) judgment, surprisingly awarded the wife a half-share in the matrimonial home, even though her original direct contribution had only amounted to 8.97 per cent of the purchase price and there was no evidence as to why the house had been put in the husband's name alone. He said,

> to my mind it is the irresistible conclusion that where a parent pays the deposit
> …on the purchase of their first matrimonial home, it is the intention of all three
> of them that the bride and groom should have equal interests in the matri-
> monial home, not interests measured by reference to the percentage half the
> deposit [bears] to the full price.[21]

This was an apparently casual but conceptually significant development. For Dillon LJ seemed to say that the contribution given on the bride's behalf towards the deposit automatically engendered a larger quantum share than the contribution bore to the purchase price.

Midland Bank plc v. *Cooke*[22] developed the theme of *McHardy*. In *Cooke*, the wife had in effect directly contributed £550 towards the total cost of the house, which was some £8,500. At first instance, the judge therefore declared, in accordance with classic resulting trust principles, that Mrs Cooke was beneficially entitled to 6.47 per cent of the property. However, the Court of Appeal then held that, once the resulting trust had been established by direct contribution, they were free to look to the whole course of dealing between the parties to determine the appropriate quantification. Thus fortified, the Court proceeded to find that Mrs Cooke was entitled to half the beneficial interest in the home – and this in the face of express evidence that at the time of parting the couple had reached no agreement at all with regard to ownership of the property. This case must have extended the ambit of a resulting trust far beyond Eyre CJ's wildest dreams.

The development of constructive trusts

An alternative (although still problematic) interpretation of both *McHardy* and *Cooke* is that the courts were imposing not resulting but constructive trusts in favour of the contributing wives. That the matter is open to doubt at all is indicative of the confusion between the two types of trust that has

---

20 [1994] 2 FLR 338.
21 At 340.
22 [1995] 4 All ER 562.

bedevilled this area over the last thirty years. Mee[23] points to Lord Diplock as the culprit, for in his seminal speech in *Gissing* v. *Gissing*,[24] Lord Diplock conflated the ideas of resulting and constructive trust, and 'hi-jacked' the resulting trust to incorporate it into his expansive description of the common foundation of all implied trusts. He thus proposed the novel theory that a resulting trust was engendered by the conduct of the *trustee*, in inducing the contribution in return for an interest in land. This is a far cry from the *Dyer* orthodoxy that merely gave effect to the presumed and unrebutted intention of the *contributor*. Thus resulting trusts became inextricably entangled within the common-intention constructive trust, and thus confusion has ensued.

The common-intention constructive trust has its origins, in effect if not in theory, in Lord Diplock's much-quoted dictum:

> A resulting, implied or constructive trust – and it is unnecessary for present purposes to distinguish between these three classes of trust – is created by a transaction between the trustee and the cestui que trust in connection with the acquisition by the trustee of a legal estate in land, whenever the trustee has so conducted himself that it would be inequitable to allow him to deny to the cestui que trust a beneficial interest in the land acquired. And he will be held to have so conducted himself if by his words or conduct he has induced the cestui que trust to act to his own detriment in the reasonable belief that by so acting he was acquiring a beneficial interest in the land.[25]

Lord Diplock proposed this formula within a case concerning a property dispute between a couple, and his attempt to provide some sort of synthesis and coherence has been rewarded by an ever increasing number of claims under constructive trust principles. Such was the avalanche of claims during the 1970s and 1980s, and so worried were some property lawyers by the juridical basis of such claims, that twenty years later, in *Lloyds Bank plc* v. *Rosset*,[26] the House of Lords deliberately attempted to clarify and restrict the law of constructive trusts. Lord Bridge divided such trusts into two categories, the first being where there was an express agreement between the parties as to the sharing of beneficial entitlement, and the second, where there was no such agreement, but a direct contribution to the purchase price. Lord Bridge's clear division highlighted the overlapping of category between resulting and constructive trusts. His implied constructive trust looks very much like a resulting trust, albeit possibly expanded by the acknowledgement that contributions to the mortgage are trust-generating.

---

[23] Mee, *The Property Rights of Cohabitees* (1999, Hart), p. 129.
[24] [1971] AC 888.
[25] [1971] AC 886, 905.
[26] [1991] 1 AC 107.

The tensions caused by the overlap were revealed in *Drake* v. *Whipp*,[27] where the arithmetical approach used at first instance to quantify the share under a resulting trust was abandoned by the Court of Appeal, who instead adopted a more free-style approach under a common-intention constructive trust analysis. But it is *Cooke* which best illustrates the theoretical difficulties that can ensue when the court is unclear as to which type of trust it is imposing. In *Cooke*, there was positive evidence before the court that Mr and Mrs Cooke had come to no agreement with regard to ownership of the matrimonial home. Yet, using either a developed resulting trust or an implied common-intention constructive trust, the Court of Appeal found an inferred agreement that Mrs Cooke should have a half-share. This agreement could not have been 'inferred' – it must have been imputed in the face of the evidence, but on what basis? It is trite law that a constructive trust is imposed to prevent a trustee from unconscionably denying the beneficiary her share. But it is difficult to see how Mr Cooke conducted himself at all inequitably, or that he in any way induced Mrs Cooke to act to her detriment. If the trust was constructive, the Court imposed it despite the lack of equitable fraud that is the underlying justification for such judicial interference in property ownership.

It remains to be seen whether and how this area will develop. One suspects that if only the courts had insisted upon a sharp distinction between the probanda for resulting and implied common-intention constructive trusts, the jurisprudence would not have become so unclear. It is also likely that the implied common-intention trust would have been subjected to more careful scrutiny. It is difficult to understand how a contribution to a purchase can, *without more*, generate a trust in a different proportion from the contribution, but this seems to be the result of the cases.

For Lord Bridge's first category of constructive trust, the claimant has to show not only the agreement, but also detrimental reliance upon this. This can be compared to the necessity for consideration to support a simple contract. In *Rosset*, Lord Bridge spoke of 'detriment' but then used the alternative phrase of significant alteration of position. Cases suggest, however, that for the actions to 'count', there must be some disadvantage to the claimant. Thus in *Hannaford* v. *Selby*[28] a father-in-law's work in the garden did not count as sufficient detriment because gardening was his one absorbing hobby. The disadvantage also seems to require at least some financial implication, even though it may not involve financial sacrifice. Thus Janet Eve's physical labour in the garden and house was sufficient to constitute detriment in *Eves* v. *Eves*,[29] even though she presumably

---

[27] [1996] 1 FLR 826.
[28] (1976) 239 *Estates Gazette* 811.
[29] [1975] 1 WLR 1338.

enjoyed the benefit of the enhanced environment. But a mere emotional investment, without financial implication, was insufficient in *Christian* v. *Christian*,[30] where the social embarrassment of living near a lover's wife was not accepted as sufficient detriment. Brightman LJ said, 'equity is concerned with the protection of property and proprietary interests, not with the protection of people's feelings'.

It is insufficient merely to show that there has been a detriment suffered by the claimant, there also needs to be a sufficient nexus between the detriment and the agreement as to the beneficial interest.[31] The nature of this nexus is, however, obscure. In *Grant* v. *Edwards*,[32] Nourse LJ and Browne-Wilkinson VC suggested very different requirements with regard to the nature of the reliance. Nourse LJ's approach was very restrictive. He considered that the only conduct which was relevant was that 'on which the woman could not reasonably be expected to embark unless she was to have an interest in the house'.[33] Browne-Wilkinson VC, on the other hand, expansively thought that any act done by the claimant to her detriment relating to the joint lives of the parties should be sufficient. Drawing guidance from the principles underlying proprietary estoppel, where 'the acts do not have to be inherently referable to the house',[34] he favoured accepting such joyful events as setting up house together, having a baby and making payments to general household expenses. It is unclear which approach is likely to be followed, although by implication Lord Bridge in *Rosset* preferred the more restrictive approach. Thus he dismissed Mrs Rosset's extensive work in furthering the restoration of the farmhouse as work upon which any wife would have embarked, and implied that for that reason alone it would not have supported a constructive trust, even if there had been an express agreement as to beneficial entitlement.

Lord Bridge went on to note, in the context of considering Mrs Rosset's alleged detriment, that the monetary value of her work was trifling compared to the cost of the house as a whole. It was, he suggested, almost *de minimis*. If the objective value of do-it-yourself work, rather than the effort expended, is to be the measure of the detriment, then that suggests that many future claimants will be disappointed. Almost inevitably the work that an amateur can do on a house is going to amount to a very small proportion of its total value.

---

[30] (1981) 131 NLJ 43.
[31] *Wayling* v. *Jones* ([1995] 2 FLR 1029) held that once detrimental conduct was proved, the burden switched to the defendant to show that the conduct had not been in reliance upon the promise.
[32] [1986] Ch. 638.
[33] Above, at 648. See Sufrin (1987) 50 MLR 94, at 99.
[34] Above, at 657.

Advantages of the present law of resulting and constructive trusts

More commentators are critical than supportive of the present law. Bailey-Harris[35] makes a brave attempt to list its advantages and comes up with four headings: formal neutrality as to family form, gender and sexuality; flexibility; moral basis; and party autonomy. The first and the last are the most persuasive.

Resulting and constructive trusts show no preference for any particular family form or type of relationship. If the criteria are met, then the claimant will succeed, whether or not she was in a heterosexual relationship, in a same-sex relationship, or indeed in a non-sexual relationship. Thus in *Tinsley* v. *Milligan*,[36] where the plaintiff succeeded in her claim for an interest under a resulting trust against her erstwhile same-sex partner, the sexual orientation of the couple was quite irrelevant. This lack of bias towards any particular living arrangement is a very welcome attribute of the law and especially appropriate now that society is so multi-faceted and diverse. And indeed, the formal neutrality of implied trusts is likely to be increasingly celebrated, now that the Human Rights Act has reinvigorated a debate about discriminatory structures in society.

The other benefit in the present law is the way in which implied trusts are justified by and premised upon the intention of the parties. Thus the claimant under a constructive trust needs to show a common intention that she would acquire an ownership share in the property – usually, in this context, the house. In this way, the common law accords primacy to individual autonomy and ensures that the role of the state is kept within traditional constraints. Liberal political theory considers that property is a private affair, and that it is up to individuals to order their property holdings as they wish. Indeed, private property can be seen as having a constitutional role in enabling the individual to resist the tyrannical democratic majority,[37] and restricting constitutional government to its proper limits. If one espouses this theory, then intention and consent are the correct bases for property holding, and whenever possible, the law should refrain from interfering between private parties and redistributing their property on another basis. From this perspective, it is perfectly justifiable that the Mrs Burnses of this world acquire property in food or furniture when they purchase the same, but that they do not thereby also acquire bricks and mortar.

---

[35] Bailey-Harris, 'Dividing the Assets on Breakdown of Relationships Outside Marriage' in Bailey-Harris (ed.), *Dividing the Assets on Family Breakdown* (1998, Family Law).
[36] [1992] Ch. 310.
[37] See McLean (ed.), *Property and the Constitution* (1999, Hart).

Disadvantages of the present law of resulting and constructive trusts

But, as many commentators have pointed out, happy couples do not think in terms of proprietary entitlement.[38] The whole process of looking for a common agreement or intention as to ownership is quite unrealistic in the context of family relationships. The rather poignant exchange between counsel and Mr Cooke[39] encapsulates the problem. When asked if he and his wife had discussed property rights, he answered, 'Not really, no. We were just happy, I suppose, you know.' The judiciary also has expressed reservations, and Waite J threw resounding scorn on the whole exercise in *Hammond* v. *Mitchell*.[40]

Unpredictable outcomes
The courts have responded to the need to identify an agreement by purporting to find agreements where none really existed, and post-*Rosset*, they have been able to take advantage of Lord Bridge's allowing that the agreement could be imperfectly remembered and imprecisely worded. The result has been cases where the finding or otherwise of an express agreement has been unpredictable, and sometimes implausible. In *Hammond* v. *Mitchell*, Waite J found a sufficient common agreement on the basis of excuses and the following assurance: 'don't worry about the future because when we are married [the house] will be half yours anyway and I'll always look after you and our child'.[41] It seems rather perverse that a promise to give the woman half when they were married was interpreted as an agreement that she should have half before the tying of the nuptial knot. And though this can provide an apparently fair outcome in an individual case, the sleight of hand and dubious logic involved in labelling an excuse an agreement does not make for a satisfactory jurisprudence.

No relationship to future needs
The court's insistence that ownership depends ultimately upon intention, which may be inferred from certain types of behaviour, means that the division of property when a cohabiting couple breaks up may bear no relationship at all to the future needs and requirements of each. The whole approach involves a retrospective assessment of what happened in the past, rather than a prospective evaluation that will provide the fairest division for the future. This has implications not only for 'fairness' and 'justice' but also, of course, for the public purse.

[38] See, e.g. Gardner, 'Rethinking Family Property' (1993) 109 *Law Quarterly Review* 263; Glover and Todd, 'The Myth of Common Intention' (1996) 16 *Legal Studies* 325.
[39] [1995] 4 All ER 562, 568.
[40] [1992] 1 FLR 229.

Devaluation of non-financial contributions

A further and related issue involves the treatment of non-financial contributions. Unless the claimant made a direct financial contribution to the purchase of the house, she is not entitled to claim under a resulting trust or an implied constructive trust. One direct payment, however small, is absolutely crucial so that the court can infer the necessary intention to own. Unless the claimant and her partner reached an express agreement as to ownership of the house, she cannot claim under an express constructive trust. Without one or other of these qualifying conditions, the claimant is debarred from claiming a share of the house under any implied trust, no matter how generous her emotional support, her home-making, her house-keeping. Both resulting and constructive trust orthodoxy devalue emotional – and physical – investment. And this even though the partner's financial investment has often only been possible because of the home-maker's presence. As Sir Jocelyn Simon memorably explained nearly forty years ago, 'The cock bird can feather his nest precisely because he is not required to spend most of his time sitting on it.'[42]

Capricious outcomes

Another marked feature of the law as it has developed is that situations which seem quite similar can produce very different outcomes. Mrs Cooke was entitled to half of the former matrimonial home just because her in-laws had given the young couple, as a wedding present, a small sum of money towards the deposit. Had exactly the same sum of money instead been given to the hopeful couple for furniture, or a car, then Mrs Cooke would have received no share of the house at all. Poor Mrs Burns received nothing, but had she used her earnings to help pay the mortgage instead of buying furniture, she might have received a share of the house. Such distinctions do not make sense to people who are going through the trauma of relationship break-up, and the outcomes seem merely capricious.

Gender bias

Finally, despite its formal neutrality, a gender bias is implicit within the present law. For it is likely to be the woman in a heterosexual relationship who provides the non-financial caring and domestic work which transforms a house into a home, and which supports a couple's relationship. This, of course, is precisely the contribution which is discounted in establishing a resulting or implied constructive trust.[43] Gender bias is also

---

[41] At 233.

[42] Sir J. Simon, *With all my Worldly Goods* (1964, Holdsworth Lecture, Birmingham), 14–15.

[43] In *White* v. *White* [2000] 3 WLR 1571 the House of Lords strongly affirmed that there should be no bias in favour of the money-earner and against the home-maker and the child-carer in relation to proceedings for ancillary relief under the Matrimonial Causes

discernible in the courts' attitude to the detrimental reliance which supports a claim under an express constructive trust. It seems that work which is outside the gender expectation is more highly regarded than work which is gender typical. This can cut both ways. The claimant, whether male or female, who acts within the gender norms may find his or her contribution considered insufficient. Thus Lord Bridge thought that Mrs Rosset had done no more than any wife would have done. On the other hand, one suspects that Janet Eve was the lucky beneficiary of this gender bias. If one looks at what she did dispassionately, it does not seem a lot, but because she had wielded a sledge-hammer, she persuaded the court that she had suffered significant detriment.

Alternatives: the remedial constructive trust in other jurisdictions[44]

It is not only in England and Wales that the common law has been called upon to respond to diversifying social norms and familial structures. The same pattern of dramatic social change is recognisable in other, comparable jurisdictions, and so the way that the common law has evolved in such countries provides a useful template for possible reform or development here. Canada, New Zealand and Australia have all developed remedial constructive trust regimes which at first glance seem to provide fairer and less capricious outcomes to the problem of property division upon the breakdown of a relationship.

In Canada, the courts have constructed a remedial trust upon the basis of unjust enrichment, so as to secure fair property division when appropriate. The jurisprudence has developed rapidly over the past quarter of a century, from Laskin J's seminal dissenting judgment in *Murdoch* v. *Murdoch*,[45] to an acceptance by the majority of the Supreme Court just seven years later in *Pettkus* v. *Becker*.[46] The dramatic possibilities of the remedy can be seen in *Peter* v. *Beblow*,[47] where a claim based on conventional domestic services succeeded in furnishing the claimant with the entire equity in the house.

But although the outcomes often seem 'fair' and to redress the economic imbalance which can result from shared lives, there are juristic problems

Act 1973. This ringing endorsement of the value of domestic contribution sits uncomfortably with the law of implied trusts.

[44] See, generally, Mee, *The Property Rights of Cohabitees* (1999, Hart) and Wong, 'Constructive trusts over the family home: lessons to be learned from other commonwealth jurisdictions?'(1998) 18 *Legal Studies* 369.

[45] (1973) 41 DLR (3d) 367 at 377.

[46] (1980) 117 DLR (3d) 257.

[47] (1993) 101 DLR (4th) 621.

with the approach and these still need to be addressed.[48] The theoretical underpinning is that if there is an enrichment, with a corresponding deprivation, and there is no juristic reason for the enrichment, then the claimant deserves a remedy, which may amount to an interest under a constructive trust over the property in question. The problem lies in the lack of juristic reason, or, in other words, what makes an enrichment 'unjust'. The conventional answer, in the context of cohabitation, is: when the donor believes that she will be rewarded for her donation and the donee, to her knowledge, knows of this belief and fails to disabuse her, or reneges on their understanding. But this does not cover the case where the donor makes her donation with no thought of reward or recompense – and that, of course, is what so often happens. Scane[49] argues that a legal presumption is developing that domestic contribution is provided in the reasonable belief that it will be recompensed and that its acceptance of itself fuels the obligation. This is possibly fair, although of course it reduces individual freedom, and is especially difficult to justify where the donee has made clear that he does not intend to share the house, and yet the donor still donates. Yet even in this situation, the Canadian courts have been prepared to find for the claimant.[50] Thus in *Harrison v. Kalinocha*,[51] the trial judge found as a fact that Ms Harrison was aware that Mr Kalinocha did not want to share ownership of the house with her (or marry her). Yet even so, the British Columbia Court of Appeal held that she was entitled to a constructive trust on the basis of unjust enrichment.

McLachlin J remarked in *Beblow* that 'there is a tendency on the part of some to view the action for unjust enrichment as a device for doing whatever may seem fair between the parties'.[52] The protest is telling. It adverts to the imposition of a value structure by the courts upon a couple, regardless of their individual intentions, and even when those intentions have been made quite clear to the other. This may be considered acceptable, but it is controversial and should at least be discussed and acknowledged.

---

[48] There are also quite separate problems of enforcement – when, in 1986, Miss Becker had still not received any money in hand after her successful claim against Mr Pettkus, she committed suicide (*Globe and Mail*, 13 November 1986).

[49] Scane, 'Relationships "Tantamount to Spousal", Unjust Enrichment and Constructive Trusts', (1991) 70 *Canadian Bar Review* 260.

[50] Sometimes, the problem is resolved by a particular interpretation of the facts. In *Sorochan v. Sorochan* ((1986) 29 DLR (4th) 1), Mr Sorochan refused Mrs Sorochan's request in 1971 that part of the land be transferred to her. Despite this, she continued to provide domestic services for a further eleven years. The refusal was then used by the court as evidence that Mr Sorochan must have known that his partner (reasonably) expected a share of his property.

[51] (1994) 112 DLR (4th) 43.

[52] (1993) 101 DLR (4th) 621, 643.

The Australian courts have adopted a different approach, and have been prepared to find a constructive trust upon the basis of avoiding 'unconscionability'.[53] They have proceeded by analogy with the rules governing a failed joint venture in commerce[54] – to the extent that, showing a sophisticated grasp of the possibilities of language, they now deal with 'joint venturers … in the journey of life'.[55] As in Canada, and as in New Zealand with its emphasis on 'reasonable expectations',[56] the discretion is wide and the outcomes often seem fair. However, a lingering doubt remains. In all of these jurisdictions, there is either a disparity or ambiguity between the ostensible principles applied and the court decisions, or there is a lack of clarity about the principles. The remedial constructive trusts which have emerged have many advantages of flexibility over the more restrictive English common-intention trusts, and it may well be that we could learn from the developments in other common law jurisdictions, but no system yet seems perfect.

The law of personal property for cohabitants

For the sake of completeness, one should also mention the law of personal property, which governs assets other than the home or land. Here again, ownership is founded on intention, but ownership is not subject to the same formality rules as in land law. This means that, for example, an oral declaration of trust is effective, as was shown in the case of a yacht in *Rowe* v. *Prance*.[57] Again, the problem is that harmonious couples do not give much thought to ownership, and disputes about items of personal property can be bitter and disproportionate to the actual value of the chattel.

Property distribution for divorcing couples

The normal common law principles of property, described above, apply to all individuals, whether married or not.[58] But spouses (or, more specifically, the economically weaker spouses in a marriage) enjoy a great advantage over their cohabiting sisters because, upon divorce, they are

---

[53] *Baumgartner* v. *Baumgartner* (1987) 164 CLR 137.

[54] *Muchinski* v. *Dodds* (1985) 160 CLR 583, per Deane J.

[55] *Bell* v. *Bell* (1995) 19 *Family Law Review* 690, 694, quoted in Mee, *op. cit.*, 264.

[56] *Gillies* v. *Keogh* [1989] 2 NZLR 327.

[57] [1999] 2 FLR 787.

[58] Separation of property between spouses dates from the Married Women's Property Act 1882. Before then, the doctrine of coverture operated – in effect to give the wife's property to the husband; in return, the husband was under an obligation to maintain the wife.

able to seek reallocation of property and maintenance under Part II of the Matrimonial Causes Act 1973. Although the statutory provisions have been amended over the years, most recently by the Welfare Reform and Pensions Act 1999, they still remain substantially the same as they were when introduced thirty years ago, and they give the court a very, very wide discretion to reorder the couple's financial affairs.

No express objective underlying the statutory discretion

The lay person would be surprised to learn that, although the discretion awarded the court is so wide, nowhere does the statute state the purpose of ancillary relief orders. When the Matrimonial Causes Act 1857 first introduced maintenance orders, the judges used them to try to preserve the standard of living for innocent wives who would otherwise be financially prejudiced by divorce.[59] At that time, marriage was still seen as a moral commitment for life, and an attempt to ensure that a wronged wife was not economically prejudiced by her errant husband's sinful ways, and that the errant husband did not escape his moral and economic obligations, was in accord with the prevailing mores. It was also essential for an ex-wife's well-being that she was supported economically, because the opportunities for a gentlewoman[60] to become financially independent were very limited. The underlying moral basis of the awards is illustrated by the reluctance of the courts to make orders in favour of 'guilty' wives – the best that such a wicked woman could hope for was a minimal order, a 'compassionate allowance',[61] to keep her from utter penury. *N* v. *N*[62] is the classic case in which Lord Merrivale P articulated that the court was trying to preserve for each party their financial position as it would have been, had the marriage not broken down.[63] And this objective – the so-called 'minimal loss principle' – was incorporated, without discussion, into the Matrimonial Proceedings and Property Act 1970, which is the basis of the Matrimonial Causes Act 1973.

But times were changing, both economically and socially. The increase in the divorce rate entailed an implicit redefinition of marriage,[64] for how

[59] See Cretney, 'Trusting the Judges: Money after Divorce', *Current Legal Problems* (1999) 286 for an excellent overview of the history of judicial attitudes to ancillary relief.
[60] Divorce was not a realistic possibility for the working classes.
[61] *Dailey* v. *Dailey* [1947] 1 All ER 847, 851, *per* Willmer LJ.
[62] (1928) 138 LT 693.
[63] See also *Sherwood* v. *Sherwood* [1928] P. 215.
[64] Smart, 'Marriage, Divorce and Women's Economic Dependency: A Discussion of the Politics of Private Maintenance' in Freeman, M. (ed.) *State, Law and the Family* (1984, Tavistock) argues that the new statutory regime revealed the marriage contract as 'an economic or financial one rather than a contract based on sexual fidelity and moral obligation', pp. 99–100.

could marriage be viewed as a life-long commitment and guarantee of economic security when more and more frequently it was ending prematurely, and people were embarking upon second marriages? This change of perspective, together with the increasing participation of women in the work force and the practical impossibility of achieving the stated objective of minimal loss, all conspired to throw the objective into disrepute. Men's groups questioned why ex-husbands should provide an ex-wife with 'a meal ticket for life' and by the early 1980s it had become obvious that the statutory attempt to preserve the pre-divorce standard of living was anachronistic.[65] The Law Commission considered the issue,[66] but in the absence of any consensus as to what the courts should be trying to achieve, decided that discretion was the better part of valour. And so the Matrimonial and Family Proceedings Act 1984 excised the reference to purpose, but failed to replace it with any other objective. Instead, it merely adjured the court to give first consideration to the welfare, whilst a minor, of any child of the family under 18 and to consider the possibility of a 'clean break'. In furtherance of the latter, it suggested limiting maintenance payments for a period of readjustment.

The 'needs' approach

So section 25 fails to give a clear lead as to the purpose of ancillary relief, but provides a generous and wide-ranging list of considerations. Although it is possible to distil differing theoretical models from these guidelines[67] – for example needs-based or compensatory – until very recently the predominant discourse was firmly needs-based. Most practitioners agreed that the purpose of ancillary relief was to provide for the reasonable requirements of the parties.[68]

The practical result of this approach varied according to the wealth of the couple. In 'big money' cases, the court would only disturb the individual formal property entitlement of each to the extent necessary to meet the requirements of the more needy, less affluent partner – usually, of course, the wife. So the woman would only be awarded a small proportion of the assets. In *Dart* v. *Dart*,[69] both Peter Gibson LJ and Butler-Sloss LJ

---

[65] See Cretney, 'Trusting the Judges: Money after Divorce', *Current Legal Problems* (1999) 286.

[66] Law Commission, *The Financial Consequences of Divorce: The Basic Policy* (1980), Law Com. No. 103. This was the first official attempt to consider underlying principle.

[67] Diduck identifies the following models: subsections 25(2)(a)-(e) illustrate a needs-based or insurance model, subsections (f)-(h), a compensatory model and section 25A, a pure clean break. (Note that the last is not commensurate with the first two.) See Diduck, 'Dividing the Family Assets' in Day Sclater and Piper (ed.), *Undercurrents of Divorce* (1999, Ashgate), p. 211.

[68] *Ibid.*

[69] [1996] 2 FLR 286, 303, 305, CA.

expressed doubts about the fairness of limiting Mrs Dart's claim to her 'reasonable requirements', but they thought that this was necessary, and so they only awarded her £10 million, which was a mere 2.5 per cent of her husband's wealth. In *Conran* v. *Conran*,[70] the judge decided that the wife's contribution was so outstanding that it deserved recognition over and above her reasonable requirements – but the concept was still used as a benchmark, and she still only received a 10 per cent share of the husband's wealth.

But of course such 'big money' cases are the exception rather than the rule. In the vast majority of cases, the needs of the wife/mother – especially the pressing need for a roof – absorb most of the marital assets. In this situation, the 'needs' objective was moderated by a further, often unarticulated, objective to *share* the marital property rather than allocate it *all* according to need. This explains *Martin*[71] and *Mesher*[72] orders. It also explains the finding in a recent Cardiff study[73] that women often traded their long-term financial security – a claim against the male's pension – in return for the present security of the house. Such an arrangement cannot be explained purely on the theory that need was being met: it seems that in fact, need was only determinative to the extent that it entailed the transfer of a proportion, but not all, of the couple's assets.

White v. *White*[74]

But the House of Lords has now criticised the 'needs' approach, and its future is in doubt. In *White*, the House of Lords was called upon to consider the broad application of section 25 for the first time in the provision's thirty-year history.[75] And so the case is of great significance for the future, though of course the speeches are open to different interpretations, and the nature of the case's influence will only become apparent with time.

The first issue involves the future of the 'needs' approach. And here Lord Nicholls was very clear. He stated '[t]he statutory provisions lend no support to the idea that a claimant's financial needs, even interpreted generously and called reasonable requirements, are to be regarded as

---

[70] [1997] 2 FLR 615.

[71] [1978] Fam 12, CA.

[72] [1980] 1 All ER 126, CA.

[73] Perry *et al*, *How Parents Cope Financially on Marriage Breakdown* (1999, Family Policy Studies Centre).

[74] [2000] 3 WLR 1571.

[75] In *Piglowska* v. *Piglowski* ([1999] 1 WLR 360), the House of Lords also considered an application for ancillary relief, but the main issue there concerned how appellate courts should approach appeals from trial judges' decisions.

determinative'. He emphasised that the statutory scheme involved consideration of other factors as well, such as the available resources and the parties' contributions.

Whether or not this will prove the death-knell of the 'needs' approach is uncertain. For Lord Nicholls prefaced his speech with the *caveat* that the Whites were a couple with plentiful assets, and that his general observations should be read with this in mind. So while it seems clear from *White* that neither needs nor reasonable requirements will be limiting factors in 'big money' cases, it is not clear how need will be treated in the more usual case where the requirements of the primary carer would take the major share of the available assets.

In particular, it is unclear how need will interact with equal sharing. For Lord Nicholls and Lord Cooke, who delivered the two reasoned speeches, both strongly endorsed the idea that equality of division should be a yardstick against which any proposed order for ancillary relief be measured. Lord Nicholls was obviously concerned lest he strayed beyond the bounds of proper statutory construction, and so he rivalled medievalists in the subtlety of his distinction between a yardstick, which he felt was permissible, and a starting-point or a presumption, which he considered impermissible. Lords Hoffman, Hope and Hutton were content to agree with Lord Nicholls' contortions, but Lord Cooke was made of sterner stuff, and bravely doubted whether there was much difference between a yardstick and a starting-point. The bold reader may agree. But despite these linguistic shenanigans, the House of Lords has now given a ringing endorsement to equality of division in respect of ancillary relief. It remains to be seen whether or not the courts and practitioners will enthusiastically follow the lead that has been given to them. If they do, then some settlements in the future may be much larger and more generous than anything hitherto. The effect of *White* could be minimised, however, if future courts interpret the speeches restrictively, as only relevant within the particular context of both abundant wealth and a long-term equal farming partnership.

In considering section 25, Lord Nicholls also emphasised that contributions were relevant, and here a significant aspect of his speech was his insistence that, in evaluating contributions, there should be no bias in favour of the money-earner and against the home-maker and the child-carer. He has thereby provided a useful gloss on the section, and no doubt many stay-at-home wives (or at least their advisors) will quote his words to their recalcitrant ex-husbands during negotiations as to quantum.

Satisfaction with Part II of the Matrimonial Causes Act 1973

The remarkable sea-change in judicial policy heralded by *White* shows just how flexible section 25 is. Many practitioners like the flexibility, and are content with the present system.[76] They think that it works and – on the basis that 'if it ain't broke, don't mend it' – does not need fundamental reform. Similarly, albeit more elegantly, some of the foremost academics working in this field favour the wide discretionary approach. Dewar, for example, argues that the contradictory, indeed antinomous, nature of family law reflects the normal chaos of our private lives, and enables the judges to deal fairly and appropriately with individual cases.[77] When one considers the infinite number of different situations and all the variables which need to be taken into account when dividing property, the complexity of the task is obvious. And any more rigid or formulaic or hierarchical approach could lead, paradoxically, to more litigation, to address definitional problems or apparent unfairness of outcome. The unhappy record to date of the rule-based Child Support Agency lends added weight to the argument in favour of discretion.

Criticisms of Part II of the Matrimonial Causes Act 1973

But others criticise the present statutory provisions for both theoretical and practical reasons.

Unpredictable outcome
A recurrent complaint is that the wide judicial discretion, which is not underpinned by any clear statutory purpose, gives advisors and indeed the parties themselves little guidance as to likely outcome.[78] This difficulty is exacerbated by the judicial insistence that previous cases provide mere guidelines, but not precedents, because every case has to be decided upon its particular facts.[79] And so many issues – for example, the effect of post-divorce changes in circumstance, and the effect of social security payments – can apparently be answered in quite opposite ways so long as 'all the circumstances of the case' are taken into account.[80] A recent empirical study by Davis and others[81] shows that although the broad outlines of the eventual 'solutions' were predictable, the details were infinitely variable. Critics argue that such unpredictability offends against underlying principles of justice, which require broad consistency of outcome in

---

[76] The practitioners who responded to the Ancillary Relief Advisory Group, *Report to the Lord Chancellor by the Ancillary Relief Advisory Group* (London, 1998) were opposed to change.

[77] Dewar, 'The Normal Chaos of Family Law' (1998) 61 *Modern Law Review* 467.

[78] Davis, Cretney and Collins, *Simple Quarrels* (1994, Clarendon Press); *Supporting Families: A Consultation Document* (1998, Stationery Office), para. 4.46.

[79] *Gojkovic* v. *Gojkovic* [1990] 1 FLR 140 (CA).

[80] Contrast *Whiting* v. *Whiting* [1988] 2 FLR 189 and *Fisher* v. *Fisher* [1989] 1 FLR 423, *Smith* v. *Smith (Smith Intervening)* [1991] 2 All ER 306, *Schuller* v. *Schuller* [1990] 2 FLR 193.

[81] Davis *et al*, 'Ancillary relief outcomes' [2000] CFLQ 43.

decisions.[82] It also means that individuals may feel dissatisfied with the legal process, when they discover that their advisors cannot clearly predict a likely outcome of litigation.

The unresolved question of 'fault'

Related to the above, but deserving of separate treatment, is the uncertainty surrounding the relevance of the parties' conduct in ancillary relief proceedings. When marriage was viewed as a moral undertaking, and divorce was based upon matrimonial fault then, indeed, it was perfectly appropriate to take matrimonial conduct into account, and to reward the innocent and penalise the guilty. But when 'no fault' divorce was introduced,[83] the relevance of conduct to a financial settlement became difficult to justify both intellectually and practically. And so it was no surprise when Lord Denning MR announced in *Wachtel* v. *Wachtel*[84] that conduct should no longer be relevant to ancillary relief proceedings, other than in exceptional cases where the conduct was both obvious and gross. In 1984, when the minimal loss objective was excised, conduct had to be given its own separate heading under section 25, but this did not seem to make any difference to judicial attitudes. However, as any family lawyer can confirm, unhappy individuals in the throes of divorce think that the (wrongful) conduct of their spouses most certainly should be taken into account, and they rail against the apparent injustice of the present policy. Indeed, it was public pressure, as mediated through MPs, which forced additional wording upon a reluctant government in the Family Law Act 1996, to suggest that conduct should play a more prominent part in reaching financial settlement. Whether or not the additional words will ever be implemented is unclear, but in the meantime, there is much lay bitterness and resentment surrounding this issue, and this undermines confidence in the whole judicial process.

Encouragement of litigation

The 1998 government consultation document *Supporting Families* considers that the uncertainty of outcome discussed above encourages litigation.[85] If this is true, then such an outcome may seem undesirable on the grounds that litigation is so stressful for the parties involved, and takes such a heavy emotional toll from them. Court proceedings may exacerbate already painful situations, and the resultant bitterness may impinge upon any children of the family. This argument needs to be treated with some caution, however. Dewar points out that 'there is no hard evidence that

---

[82] Eekelaar, 'Should Section 25 be Reformed?' [1998] Fam. Law 469.
[83] By the Divorce Reform Act 1969.
[84] [1973] Fam 72 (CA).
[85] *Supporting Families: A Consultation Document* (1998, The Stationery Office) para 4.47.

firmer rules make it easier to reach agreements'.[86] Indeed, and on the contrary, Davis, Cretney and Collins[87] found that some solicitors positively welcomed the unpredictability of the law because it promoted settlement. A further point to bear in mind when considering this particular issue is that for some, litigation may seem therapeutic, and for others, litigation is driven by deep emotional impulses rather than any reasonable assessment of likely benefit. Thorpe LJ has commented that no amount of statutory reform will eradicate the psychological disturbance that fuels such litigiousness.[88]

Cost

No doubt the government has the psychological well-being of its citizens in mind when it expresses concern about the amount of litigation in this area, but one suspects that the financial cost of litigation, in the maintenance of the courts, to the legal aid system and to the parties themselves, is its major concern. And no wonder – the present system is very expensive. The requirement that the judges should take all the circumstances into account means that solicitors have embarked upon thorough and wide-ranging investigations into the financial positions of the parties, past, present and future; such investigations can prove very time-consuming, and so enormously costly to the parties or the legal aid system.[89] The findings can then result in complex and long drawn-out hearings, which are very expensive for the courts. The Lord Chancellor cannot even try to economise on the judges who hear these cases, because the wideness of the discretion means that the judges need to be of the highest possible calibre. The government is desperate to try to reduce the escalating costs in this area.

Suggestions for reform: cohabitants and divorcing couples

And thus the present state of the law, both for the married and the unmarried, causes concern to many. It is easy to identify areas of weakness, rigidity and inconsistency in the law and its application; and the outcomes can seem inappropriate, both for cohabitants and divorcing couples, and provide ready ammunition for critics of family and property law. But of course it is always so much easier to criticise than to reform. How the law should be reformed is problematic. There is general consensus that the

---

[86] Dewar, 'Reducing Discretion in Family Law' (1997) 11 *Australian Journal of Family Law* 309.

[87] Davis, Cretney and Collins, *Simple Quarrels* (1994, Clarendon Press), p. 108.

[88] Thorpe LJ, 'The English system of ancillary relief' in Bailey-Harris (ed.), *Dividing the Assets on Family Breakdown* (1998, Bristol, Family Law).

[89] Davis, Cretney and Collins, *Simple Quarrels* (1994, Clarendon Press), p. 256. Possibly the strictures in *White* will reduce some of these costs.

welfare of any relevant children should at least be a first priority, but beyond this, there is no generally agreed objective. Some have proposed models in the context of reforming the Matrimonial Causes Act, while others have sought a formula which is equally applicable to cohabitants and divorcing couples.

Articulation of objectives

A preliminary challenge is to articulate what the law is trying to achieve in this area. The theoretical issue is the extent to which, beyond securing the welfare of children, the former partners to a marriage or relationship should share their property and maintain each other, and this one is tricky. So suggestions tend to be of the 'to do that which is fair and reasonable between the parties and any child of the family'[90] variety. Of course the great merit of this type of formulation is that no-one can argue against it – unfair and unreasonable aims not being fashionable at present – but a disadvantage is that it is utterly meaningless.

There are several possible theoretical objectives. The four most commonly discussed are: (1) to compensate the parties for their contributions to the marriage/relationship, (2) to equalise the economic *position* of each party, (3) to equalise the economic *effect* of the marriage/relationship or (4) to meet the future needs of the parties (which prior to *White* was the favoured model in ancillary relief).

Compensation model

The compensation approach has the merit that in broad outline it is understandable; also, and very importantly, it can be explained to the individuals involved in the process in a way that makes it seem fair. Eekelaar[91] has recently suggested that the compensation (he calls it the contribution) approach is appropriate for a childless couple. But of course there are huge problems in the detail. How does one weigh domestic endeavour against the grind of wage-earning? And what if the outcome, based as it will be on a retrospective assessment of the marriage or relationship, bears no relationship to future need? Despite these difficulties, it is possible to see within some of the reform suggestions discussed below, the seeds of a compensatory approach.

Equal division of property model

This in effect calls for equal sharing. Various jurisdictions have introduced community of property regimes, of varying breadth, complexity and

---

90   *Supporting Families: A Consultation Document* (1998, The Stationery Office).
91   Eekelaar, 'Should Section 25 be Reformed?' [1998] Fam Law 469.

sophistication.[92] In Scotland, for example, a type of deferred community of property regime applies to spouses,[93] with a statutory presumption in favour of equal division upon divorce unless there are special circumstances.[94] The underlying premise of this model is that marriage (and possibly cohabitation) is a joint cooperative endeavour in which equal sharing of the couple's assets is fair and appropriate. Some interesting proposals for a modified community of property regime in England and Wales have surfaced in recent years. In 1993 Gardner published *Rethinking Family Property* which has proved very influential in further debate. Gardner argued that when a relationship (whether married or cohabiting) is truly committed, the partners pool their efforts and resources towards a shared well-being, without any thought as to formal ownership. If such a relationship subsequently breaks down, it is right and appropriate that the property is shared equally. His suggestion that the degree of commitment in a relationship – not, note, a marriage certificate – should govern the property distribution has been very influential in further debate, and has led to proposals involving sliding scales, conditional upon the length of the relationship. Thus Barlow and Lind[95] suggest that, subject to contrary agreement, a family home should be owned by both parties, whether married or cohabiting, in shares determined by the length of the relationship and rising from 10 per cent for the non-owner after one year of 'qualifying relationship ' up to 50 per cent after five years. They include an escape clause – the couple should be able to contract out of the presumptions by formal agreement entered into prior to marriage or within the first two years of cohabitation, but there should be a residual discretion for the court to adjust the parties' property rights in cases of manifest injustice.

Eekelaar has also recently proposed a solution which is based upon the length of the marriage or relationship, although his is firmly placed in the context of parenthood.[96] He considers that the present practice of giving priority to the accommodation needs of the parties should remain. Subject to that, he suggests that, if the parties have lived together for 15 years *and* have brought up a child together, then all property, whenever acquired, should be subject to a presumption of equal sharing. If however the couple have lived together for a lesser period, the allocation would be in lesser proportions. Eekelaar thinks that his time period guidelines could reduce conflict, by giving clear and consensual guidelines.

[92] For example, New Zealand, Ontario, Quebec.
[93] In an unqualified community of property regime, the couple share their property during as well as after their relationship. In a deferred system, the sharing is imposed on the couple at the time of their break up.
[94] Family Law (Scotland) Act 1985, s. 9 (1), 10(1).
[95] Barlow and Lind, 'A matter of trust: the allocation of rights in the family home' (1999) 19 *Legal Studies* 468.
[96] Eekelaar, 'Should Section 25 be Reformed?' [1998] Fam Law 469.

An advantage of equal sharing is that it is easily understood in general terms, and, superficially at any rate, seems fair. If this were the template against which couples had to negotiate, at least they would have a basic starting-point for their discussions. A further, and very attractive aspect of the schemes proposed by Barlow and Lind and Eekelaar is that they recognise, and translate into action, the generally understood alchemy whereby with time and commitment relationships generate of their own accord, and even against the wishes of the participants, obligations and responsibilities.

The difficulty is that, paradoxically, community of property regimes can be very complex, with detailed rules to define the property which is subject to the equal division, and this can in itself lead to litigation.[97] The difficulty is not insuperable, but obviously means that any scheme is only as good as its detail and drafting permits.

Reallocation to equalise economic effect of relationship

A more subtle approach, favoured by both academics and professional bodies,[98] and also encapsulated in the Scottish Family Law Act, is to try to equalise the economic *effect* of a relationship. The aim is that 'fair account should be taken of any economic advantage derived by either party from contributions by the other, and of any economic disadvantage suffered by either party in the interest of another party or the family'.[99] This covers not only the spouse who stays at home or works part-time to care for the children, but also the wife who supports her husband through college, or who leaves her job to follow her husband around the world, or who refuses promotion so as not to disrupt the family. The great merit of equalisation of effect is that it accords with contemporary emphasis upon substantive equality rather than the more specious formal equality. Formal equality, unless then matched with continuing maintenance for the partner who chose to put family and home before a career trajectory, merely perpetuates an economic inequality for the future. But if one attempts to equalise the *effect* of the relationship, then such sacrifices and the value of unwaged contributions enter the equation, and the division of property can reflect the choices which may have led to depressed economic prospects for one of the partners. This objective could be used to govern property division between former spouses and former co-habitants. Its main difficulty (again) is that it would involve quite complex

---

[97] See Eekelaar, *Financial and Property Adjustment after Divorce* (1998, Centre for Socio-Legal Studies, Oxford).

[98] Bailey-Harris R, *Third Stonewall Lecture – Lesbian and Gay Family Values and the Law* [1999] Fam. Law 560, The Solicitors Family Law Association, Rodgers, 'Cohabitation Committee Report to the National Committee' SFLA Review, Issue 79, June 1999 (The Law Society, September 1999).

[99] Family Law (Scotland) Act 1985, s. 9 (1) (b).

issues of application and quantification. How in practice would one determine the effect of a relationship where one party had willingly chosen to forego a career, or even further education, to put family or other interests first? But any scheme of general application is going to need to be very carefully thought out in the detail, and will inevitably involve complex assessment. Simplicity tends always to be purchased at the cost of fairness. The alternative to such complexity is a Child Support type scenario, with its only too obvious shortcomings and injustice.

Needs model

The needs model has already been considered, as the prevailing model prior to *White*. This model has the great merit of looking at prospective requirements and trying to meet these appropriately. In that respect, the needs model seems an improvement on the rather unsatisfactory investigation into past representations and promises which the common law requires. Indeed, in so far as this approach may involve the least interference with existing property rights of all the models, it could be considered particularly appropriate for cohabitants.

Practical reform of ancillary relief

The above theoretical models are all vulnerable to the criticism that it is ultimately unrealistic to try to decide upon one single theoretical model, or even a hierarchical system, when individual circumstances are so diverse. This rather pessimistic but superficially persuasive view tends to discourage general theoretical debate. Also, as a society, we seem far from any consensus as to what is 'fair' or 'just'. Certainly, key concepts such as 'equality' and 'non-discrimination' are agreed and accepted, but how these translate into practice is not agreed, and indeed the goalposts of discussion are still shifting as society continues to transform itself at ever-increasing speed. So an easier focus for effective reform is the *process* by which property disputes are resolved, and here, surprisingly, there has been a consistent policy promoted by both the previous and now the present government. The policy is to withdraw the state from involvement in the ordering of property upon divorce, and to encourage the parties themselves to come to their own appropriate agreement. Clearly, the political motivation is cost-driven, but the supporting rhetoric is classically liberal. Thus, *Supporting Families* talks about 'giv[ing] people more choice' and 'allow[ing] them to take responsibility for ordering their own lives'. The two planks of this programme are mediation and the recognition of pre-nuptial agreements. A related initiative has been to reform the judicial process related to ancillary relief, in line with the Woolf reforms to streamline and modernise the civil law.

Mediation

Mediation sounds sensible. It conjures up ideas of calm, reasonable discussion with a wise, sensitive (and not too expensive) chairperson, leading to an agreement which the parties have reached themselves, and so which they consider fair and appropriate. At its best, mediation can approach this ideal. However, it is not a panacea. One must remember that, just as litigation is merely a procedure, so is mediation. Proponents are in danger of defining success in terms of process – mediation – rather than in terms of outcome – an appropriate division of property. Such a sleight of hand is very convenient for evaluators and quality assessors, but it is a magic trick. Yes, the process is important, and should be as stress-free and economically efficient as possible, because the process itself contributes to the outcome, but it is the final result in its entirety which is crucial.

Mediation can be useful and comparatively stress-free for those couples who are generally well disposed, the one to the other, and have had a relationship of mutual respect and esteem. But, sadly, not all couples fit this description. And for other couples, mediation can be criticised because it tries to reach a solution without those essential safeguards, as to procedure, disclosure, evidence, perjury, etc., which have been carefully developed by the courts to ensure a fair outcome. A possible danger is that, without these rules, an agreement will be reached without full knowledge of the facts or, indeed, on erroneous or downright false information. Also the lack of a formal structure and the emphasis upon agreement may perpetuate a power or economic imbalance and enable the dominant partner to impose his solution upon his scared/conciliatory/self-deprecating partner. Certainly, there is some evidence that women tend to do less well financially from mediated settlements.[100]

Pre-nuptial agreements

Another aspect of the government's promotion of private ordering is its recommendation, in *Supporting Families*, that pre-nuptial agreements should be enforceable.[101] Separation agreements between cohabiting couples have always been enforceable (although they are rare) but traditionally, pre-nuptial agreements have not been enforced because they are thought to undermine the concept of marriage as a lifelong union.[102] However, such an ideal is now so far from the reality of modern

---

[100] Diduck, 'Dividing the Family Assets' in Day Sclater and Piper (ed.), *Undercurrents of Divorce* (1999, Ashgate), p. 212.

[101] See Leadercramer, 'Prenuptial Agreements – an idea whose time has come?, [2000] Fam Law 359.

[102] N v. N *(Jurisdiction: Pre-Nuptial Agreement)* [1999] 2 FLR 745.

marriage[103] that this argument has lost its persuasiveness. *Supporting Families* endorses pre-nuptial agreements subject to protecting the interests of any children and preventing 'significant injustice' (which, wisely, the consultation document does not try to define or explain). Stated reasons for this change in policy reveal a political desire to promote marriage rather than any persuasive psychological insight – apparently enforceable pre-nuptial agreements would strengthen marriage because they would encourage people to think about their finances beforehand, and persuade people to marry rather than simply live together.

There are perhaps more difficulties with pre-nuptial agreements than the government has acknowledged. From a moral point of view, Eekelaar[104] expresses grave doubts about holding people to an agreement they may have made years earlier and concerning deeply personal matters. And from an economic perspective, it is possible that pre-nuptial agreements may only serve to add to the cost of divorce. In the United States, the net result has been further opportunities for dispute,[105] and it seems quite likely that they could have the same effect here. So then litigation upon divorce would involve not only claims under the Matrimonial Causes Act 1973 or its successor, but also claims that the pre-nuptial agreement was invalid, or that it should be construed in one particular way, or that it should not be enforced because of children or because significant injustice would ensue. The avalanche of cases following *Barclays Bank plc* v. *O'Brien*[106] well illustrates the pitfalls and difficulties inherent in enforcing agreements which are apparently more advantageous to one person in a relationship than the other, and the government's 'protection' of independent legal advice may not prove as cast iron as it would hope.[107]

Changes in procedure

A further response to the perceived problems of cost and delay in ancillary relief proceedings has been to reform court procedures,[108] in line with the Woolf reforms, so as to allow active case management and promote negotiated settlements. Strict timetables will ensure progress, and costs will be closely monitored, so that they are kept within proportionate bounds. This should avoid such horror stories as *Piglowska* v *Piglowski*,[109]

---

[103] In 1999 144,556 divorces were granted in England and Wales: *Annual Abstract of Statistics* 137 (2001, The Stationery Office), Table 5.12.

[104] Eekelaar, 'Should Section 25 be Reformed?' [1998] Fam Law 469.

[105] Katz, 'Marriage as Partnership' (1998) 75 *Notre Dame Law Rev*iew 1251.

[106] [1994] AC 180.

[107] See, for example, the comments of Millett LJ in *Credit Lyonnais Bank Nederland NV* v. *Burch* [1997] 1 All ER 144 (CA).

[108] Family Proceedings (Amendment No. 2) Rules 1999.

[109] [1999] 2 FLR 76.

to take a recent example, where costs of over £128,000 were incurred in a quarrel about assets worth £127,400 in total. If solicitors make excessive enquiries and incur heavy costs, they can be made the subject of a wasted costs order and can even be made personally liable for the costs.[110] This seems to put solicitors somewhere between Scylla and Charybdis: for they can of course be liable in negligence if they do not sufficiently investigate.[111]

Conclusions: looking to the future

There have always been many members of the general public for whom questions about property entitlement have been theoretical, just because they have owned so little. For such couples, the tenancy of the shared home has usually been the most significant asset, and generally matters have been arranged so that the primary carer of any children could keep the tenancy, or be rehoused. Social security law rather than family law has had the most impact upon such couples either in divorce or separation.

But increasingly during the last fifteen years, couples with substantial assets have also eschewed judicial involvement in the process of property division upon divorce. Barton and Bissett-Johnson have shown that the proportion of ancillary relief orders to main decrees declined from around three-quarters in 1985 to fewer than half in 1998.[112] And another trend apparent from the judicial statistics shows that those who do apply overwhelmingly reach a settlement rather than ask the court to adjudicate. The proportion of orders made by consent rose from 40 per cent in 1985 to 80 per cent in 1998. So, increasingly, judicial decision-making in this area is confined to a small minority of cases, which perhaps involve either 'big money' or especially bitter litigants. There are various possible reasons for this defection, but cost and the unpredictability of case outcome[113] seem the obvious forerunners. Whatever the cause, however, today's reality is that divorcing couples are avoiding an adjudicated solution, and settling privately either with or without the aid of solicitors. Commentators need to reconceptualise the whole process of ancillary relief as one of negotiation rather than litigation. Douglas[114] suggests that this trend should be recognised, and that a new breed of professional, not a lawyer but a divorce manager, should help a couple through all the pitfalls and changes which need to be negotiated.

[110] *Re a Solicitor (Wasted Costs Order)* [1993] 2 FLR 959.
[111] *Young* v. *Purdy* [1996] 2 FLR 795.
[112] Barton and Bissett-Johnson, 'The declining number of ancillary financial relief orders' [2000] Fam. Law 94.
[113] Davis *et al*, 'Ancillary relief outcomes' [2000] *Child and Family Law Quarterly* 43.
[114] Douglas, 'How parents cope financially on separation and divorce – implications for the future of ancillary relief', paper to SPTL conference, September 2000.

Within this context, one can look to the future to see … what? Certain glimmers of consensus are beginning to emerge. Increasingly, commentators are suggesting that some sort of adjustive regime should be available to separating cohabitants as well as married couples, and that shared parenthood is more significant for questions of property division than a marriage certificate, or even mere length of relationship. The way that domestic work has been consistently undervalued is now generally acknowledged, and the prevailing academic discourse is more about equality (whether formal or substantive) than about need. The speeches in *White* show the support of the House of Lords for these ideas and suggest the possibility of a fruitful cooperation between the judiciary and academics. That being said, there is still a long way to go, and one hopes that the discussion will continue unabated.

Finally, it is easy for students to be beguiled by the intellectual cross-currents and to forget that, at the heart of this topic, stand two couples, one married, the other unmarried, who are breaking up and having to cope with profound change and a range of deep, possibly conflicting, emotional responses. All the theoretical and practical discussions need to focus on how best to help or allow unhappy individuals deal with a period of transition and economic dislocation, so that, properly and appropriately equipped, they can move forward to the next stage of their lives.

Further reading

Bailey-Harris, 'Dividing the Assets on Breakdown of Relationships Outside Marriage' in Bailey-Harris (ed.), *Dividing the Assets on Family Breakdown* (1998, Family Law).

Barlow and Lind, 'A Matter of Trust: the Allocation of Rights in the Family Home' (1999) 19 *Legal Studies* 468.

Cretney, 'Trusting the Judges: Money after Divorce', (1999) *Current Legal Problems* 286.

Dewar, 'Reducing Discretion in Family Law' (1997) 11 *Australian Journal of Family Law* 309.

Dewar, 'The Normal Chaos of Family Law' (1998) 61 MLR 467.

Diduck, 'Dividing the Family Assets', in Day Sclater and Piper (ed.), *Undercurrents of Divorce* (1999, Ashgate).

Diduck and Kaganas, *Family Law, Gender and the State: Text, Cases and Materials* (1999, Hart).

Eekelaar, 'Should Section 25 be Reformed' [1998] Fam Law 469.

Eekelaar, *Financial and Property Adjustment after Divorce* (1998, Centre for Socio-Legal Studies, Oxford).

Freeman (ed.) *Divorce: Where Next?* (1996, Dartmouth).

Gardner, *Rethinking Family Property* (1993) 109 LQR 263.

Mee, *The Property Rights of Cohabitees* (1999, Hart).

O'Donovan, *Family Law Matters* (1993, Pluto Press).

3

Domestic violence

Joanna Miles*

1 Introduction

Domestic violence, taken here to mean 'any form of physical, sexual or emotional abuse which takes place within the context of a close relationship'[1] between adults, is more widespread than is commonly believed. It is under-reported and under-recorded, making a minor contribution to official crime figures.[2] This fosters beliefs shared by the public, agencies who come into contact with victims and victims themselves that domestic violence is rare; and that, where it does occur, it is a private matter to be resolved by the individuals concerned. And so such abuse is perceived to be something that does not warrant reporting by the victim. The 'invisibility' of domestic violence from public view is thus self-perpetuating.[3] Although both men and women are victimised, and violence occurs in both heterosexual and same-sex relationships, the prevailing view is that women in heterosexual relationships suffer far

---

* The author thanks Peter Bartlett, Stuart Bridge, Ivan Hare, Jonathan Herring, and Stephanie Palmer for comments on earlier drafts of this chapter. All errors and infelicities are entirely her own.

[1] Home Affairs Select Committee, *Report on Domestic Violence* (1993, HMSO). Some definitions include financial abuse, e.g. oppressive control of household finances.

[2] Mirlees-Black estimates that there were 6.6 million domestic physical assaults against persons aged 16–59 in 1995: *Domestic Violence: Findings from a new British Crime Survey self-completion questionnaire*, Home Office Research Study 191 (1999, Home Office). By contrast, crime statistics for the first year in which common assault became a notifiable offence recorded only 502,800 violent offences against the person (the relationship between offender and victim was not recorded) out of 5.1 million total recorded crime: Povey and Prime, *Recorded Crime Statistics, England and Wales April 1998 – March 1999* (Home Office Statistical Bulletin 18/99) (1999, Home Office).

[3] Edwards, *Policing 'Domestic' Violence: women, the law and the state* (1989, Sage), at pp. 110–13.

more, or at least more severely, than others.[4] Reflecting that belief, and for ease of exposition, this chapter will focus on abuse of women by their male partners and ex-partners.

It may be asked why *domestic* violence warrants particular consideration. It will, after all, commonly involve criminal assaults or harassment. However, the context in which those offences occur gives rise to problems not shared by other crimes. The key factor is the nature of the relationship between abuser and victim. They are not strangers to each other or mere acquaintances, but individuals whose lives are, or have been, intimately connected by sexual, emotional, economic and other familial bonds. These bonds complicate what might otherwise appear to be straightforward cases and prompt difficult questions about the appropriate response of the state. Does the fact that the abuse occurs between adults in a close relationship suggest that the decision as to how best to resolve the problem should be left to victims, rather than imposed by the state? Or should the state be entitled or obliged to prosecute such cases or to seek protection for the victim, even if she opposes such action?

Part 2 of this chapter outlines some competing theories about the causes of domestic violence. Part 3 examines some problems encountered in the law's response to domestic violence and recent steps taken to try to resolve them. Then, Part 4 explores two issues highlighted by the questions posed above: the nature and extent of the role that the state should have in responding to domestic violence; and the implications of state involvement for victims' freedom to choose their own fate and that of their abusers. Both criminal and civil laws and justice systems will be examined – the roles of police, prosecutors and courts in administering offences against the person, harassment offences and applications for civil orders under the Family Law Act 1996 and Protection from Harassment Act 1997.

It should be noted at the outset that this chapter will not discuss in detail the following issues: eligibility for and administration of welfare benefits and public housing; contact and residence arrangements in relation to children of the victim and her abuser; domestic violence between adults as a child protection issue; the special problems relating to abuse of the elderly and disabled adults. Texts discussing these topics are identified in the bibliography of suggested further readings at the end of the chapter.

---

[4] Mirlees-Black, *op. cit.* n. 2, at p. 28; Smith, *Domestic Violence*, Home Office Research Study 104 (1989, HMSO) at pp. 10 and 15; for criticism of the Conflict Tactics Scale, a model used to measure the extent of violence between partners which often suggests equal use of violence by men and women, see Dobash and Dobash, *op. cit.* n. 5, ch. 8, esp. pp. 274–81.

2 Causes of domestic violence

A proper understanding of the causes of abuse and the context in which it occurs is essential to the prescription of a suitable solution. As Hoff has observed, incorrect identification of the nature and source of the problem is likely to lead to the adoption of an inappropriate or inadequate response.[5] Some accounts of domestic violence tend to be 'reductionist', attributing the abuse to one specific cause. It may be wiser, Hoff cautions, to identify the *presence and influence* of various factors, rather than to seek one all-explaining 'cause'.[6] But it will be helpful to outline and assess some of the discrete theories that have been offered. There are essentially two schools of thought, which may be described as offering micro- and macro-level explanations respectively.[7] The former school encompasses a variety of analyses which essentially view domestic violence as an individual, private and apolitical problem. The latter, by contrast, sees domestic abuse as being symptomatic of a systemic, public and political problem implicating society at large.

Micro-level explanations of domestic violence: a private ill[8]

The micro-level explanations conceive of domestic violence variously as a problem confined to deviant individuals or families, arising from psychiatric, psychological or other characteristics of those individuals and from their personal relationships, or from their socio-economic circumstances. For some commentators, the violence originates in characteristics of individual abusers, which predispose them to assault or otherwise to abuse their partners. Violence may be a learned behaviour transmitted from one generation to the next, the perpetrator having witnessed or experienced abuse as a child. Alternatively, the source, or perpetuation, of the problem is explained as a feature of *victims'* background and psychology. Women subjected to abuse are said to become trapped by perceptions of their role as victim and passively submit to the violence. Some writers even suggest that women subjected to abuse are from the outset more prone to it than others, subconsciously and masochistically seeking out violent relationships. Others see domestic violence not as the

---

[5] *Battered Women as Survivors* (1990, Routledge), at pp. 73–7; see also Dobash and Dobash, *Women, Violence and Social Change* (1992, Routledge), at p. 112.

[6] Hoff, *op. cit.* n. 5, at pp. 5–9.

[7] This language is borrowed from Buzawa and Buzawa, *Domestic Violence: the Criminal Justice Response* (2nd ed.) (1996, Sage), ch. 2.

[8] The following account and criticisms of it are derived from Buzawa and Buzawa, *op. cit.* n. 7, ch. 2; Dobash and Dobash, *op. cit.* n. 5, ch. 7; Edwards, *op. cit.* n. 3, pp.164–70; Hoff, *op. cit.* n. 5, ch. 2 and 3; Morley and Mullender, *Preventing Domestic Violence to Women* (1994, Home Office), at pp. 6–7.

product of the problems of one individual, but of the dynamics between family members, whereby both parties may be viewed as equally culpable, provoking each other, lacking anger-management and inter-personal skills. The likelihood of violence is said also to be increased by the stress of deprived socio-economic conditions, alcoholism or other substance abuse, where the abuser will often resort to violence in the absence of other mechanisms for obtaining control over the victim. But under a broad definition of domestic abuse such as that adopted here, non-violent means of abuse, such as economic control of the victim, are equally concerning.

Some of these micro-level analyses can be used to support therapeutic responses to domestic violence, designed on the basis that the abuse is not primarily a crime which should be punished, but a 'value-free' conflict arising from the psychological problems of the individuals involved which needs to be 'solved'.[9] On this understanding, perpetrators need to identify and understand the source of their personal difficulties and to deal with their anger. Victims' psychological problems need to be tackled so that they acquire the insight required to end the cycle of violence. Women driven to kill their abusers may be best dealt with by therapeutic means.[10] Families need to unlearn destructive patterns of behaviour and acquire better communication skills. Both criminal and civil justice systems may thus contribute most effectively to combating domestic violence by channelling individuals towards appropriate non-legal professionals and non-punitive outcomes. Traditional methods of law enforcement and sanctions should on this basis be a last resort. Police called to violent homes should adopt a 'social work' as opposed to a 'law enforcement' role, seeking to mediate between the parties and advise them of counselling and support services rather than to arrest and pursue 'the guilty party' through the criminal justice system. Participation in therapy programmes may be a suitable disposal method, pre-trial or on conviction, for those individuals brought to the attention of the criminal justice system. In the civil law context, mediation and family counselling may be the most appropriate forum in which to address the problems of couples. Where a case does proceed through the traditional channels, then, in so far as these analyses impute equal blame for the violence to both parties, they may support arrest or binding over[11] of both, or the

---

[9] This uses the language of Buzawa and Buzawa, *op. cit.* n. 7, ch. 11; much of the following is derived from this source.

[10] The medicalisation of victims' problems is exemplified by use of mental abnormality defences to murder: O'Donovan, 'Defences for Battered Women who Kill' (1991) 18 *Journal of Legal Studies* 219; McColgan, 'In Defence of Battered Women Who Kill' (1993) 13 *Oxford Journal of Legal Studies* 508.

[11] Binding over to keep the peace or to be of good behaviour – a sanction which may be imposed by criminal courts on defendants, complainants and witnesses without a conviction for any offence.

acceptance by the civil courts of mutual non-molestation undertakings from both.[12]

Criticisms of the micro-level analyses

These analyses of domestic violence have been criticised for their lack of empirical support, their choice of perspective and their ideological implications. Programmes founded on the premises of these theories have not been demonstrably successful in reducing violence.[13] They may in fact further endanger victims. No profile of the 'typical' perpetrator or victim has been assembled. While alcohol features in many cases, it does not always do so, and, where it is present, it is difficult to discern its relevance, whether it be a cause, proffered excuse (and so, implicitly, a denial of individual responsibility) or mere context. Likewise, a perpetuation of violence between generations of a family, as abuser or victim, appears in only some cases. Nor is domestic violence confined to any particular socio-economic group. It has been suggested that perceptions to the contrary may be generated from the greater visibility of abuse in poorer families; lower-class victims are thought to be more likely to come to the attention of police, welfare agencies and refuges – and so of official statisticians and researchers – than middle-class victims, who may have the resources to cope without seeking public assistance. Moreover, social theories fail satisfactorily to explain the prevalence of male violence against women.

Theories focusing on the victim are particularly controversial in so far as they deflect attention from the perpetrator and his responsibility for his actions, tending instead to attribute the continuing abuse to features of the victim's psychology. The question becomes 'why didn't she leave?', rather than 'why was *he* not held responsible?'[14] Yet suggestions of victim passivity, or more controversially of masochism, ignore the various coping strategies reported by researchers to be adopted by victims, and the economic and social pressures and further threats of violence that in practice prevent many victims from leaving. The notion that simply leaving will cure the problem is belied by evidence that abuse often worsens on and after separation. Moreover, victims are encouraged by the currency of such theories to blame themselves for the abuse and so to seek 'remedies' in modifications of their own behaviour, which will necessarily be ineffectual if the true cause of the problem is external to them.[15] And if

[12] See Kewley, *op. cit*. n. 69.

[13] Buzawa and Buzawa, *op. cit*. n. 7, chs. 11 and 17; Morley and Mullender, 'Hype or Hope? The importance of pro-arrest policies and batterers' programmes from North America to Britain as key measures for preventing violence to women in the home' (1992) 6 *International Journal of Law and the Family* 265, at pp. 284–5.

[14] Mahoney, 'Legal Images of Battered Women: redefining the issue of separation assault' (1991) 90 *Michigan Law Review* 1, at pp. 61–4; Edwards, *op. cit*. n. 3, at p. 164.

[15] Hoff, *op. cit*. n. 5, at pp. 73–7.

victims as a class exhibit certain psychological characteristics at all, these are as likely to be the *result* of the abuse as its initial *cause*.

The most fundamental objection levelled at these explanations is that, reference to socio-economic factors aside, micro-analyses medicalise and so depoliticise what for their critics is an essentially political issue demanding systemic reform of *society*, and not just tinkering with the psychology and socialisation of a few apparently dysfunctional in-dividuals or families. In order to appreciate this objection, the theoretical explanation offered by these critics must be examined.

Macro-level explanations of domestic violence: a public health problem[16]

Macro-level explanations of domestic violence proceed from a very different point of departure from that of the micro-level analyses. Rather than focusing on the problems of particular abusive relationships in isolation, this approach examines those relationships in the context of society's treatment of women generally. Domestic violence is viewed by feminist scholars not as a problem confined to a few *deviant* individuals, but as being one *rational* corollary of a larger phenomenon – the inferior status of women within a male-dominated society.

The subordination of women, it is claimed, has been and is still manifested in various spheres of life, and is (albeit less so than formerly) sustained by the law and other public institutions and ideologies.[17] Until the end of the nineteenth century, the law (more or less) condoned 'reasonable chastisement' of wives by their husbands.[18] The right of husbands to beat and confine their wives was explained as a necessary consequence of the doctrine of coverture, whereby a woman's legal identity was on marriage largely subsumed within that of her husband who became responsible for her, her property and her behaviour. He was accordingly granted the power to discipline her.[19]

However, Doggett argues that this doctrinal 'justification' was no more than a rhetorical device used to disguise the less palatable reality of male

---

[16] *Ibid.*, at p. 241.

[17] Freeman, 'Legal Ideologies: patriarchal precedents and domestic violence', in *The State, the Law and the Family: critical perspectives*, Freeman (ed.) (1984, Sweet and Maxwell); for legal developments since 1984, see n. 23.

[18] *Jackson* (1891) 1 QB 671 finally confined the rights to beat and confine to history (though some commentators persisted in claiming the existence of more limited rights): see Doggett, *Marriage, Wife-beating and the Law in Victorian England*, (1992, Weidenfeld and Nicholson), ch. 1 and at pp. 134–9.

[19] Blackstone, *Commentaries on the Laws of England*, 21st ed. (1844, London), ch.15, esp. p. 444. For detailed discussion of the effects of marriage on wives' legal status., see Doggett, *op. cit.* n. 18, ch. 2.

power.[20] Although the use of physical (and, eventually, sexual)[21] force by husbands came officially to be outlawed, and although the formal status of women improved – eventually acquiring equal civil and political rights in relation to the vote, property ownership, etc., despite marriage – women remained in an inferior position. The influence of Victorian ideologies of family life and proper gender roles – the bread-winning male in the public world, the home-making, child-rearing, dependent female in the private world – meant that many women were *in practice* denied the opportunity to acquire the wealth and power which could now *in theory* be theirs.[22] If no longer lawfully subjected to their husbands' physical force, many women remained lawfully subject to their *de facto* economic authority.

Indeed, Freeman has argued that many fiscal and welfare laws have (until recently) been premised on women's economic dependence on their male partners, thereby reinforcing a patriarchal ideology and social structure.[23] Yet at the same time, he notes, although it imposes on spouses (but not cohabitants) duties to maintain each other, the law is reluctant while the parties live together to enforce those duties, thereby leaving (usually) women at the mercy of their partners' benevolence.[24] This failure of the law adequately to protect those women whose dependence it presumes and arguably reinforces reflects the problematic influence on family law of liberal ideology – that the family should be free to order its private affairs without state interference until something is perceived to 'go wrong'. However, to adopt O'Donovan's thesis, in so far as the law has the power to define what counts as 'going wrong' and so merits corrective

[20] Doggett, *op. cit.* n. 18.

[21] Rape within marriage was acknowledged as criminal in *R* v. *R* [1992] 1 AC 599.

[22] Doggett, *op. cit.* n. 18, at pp. 98–9, 139–40.

[23] *Op. cit.* n. 17, Freeman, 'Violence against women: does the legal system provide solutions or itself constitute the problem?' (1980) 7 *Journal of Legal Studies* 215; Douglas, 'The Family, Gender and Security', in Harris, ed., *Social Security Law in Context* (2000, OUP). On taxation, see Tiley, *Revenue Law* (2000, Hart), esp. ch. 8, 9 and 11. Fiscal and welfare law is now formally gender neutral. Either party to a relationship may now claim means-tested benefit or tax credit for that family unit. The Finance Act 1999, sections 30–35, replaces the married persons' allowance with the new Children's Tax Credit. Preference is sometimes given to the primary child-carer: e.g. regulations for the Working Families Tax Credit, SI 1999/2572, provide that the credit may be paid to the primary child-carer (even if not earning) if the parties disagree about which should receive it.

[24] Freeman, *op. cit.* n. 17, at pp. 64–5. On duties of maintenance, see Lowe and Douglas, *Bromley's Family Law*, 9th ed. (1998, Butterworths), at pp. 715–19, *et seq*. Maintenance orders for spouses under the Domestic Proceedings and Magistrates' Courts Act 1978, s. 2, will not survive beyond six months of the parties' cohabitation: section 25; prior to that Act, the courts had no jurisdiction to make orders while the parties were cohabiting. If the dependant spouse claims welfare benefits where their absent partner fails to provide for them or their children, the state is more concerned: see the liable relative procedure for recovery of some means-tested benefit payments under the Social Security Administration Act 1992 and the Child Support Act regime, discussed in Douglas, *op. cit.* n. 23, at pp. 271–80.

state intervention, it implicitly defines what constitutes a properly functioning family and can indirectly regulate the private sphere in endorsing by purposeful non-intervention whatever order happens to prevail there.[25] So, for example, it could be inferred from the current state of the law that although the state now officially abhors domestic violence, it is at best equivocal about economic domination of one partner by the other. Yet the state endeavours by invoking the privacy mantra to claim that it does not regulate on-going family life. The concept of privacy is thus a double-edged sword: although it may legitimately protect families from state intrusion, it may equally be deployed to justify the state's failure to protect weaker individuals from the abuse of private power within the family;[26] and it distracts attention from those legal structures which in fact seek to construct a particular model family life.

The ideology of male superiority within the family is said to exert a malevolent influence over gender relations today and to exacerbate the problems encountered by victims of domestic violence. Even though the common law no longer upholds the right of husbands to beat their wives, 'folk law' in some quarters appears still to support it. Many men resort to abuse in an effort to control 'their' women, which helps to explain why abuse often worsens when the woman asserts her independence by leaving or trying to leave the relationship.[27] Violence is often precipitated by the 'failure' of the woman to perform 'her' domestic duties to the satisfaction of her partner. By placing primary responsibility for maintaining a happy home life on wives and mothers, the social order encourages self-blame amongst victims, who consequently engage in repeated but futile efforts to prevent the violence by modifying their own behaviour.[28] Although in reality working patterns within the family often differ from the stereotypical view, many women still find themselves in economically inferior positions to their partners. The dearth of child-care facilities and the unequal distribution of responsibility for child-care within most families confines many women for at least part of their working lives to part-time and low-paid employment, which limits their choices when they find themselves in a violent relationship.[29] Moreover, the administration of legal remedies and public resources able to deal with domestic violence

---

[25] *Sexual Divisions in Law* (1985, Weidenfeld and Nicholson); see also Schneider, 'The Violence of Privacy' in Fineman and Mykitiuk (eds), *The Public Nature of Private Violence* (1994, Routledge).

[26] Pahl (ed.), *Private Violence and Public Policy: the needs of battered women and the responses of the public services* (1985, London), at p. 191.

[27] Mahoney, *op. cit.* n. 14.

[28] Dobash and Dobash, *op. cit.* n. 5, at p. 232–4.

[29] Hoff, *op. cit.* n. 5, ch. 12. On women's contribution to and the management of family income, see Douglas, *op. cit.* n. 23, pp. 280–1; Diduck and Kaganas, *Family Law, Gender and the State* (1999, Hart), at pp. 90–5, 168–73; Pahl, 'The Allocation of Money within the Household', in Freeman (ed.), *op. cit.* n. 17.

and its consequences is said to be affected by the enduring influence among responsible agencies of traditional ideologies about gender relations, or at least by unease about violating family privacy.[30]

Given a diagnosis of domestic violence as one manifestation of a deep-seated social, political and *public* problem, rather than one peculiar to certain individuals, the cure is necessarily complex. If domestic violence is a consequence of the general subordination of women within society, it may never be eradicated until women attain equal status with men within society at large, and within the family, not simply in *formal* terms, but in *substance*. For some feminists, the law's historical complicity in the subordination of women makes its use in any reforming campaign problematic; it is regarded as an inherently patriarchal institution.[31] But it may be possible, with due caution, to use law and the legal system to help effect the changes in ideology and social structures needed to combat gender inequality and domestic violence. Just as law historically sustained women's subordination to men, so it can be used to help dismantle that ideology.

In so far as the ideology manifests itself in the actions of individual abusers, the law can be employed to send a clear message that violence and harassment in the domestic context are serious crimes and to affirm the right of women to live free from abuse. Furthermore, feminist appreciation of the imbalance of power within abusive relationships suggests that remedies dependent on the victim initiating proceedings or on mediation between the couple may be ineffective, so proactive *public* intervention to protect the victim should be considered. Any counselling of abusers, used perhaps as a diversion from the ordinary criminal process, or as an aspect of sentencing, should proceed from a feminist standpoint. The law can also supply a framework for public provision of the *material* support (such as welfare benefits and housing) needed to enable victims to leave their violent relationships. However, focusing exclusively on individual cases of violence and the immediate crises they precipitate for victims and their families to the neglect of reform of the social structures and ideologies which foster the inferior status of women will have only a superficial impact.[32] Pursuit of individual cases must be accompanied by implementation of social and economic policies and

---

[30] On police, prosecutors, courts: Edwards, *op. cit.* n. 3; on court welfare officers and mediators: Hester and Pearson, 'Domestic Violence and Children – the practice of court welfare officers' (1997) 9 *Child and Family Law Quarterly* 281 and texts in note 94; on social workers: Maynard, 'The Response of Social Workers to Domestic Violence' in Pahl (ed.) *op. cit.* n. 26; on housing officers: Binney, Harkell and Nixon, 'Refuges and Housing for Battered Women', in Pahl (ed.), *op. cit.* n. 26; Thornton, 'Homelessness through Relationship Breakdown: the local authorities' response' (1989) 11 *Journal of Social Welfare Law* 67 and texts in suggested further reading.

[31] Smart, *Feminism and the Power of Law* (1989, Routledge).

[32] Hoff, *op. cit.* n. 5, ch. 12.

educational programmes in a wider project of substituting for patriarchal ideology an egalitarian view of gender relations.

3 The criminal and civil justice systems' responses to domestic violence

This section identifies some of the problems that have characterised the criminal and civil justice systems' responses to domestic violence, and the efforts made to overcome these deficiencies. As will be seen, recent attention to domestic violence has focused on enhancing the response of the criminal justice system to domestic violence, based on a feminist-inspired understanding that the state has a central responsibility to deal proactively with domestic violence, holding offenders *publicly* to account for their behaviour. Meanwhile, the traditional view of the civil justice system as a forum for the *private* resolution of disputes with no state involvement is being challenged by moves to allow state applicants to seek protective orders on behalf of victims. Such proactive involvement of the state raises questions about the status of the victim in the criminal and civil justice systems, and the extent of control that she may legitimately exert over 'her' case.

The criminal justice system[33]

Previous perceived failings

Historically, the criminal law has been little used as a means of dealing with domestic violence. Research conducted into the operation of the criminal justice system has suggested that this limited use has derived in large part from the manner in which police, prosecutors and courts have exercised their discretionary powers in these cases. The discretion enjoyed by police officers in dealing with domestic violence has often been exercised in a manner which seems prejudicial to victims: failing to record

---

[33] The following is derived from several sources: Edwards, *op. cit.* n. 3; Faragher, 'The Police Response to Violence against Women in the Home' in Pahl (ed.) *op. cit.* n. 26; and more recent research, undertaken since the introduction of new policies by Home Office Circular 60/1990, the effects of which are discussed later in the text: Grace, *Policing Domestic Violence*, Home Office Research Study 139 (1995, Home Office); Morley and Mullender, *op. cit.* n. 8; Cretney and Davis, *Punishing Violence* (1995, Routledge); Hoyle, *Negotiating Domestic Violence: Police, Criminal Justice* and *Victims* (1998, Clarendon Press); Kelly *et al.*, *Domestic Violence Matters: an evaluation of a development project*, Home Office Research Study 193 (1999, Home Office); Burton, 'Prosecution decisions in cases of domestic violence involving children' (2000) 22 *Journal of Social Welfare Family Law* 175; Edwards, *Sex and Gender in the Legal Process* (1996, Blackstone), at pp. 192–213. For North America, Buzawa and Buzawa, *op. cit.* n. 7.

incidents as crimes and failing to arrest offenders even where there were legal and evidential grounds for doing so, or 'down-criming' (i.e. charging a lower level of offence than the extent of the injuries and other evidence warrants). Similarly, prosecutors and courts have appeared to play down domestic violence: discontinuing cases, prosecuting on less serious charges than the evidence allows, and imposing low or non-custodial sentences. There are several factors which may explain this behaviour; but note that not all complaints made here are unique to cases of domestic violence.

The approach of the police and others has been accounted for in part by their failure to appreciate the context of domestic violence cases. Police called to an incident might assume that it was an isolated, one-off event and deal with it accordingly, when in fact there was an established pattern of abuse within the relationship. This ignorance would often be the result of organisational problems: failure to record incidents carefully or at all, and inadequate communication of information to officers attending the scene after an emergency call. Or, if this was the first time that the particular victim had sought outside help, the police might wrongly infer that it was the first time that she had been assaulted.[34] These misperceptions have been reflected in courts' decisions about breach of bail, remand and sentencing, failing to recognise that domestic violence may become increasingly severe if not stopped early on.

The negative attitudes towards these cases have also been attributed to frustration at the perceived 'fickleness' of domestic violence victims, who one minute seek police protection, but the next refuse to cooperate in criminal proceedings. Given the centrality of victim testimony to otherwise unwitnessed crimes, this refusal may doom a prosecution to failure.[35] Many police officers find themselves called repeatedly to the same household without getting 'a result', i.e. an arrest leading to a successful prosecution. Given this experience, police may be reluctant to proceed with a case unless they can be sure of the victim's commitment to prosecution. But in seeking to test that commitment – in particular, by asking the victim if she wants to make a complaint, thereby implying erroneously that further action in the case is dependent upon her wish for it to proceed – they may only succeed in having their expectations of the victim fulfilled. In their anticipation of the victim withdrawing her

---

[34] Or harassed; efficient use of the new harassment offences demands careful recording to establish the 'course of conduct' necessary to bring a charge: Protection from Harassment Act 1997, section 1; see Harris, *An evaluation of the use and effectiveness of the Protection from Harassment Act 1997*, Home Office Research Study 203 (2000, Home Office).

[35] It is not clear that perceptions of domestic violence victims as being especially prone to withdraw their cooperation from prosecution are well-founded; it is likely to occur wherever victims and offenders are acquainted and there is a power imbalance in their relationship: Cretney and Davis, *op. cit.* n. 33, at pp. 84–6, 99–100.

cooperation, police and prosecutors can by their handling of the case themselves precipitate that outcome, where a more sensitive and supportive approach might encourage the victim to proceed.

Overall, the system has appeared to trivialise domestic violence. The very labelling of a case as 'a domestic' carries with it an 'implicit case management prescription':[36] this is a minor matter, probably involving fault on both sides and the victim will probably withdraw her complaint sooner or later, so it should not take up valuable police time. Indeed, each agency within the system has seemed to encourage the others to persist in this view. For example, police attitudes are in part influenced by prosecutors failing to proceed with cases where the victim is unco-operative or prosecuting lesser offences, and by low, often non-custodial sentences being imposed by some courts, and by the use of bind-overs, in the few cases that have reached that stage.[37]

At worst, these practices may have been attributable to a patriarchal culture which condoned or at least tolerated the abuse by men of their partners. Alternatively, they may have reflected variously: concern to preserve the parties' privacy and reunite the family; an awkwardness in dealing with emotionally charged situations; a perception, often generated by hostility from the victim, of fault on both sides; officers' fears for their own safety, even from the 'victim'. Even where the police have been willing to help, ignorance among some officers of their powers has prevented them from taking effective action. But some research suggests that domestic assaults may be treated no less seriously than other assaults.[38] And it has also been suggested that these apparently unhelpful attitudes are the product of what may be a well-founded perception that the criminal justice system is ill-suited to meet the needs of domestic

---

[36] Cretney and Davis, *op. cit.* n. 33, at p. 125; see ch. 6 generally on police case construction. These authors emphasise that police practices are as much influenced by prosecutors' decisions as prosecutors' practices are affected by those of the police: ch. 8, pp. 164–5.

[37] Bind-overs are often used where the victim refuses to testify, instead of prosecuting the substantive charge on other evidence: Cretney and Davis, 'Prosecuting "Domestic" Assault' [1996] *Criminal Law Review* 162, at pp. 170–1. For criticism of binding-over, see Law Com. 222, *Binding Over* (1994), para 6.9–6.19.; see also remarks of Thorpe LJ in *Foulkes* v. *Chief Constable of Merseyside Police* [1998] 2 FLR 789, at 797–98 concerning arrest for breach of the peace.

[38] The notion that police treatment of domestic violence cases is the result of patriarchy is disputed. They, like other assaults between acquaintances, may be regarded as merely private quarrels, ordinarily warranting only a 'cooling-down' police intervention, at least where the victim does not want prosecution (as to which, see Part 5 below): Cretney and Davis, *op. cit.* n. 33, at p. 77. Sanders' research suggests that without a threat to public order or police authority, arrest in domestic and non-domestic situations is equally (un)likely. It is because those public factors are more common in non-domestic cases, rather than downgrading of domestic cases *per se*, that arrest there is more likely: Sanders, 'Personal Violence and Public Order: the prosecution of "domestic" violence in England and Wales' (1988) 16 *International Journal of the Sociology of Law* 359.

violence victims, not least where the victim herself opposes prosecution.[39] This idea will be explored below in Parts 4 and 5.

These 'failures' in the operation of the criminal justice system are counter-productive. Abusers may have been encouraged by the apparent impotence, lack of interest or implicit support of the police and the courts to repeat their conduct with renewed vigour, or with a view to retaliation for having been exposed by the victim to police attention. Some offenders have been arrested and charged for public order offences which are often easier to prosecute given the available evidence but which do not obviously relate to the domestic violence, and so fail to send a clear message about the criminality of *that* behaviour.[40] Victims may have been left feeling isolated, helpless and in greater danger than ever, having received little or no support on what may have been the first occasion on which they had disclosed the abuse to any formal agency.

New approaches to the problem

In response to the criticisms of some feminist reformers, official policy relating to domestic violence now expressly encourages arrest and prosecution, affirming the central role of the police as impartial law-enforcers. The most recent Home Office circular on domestic violence, issued in April 2000, is particularly emphatic about the importance of arrest which should 'normally' occur where an offence is committed, and charging, which it envisages occurring in all but exceptional cases.[41] Some American jurisdictions have even introduced *mandatory* arrest legislation which *requires* police officers to arrest perpetrators where there are legal and evidential grounds for doing so, thereby attempting (not necessarily successfully) to remove a large part of police discretion.[42] These new policies rest on the belief that 'arrest of an alleged assailant may act as a powerful deterrent against his re-offending – at least for some time – and it is an important means of showing the victim that she is entitled to, and will receive, *society's* protection and support',[43] sentiments which clearly reflect an appreciation of domestic violence as a public, rather than a purely private, matter. However, it is recognised that arrest alone may not be effective in preventing repeat victimisation. It must be accompanied by further action throughout the system – not least charge and prosecution – to control the offender and to protect and support the victim. Police are

---

[39] Cretney and Davis, *op cit.* n. 33, at p. 84; Hoyle, *op. cit.* n. 33, at p. 169.

[40] See Sanders, *op. cit.* n. 38.

[41] *Domestic Violence: Revised Circular to Police*, Home Office Circular 19/2000, replacing and in significant respects changing in emphasis from HOC 60/1990; *Crown Prosecution Policy for Prosecuting Cases of Domestic Violence* (1995) – new edition due end 2001. Contrast earlier Home Office policy, discussed by Dobash and Dobash, *op. cit.* n. 5, at pp. 195–6.

[42] Buzawa and Buzawa, *op. cit.* n. 7, ch. 13.

[43] *Domestic Violence*, Home Office Circular 6/1990, para. 16, emphasis added.

urged to give serious consideration to use of remand and conditional bail.[44] Sentencing too is important; the Court of Appeal has emphasised that the domestic context does not excuse or mitigate the criminality of the behaviour.[45]

The prosecution of domestic violence cases has been facilitated by changes to evidential rules relating to spouses, who may be compelled to testify against their partners in cases of assaults, injury or threats against them, on pain of punishment for contempt if they fail to cooperate.[46] This change overruled the common law, which sought to protect the sanctity and privacy of marriage by refraining from taking the 'repugnant' step of forcing a victim reconciled with her abusive husband to testify against him.[47] Moreover, if a victim is absent from the trial through fear, the prosecution may apply to admit her written statement in evidence in lieu of oral testimony.[48] Should a victim wish to withdraw her complaint, she will be required to make a full withdrawal statement to the police, detailing her reasons and, if she does not deny the truth of her original complaint, may be required to explain her withdrawal in court.[49] Crown Prosecution Service policy states that where a victim wishes to withdraw her complaint, full consideration will be given to continuing without oral or any victim testimony, or 'sensitively' compelling the victim to give evidence. It makes clear that a prosecution may be taken in the public interest in spite of the victim's wishes.[50] In anticipation of this possibility, police are encouraged at the outset to engage in a comprehensive evidence-gathering process, rather than focusing exclusively on obtaining the victim's statement, to increase the chances that a charge can be preferred and prosecution pursued without victim testimony if necessary.[51] Indeed, the recent guidance to police states that where there is enough evidence to do so, they should charge the suspect in all but exceptional circumstances. The question of victim cooperation and its

---

[44] HOC 19/2000 para.8 (n. 41). Court (but not police) bail can require the defendant to reside at a bail hostel pending trial; see Zander, *Cases and Materials on the English Legal System* (1999, Butterworth), at pp. 238–44. On reducing repeat victimisation: Kelly *et al., op. cit.* n. 33; Hanmer, Griffiths and Jerwood, *Arresting Evidence: domestic violence and repeat victimisation*, Police Research Series 104 (1999, Home Office); Lloyd, Farrell and Pease, *Preventing Repeated Domestic Violence: a demonstration project on Merseyside*, Police Research Group, Crime Prevention Unit Series 49 (1994, Home Office); Morley and Mullender, *op. cit.* n. 13.

[45] *R* v. *Cutts* (1987) 17 FL 311, *per* Michael Davies J.

[46] Police and Criminal Evidence Act 1984, s. 80.

[47] *Hoskyns* v. *Metropolitan Police Commissioner* [1979] AC 474.

[48] Criminal Justice Act 1988, s. 23, interpreted broadly in *R* v. *Ashford Magistrates Court, ex p Hilden* (1993) 96 Cr. App. Rep. 92.

[49] See HOC 19/2000 para.11 (n. 41) for the suggested contents of withdrawal statements.

[50] CPS *op. cit.* n. 41, paras. 4 and 5.

[51] HOC 19/2000 para. 4 (n. 41).

necessity for a successful prosecution is not to be pre-judged by the police.

Another aspect of the new proactive policy has been the introduction of dedicated Domestic Violence Units within some police forces. These units can play a vital role in supporting victims throughout the criminal process, enhancing the prospects for their participation in a prosecution. They also endeavour to improve the overall police response to domestic violence through training programmes and the introduction of improved data-management systems. These seek to ensure that officers attending emergency calls have relevant background information (e.g. of civil orders under the Family Law Act to which powers of arrest have been attached) and a more sympathetic appreciation of the situation of victims of abuse generally. DVUs can also perform a valuable task in referring victims to state and voluntary agencies equipped to cater for their wider socio-economic and emotional needs. The importance of this function will be discussed in more detail below in Part 4.

However, research by Grace and by others suggests that although police attitudes to domestic violence are improving, arrest rates remain relatively low.[52] And there is still evidence of bad practice among some officers, which can make calling the police a lottery for the victim. Police may be more interventionist where there are children who may be regarded as indirect victims of the violence; the threat to the children rather than the victim herself seems to provide the impetus for action.[53] But they may be more concerned to ensure the safety of victim and child than to arrest the abuser. As for prosecutors, even if arrest and charge rates might be improving, there is still a high discontinuance rate for domestic violence prosecutions. It seems that prosecutions tend to be dropped if the victim withdraws her cooperation, even where there is other evidence available and even where there are children involved.[54] The power to compel victims to testify is rarely used. The opportunity to admit written evidence in lieu is also seldom taken by the prosecution, though some victims may be absent through a desire for reconciliation rather than fear. The CPS Inspectorate has found that significant numbers of decisions both to prosecute and to discontinue cases are taken without the benefit of key information and fail to comply with CPS policy.[55] Despite Court of Appeal

---

[52] Grace, *op. cit.* n. 33; Hoyle, *op. cit.* n. 33, ch. 4. Even mandatory arrest legislation seems not to increase arrest rates significantly: Buzawa and Buzawa, *op. cit.* n. 7, ch.13.

[53] Burton, *op. cit.* n. 33.

[54] *Ibid*; Cretney and Davis, *op. cit.* n. 37; and 'The Significance of Compellability in the Prosecution of Domestic Violence' (1997) 37 *British Journal of Criminology* 75.

[55] Crown Prosecution Service Inspectorate, *The Inspectorate's Report on cases involving domestic violence*, Thematic Report 2/98 May (1998), cited by Edwards, 'Use of the Criminal Law', *Briefing Note: Reducing Domestic Violence … What works?*, Policing and Reducing Crime Unit (2000, Home Office).

pronouncements about appropriate sentencing, commentators remain critical of sentencing practice.[56] Conditional bail and remand are not always used as effectively by police and courts as they might be to protect victims from intimidation prior to trial. Domestic Violence Units have not been established in all forces, their resourcing and status within the force has been low and their remits vary. Indeed, the appropriate role of these officers remains controversial – should they be aiming specifically to encourage the victim to cooperate with prosecution, or offering neutral support?[57] Reasons for this apparent failure of the new policies to be translated fully into practice thus far will be explored below.

It is perhaps worth noting that the research discussed here is based on practice in the 1990s. The latest police circular's espousal of more thorough evidence-gathering might encourage prosecutors to pursue more cases without the victim's involvement; armed with sufficient evidence even without victim testimony, the only remaining issue would be whether prosecution were required in the public interest despite, in many cases, the victim's opposition. The stronger pro-arrest emphasis of the latest police circular may prompt the making of more arrests. So too may the possibility of litigation by aggrieved victims under the Human Rights Act 1998, or in negligence.[58] The Act generally requires public authorities, courts included, to act compatibly with the rights protected by the European Convention on Human Rights and provides a cause of action and remedies for victims.[59] As well as requiring the state not to interfere with individual rights itself, the Convention imposes positive obligations on the state to take steps to protect individuals' rights from interference by others. Some cases have examined the extent of these obligations in relation to the rights to life and freedom from inhuman and degrading treatment under Articles 2 and 3.[60] The right to respect for

---

[56] Edwards, *op. cit.* n. 33 (1996), pp. 208–12; on sentencing of marital and other relationship rape post-*R* v. *R*: Rumney, 'When Rape isn't Rape: Court of Appeal Sentencing Practice in Cases of Marital and Relationship Rape' (1999) 19 *Oxford Journal of Legal Studies* 243.

[57] Grace, *op. cit.* n. 33, ch.5; Morley and Mullender, *op. cit.* n. 8, pp. 17–23; Plotnikoff and Wilson, *Policing Domestic Violence: effective organisational structure*, Police Research Series 104 (1998, Home Office).

[58] The somewhat problematic decision of the European Court of Human Rights in *Osman* v. *UK* [1999] 1 FLR 193 may facilitate negligence actions against police, in so far as it suggests that such actions cannot be struck out on the basis of a 'class immunity' without any consideration of the merits of the individual case. US mandatory arrest laws were in part prompted by successful civil rights actions brought against the police by victims who had been left inadequately protected: see Dobash and Dobash, *op. cit.* n. 5, p. 198. Decisions not to prosecute are susceptible to judicial review: *R* v. *DPP, ex parte C* [1995] 1 Cr App R 136.

[59] Sections 6–9; note section 6(2) for cases where incompatible action is not unlawful.

[60] Art. 2: *Osman* v. *UK* [1999] 1 FLR 193; Art. 3: on state intervention for child protection: *Z* v. *UK* [2000] 2 FCR 245; see generally Starmer, *European Human Rights Law* (1999, LAG), ch. 5, and paras. 19.50–19.52.

private and family life under Article 8 has also been interpreted to impose positive obligations on the state, and in the *Whiteside* case, the Commission held that this included an obligation to protect individuals from harassment within their home.[61] That said, while it is clear that 'unreasonable' demands will not be made of the state – it is certainly not required to offer an absolute guarantee of rights protection – the parameters of its positive obligations under the Convention and under common law negligence are uncertain, and will vary from case to case. While some cases before the European institutions have addressed the state's obligations in child protection cases, it appears that no case has directly considered the state's obligations in relation to the policing and prosecution of domestic violence.[62] But they may nevertheless encourage more robust policing and prosecution of domestic violence, at least in those cases where the victim wants it. Cases where the victim opposes such action raise rather different considerations, and these are considered in Part 4.

The civil justice system

Previous perceived failings

Civil remedies potentially provide benefits not traditionally available from the criminal system, focusing on the protection and needs of the victim rather than condemnation of the abuser, and being available on a lower standard of proof. Civil remedies can specify when and how the abuser is allowed to contact the victim, if at all, and remove the abuser from his own property to provide the victim with a secure home, even if she otherwise has no entitlement to occupy it.[63] They have a less detrimental impact on the abuser than criminal conviction, and avoid the indirect harm suffered by a victim and her children where the abuser is fined or imprisoned. The abuser may be ejected from the home, but both he and his victim will be saved the public ordeal of a criminal trial. Moreover, many victims prefer seeking civil remedies to participating in a prosecution because they and their own legal representative will control the proceedings, which are held in private. On the other hand, further reductions in legal aid eligibility are

---

[61] *Whiteside* v. *UK* (1994) 76–A DR 80, 86, but found no violation on the merits; see also *Airey* v. *Ireland* (1979) 2 EHRR 305; *X and Y* v. *Netherlands* (1986) 8 EHRR 235; the applicant in *Whiteside* also argued that Article 1 of Protocol 1 imposed a positive obligation on the state.

[62] *Whiteside* and *Airey* both concerned the state's obligations to ensure individuals' access to private law remedies in relation to domestic violence.

[63] Bail conditions can control the defendants' contact with victims and require them to live away from home, but apply only pending trial and give victims no corresponding right to occupy. Contrast the new restraining orders available to dispose of criminal harassment cases, discussed in the text at note 111.

rendering costly civil remedies inaccessible to many victims.[64] Most fundamentally, traditional civil law responses necessarily cast the problem of domestic violence as one that is *private* to the parties, and not a matter for public, or police, concern.[65]

As is the case with the criminal law, the ability of the civil justice system to deal satisfactorily with domestic violence depends upon the ideology and understanding of agents operating within it. The 1970s legislation which enhanced civil remedies for domestic violence was the product of pressure by women's groups to bring domestic violence onto the political agenda.[66] However, many writers report that victims who sought non-molestation injunctions and orders regulating the occupation of the family home under this legislation were often disappointed. The legislation's ostensible objectives were frustrated by various problems. It had a narrow scope, applying only to spouses and heterosexual cohabitants. The array of statutes creating different jurisdictions for different courts did not aid clarity. Since the courts had no power to make incidental orders relating to household items, some otherwise successful applicants found themselves occupying homes vindictively stripped of their furnishings.[67] Courts were extremely reluctant to make *ex parte* and interim ouster orders that could, in theory, have provided timely relief.[68] Ouster orders tended to be short, the norm being three months, even where the applicant was herself entitled to live in the property.[69] Undertakings were frequently accepted in lieu of orders, despite the fact that no power of arrest can be attached to undertakings, so that the onus is on the victim to return to court to trigger its enforcement powers. When orders were made, the courts were reluctant to impose powers of arrest, and when they did so, the police were too often ignorant of the existence of orders to make the powers of arrest useful. Even if the police were aware, the problems relating to police enforcement of the criminal law applied here. And if an abuser ever were brought before court to be punished for breaching an order, the penalties

---

[64] Morley and Mullender, *op. cit.* n. 8, at p. 30; Hester and Radford, *Domestic Violence and Child Contact Arrangements in England* and *Denmark* (1996, Policy Press), at p. 17.

[65] See Dobash and Dobash, *op. cit.* n. 5, discussing findings of Cleveland Women's Aid and National Women's Aid Federation research, at pp. 192–3.

[66] This legislation and that increasing local authorities' duties towards the homeless was enacted following the Report from the Select Committee on Violence in Marriage (1975, HMSO); Dobash and Dobash give an account of the hearings preceding this report, *op. cit.* n. 5, at pp. 112–28, 149–52.

[67] See Cretney and Masson, *Principles of Family Law*, 5th ed. (1990, Sweet and Maxwell), at p. 201.

[68] *G v. G (Ouster: ex parte application)* [1990] 1 FLR 395; *Tuck v. Nicholls* [1989] 1 FLR 283; see generally Hayes and Williams, *Family Law: Principles, Policy and Practice*, 2nd ed. (1999, Butterworth), at pp. 457–9.

[69] Practice Note (Family Division: Injunction: Exclusion from the family home) [1978] 2 All ER 1056; see Hayes and Williams, *op. cit.*, 1st ed. (1995) at p. 345 *et seq.*

imposed, like the sentences dispensed by the criminal courts, tended to be lenient.[70]

Perhaps most importantly, the judiciary's reluctance to make 'draconian' occupation orders often appeared to prioritise the property rights of abusers over the needs of victims and their children.[71] Some early decisions of the Court of Appeal, overturned by the House of Lords in *Davis* v. *Johnson*,[72] construed the legislation narrowly, denying the existence of a power to oust abusers from homes that they owned either solely or jointly with their unmarried victims, thereby undermining the legislative purpose.[73] Conversely, in *Richards* v. *Richards*,[74] the House halted a tendency that had developed amongst many judges invariably to oust respondents wherever that met the best interests of any children as the optimum housing solution, holding that the welfare of any children was not the paramount consideration.[75] But, as Hayes and Williams record, that pro-order tendency was soon replaced by one, not required by the decision in *Richards*, which prioritised the property-owning respondent's interests, permitting ousters only where there was a 'real necessity' to do so given his conduct.[76] Ousters were rare in the absence of proven physical violence by the respondent, disregarding other forms of abusive, controlling behaviour.[77] And, perhaps in response to these judicial attitudes, solicitors failed fully to exploit the potential of the legislation for their clients.[78]

---

[70] Kewley, 'Pragmatism before Principle: the limitations of civil law remedies for the victims of domestic violence' (1996) 16 *Journal of Social Welfare Law* 1; on enforcement of civil orders generally see Hayes and Williams, *op. cit.* n. 68, at pp. 459–67.

[71] McCann, 'Battered Women and the Law – the limits of the legislation', in Brophy and Smart (eds.), *Women in the Law: explorations in law, family and sexuality* (1985, Routledge); Edwards, *op. cit.* n. 3, at pp. 70–4; Dobash and Dobash, *op. cit.* n. 5, at pp. 186–90; for a fuller review of the case law (in the context of the Family Law Act 1996), see Hayes and Williams, *op. cit.* n. 68, at pp. 427–41.

[72] [1979] AC 264.

[73] Spouse victims had been given that right by the 1976 legislation in response to restrictive judicial interpretation of the Matrimonial Homes Act 1967: *Tarr* v. *Tarr* [1973] AC 254.

[74] [1984] AC 174.

[75] Several commentators suggest that victims were protected as *mothers*, not in recognition of their personal needs: McCann, *op. cit.* n. 70; Dobash and Dobash, *op. cit.* n. 5, at p. 187. This is also reflected in the activities of police: see Burton, *op. cit.* n. 33.

[76] Hayes and Williams, *op. cit.* n. 68, at pp. 427–41; Hayes, 'The Law Commission and the Family Home' (1990) 53 *Modern Law Review* 222, at pp. 223–4; Hayes criticises courts' emphasis on violence for severely limiting the utility of ousters in cases of non-violent relationship breakdown.

[77] *Blackstock* [1991] 2 FLR 308 – the court refused an ouster where it was unable to allocate blame for an incident involving serious violence; contrast *Brown* [1994] 1 FLR 233, for award of an ouster where the respondent exhibited strict, jealous, but not violent, behaviour towards the applicant.

[78] Kewley, *op. cit.* n. 69.

New approaches to the problem

The 1970s legislation has now been replaced by Part IV of the Family Law Act 1996, which provides a more coherent and comprehensive, if somewhat complex, scheme for civil orders. It is supplemented by the new civil remedies for harassment, created by the Protection from Harassment Act 1997. Like those under the old legislation, proceedings under the 1996 Act are included in the category of 'family proceedings' identified in section 63(2), in which any order available under the specified jurisdictions may be sought by the parties. This enables one set of proceedings to deal with applications for most orders relating to the violence and the needs of any children. The Act applies to a far wider range of applicants than the old statutes. The courts are empowered to make occupation and non-molestation orders between 'associated persons'. This concept includes both current and former spouses and heterosexual cohabitants, fiancés past and present, relatives and some persons who live or have lived together, such as same-sex couples who cohabit and even platonic home-sharers.[79] The harassment legislation is even more inclusive, having no standing requirement for applicants. The 1996 Act enables the courts to make orders incidental to occupation orders, concerning obligations to pay rent and mortgage, repairs, use of furniture and so on, which can provide valuable protection to the interests of both occupying and excluded parties.[80] New provisions governing duration of orders may encourage greater generosity from the courts than under the old law, at least in the case of applicants entitled to occupy the property.[81] Further provisions improve the enforceability of orders, guaranteeing the imposition of arrest powers in appropriate cases and guarding against the inappropriate acceptance of undertakings.[82] The harassment legislation provides an even more robust enforcement regime for its civil orders, rendering breach of orders an arrestable offence, as an alternative to allowing applicants to seek a warrant for arrest for contempt.[83]

---

[79] Family Law Act 1996, section 62(3).

[80] *Ibid.*, section 40. Previously, courts only had jurisdiction to make ancillary orders relating to payment of rent, mortgage and other outgoings in proceedings under the Matrimonial Homes Act 1983.

[81] In the case of applicants who are not entitled to occupy the property, the Act sets a maximum duration for orders (sections 36(10) and 38(6)), though the position of former spouse applicants is somewhat different, with potential for long-term protection, but only on repeated six-monthly application (sections 35(10) and 37(5)); contrast entitled occupants who may in theory acquire protection of unlimited duration: section 33(10). See Hayes and Williams, *op. cit.* n. 68, pp. 444–6.

[82] *Ibid.*, sections 46(3) and 47.

[83] Protection from Harassment Act 1997, section 3; Police and Criminal Evidence Act 1984, section 24. See Lawson-Cruttenden and Addison, 'Harassment and Domestic Violence' (1997) 27 *Family Law* 429.

Central to the Family Law Act scheme is the 'balance of harm' test,[84] which governs the courts' power to make occupation orders. This test is weighted more explicitly than were the criteria of the old legislation in favour of protecting applicants and any relevant children, obliging the court to make an order in certain cases. But the precise formula of the test, focusing courts' attention exclusively on that harm which is likely to be suffered by the applicant or any relevant child which is *attributable to the respondent's conduct*, may reduce the number of cases where applicants will win the balance of harm contest. The attributability test is problematic. Whether a given harm can be said to be attributable to the respondent's conduct is not straightforward. Can the harm suffered as a result of poor quality accommodation to which the victim and her children have been forced to resort be attributed to the behaviour of the respondent which drove them there?[85] Moreover, in order to *oblige* the courts to make orders on the basis of the balance of harm, the applicant must be (or have been) married to the respondent, or, in the case of otherwise 'associated' applicants, be entitled to occupy the property over which the order is sought.[86] In other cases, the judges may choose not to make an order *despite* the applicant winning the balance of harm test. This structural preference within the Act for marriage and property owners potentially limits the scope of the advantages gained by the introduction of the test; whether it makes any difference in practice will depend on the attitude of the judges towards those cases where they are left a discretion.[87]

It is too early to judge whether these legislative changes will encourage changes in judicial ideology. The few reported decisions of the higher courts suggest that orders ousting abusers from their homes continue to be viewed as draconian: they should be restricted to 'exceptional' cases (especially where sought on an interim basis), where warranted by the character of the violence or risk of it, or the harm to the victim or risk of

---

[84] See, for example, section 33(7).

[85] Butler-Sloss LJ seems to have thought so in *B* v. *B* [1999] 1 FLR 715, at p. 723, but commentators are less confident; see Cretney and Masson, *Principles of Family Law* 6th ed. (1997, Sweet and Maxwell), at pp. 250–1; Hayes and Williams, *op. cit.* n. 68, at pp. 443–4. Attributability does not require intention: *G* v. *G* (*Occupation order: conduct*) [2000] 2 FLR 36.

[86] The extension of the duty to make an order to any entitled person, whatever the nature of their 'associated person' relationship, is a striking instance of prioritisation of property rights, even over sexuality. Same-sex partners who are entitled to occupy the property in which they live with their partner will enjoy the same degree of protection as spouses. Associated persons who are not so entitled and who are neither (ex-)spouses or (ex-)cohabitants only qualify for non-molestation orders.

[87] Family Law Act 1996, sections 33, 35 and 37; compare sections 36 and 38; see also factor (c) in the checklist that guides the courts' discretion in each section. Note also the different provisions relating to the maximum duration of orders.

it.[88] However, research suggests that more occupation orders are being granted now than under the old legislation; which may suggest that the balance of harm test is doing its job, or that lower courts may not share the views of their High Court colleagues.[89] Powers of arrest are being more frequently imposed; in the first year of the operation of the Act, 80 per cent of non-molestation orders and 75 per cent of occupation orders had such powers attached.[90] Recent Court of Appeal cases advocate a tough attitude towards those who breach orders,[91] and the increase in the number of committal proceedings since the introduction of the Family Law Act suggests that a more robust approach to breach is being taken. However, undertakings are also increasingly being used, which prompts concern as to whether those provisions designed to restrict the use of undertakings in cases where violence has been used or threatened are achieving their objective. And despite its potential relevance to domestic violence cases and the strength of its enforcement provisions, the civil law aspects of the harassment legislation appear to have been used far less than its criminal counterparts.[92]

In addition to improving the availability and enforcement of familiar forms of civil remedy, the Family Law Act offers the potential to break new ground in the civil law's response to domestic violence. In the light of the fact that some victims are inhibited for various reasons from seeking relief for themselves, some provisions of the Act offer protection to victims who have not themselves sought an order. The Act empowers the courts of their own motion to make non-molestation orders in any family proceedings. So, for example, if violence comes to light during an abuser's application for contact with a child of the couple, the court can make a non-molestation order without application by the victim.[93] Moreover, section 60 of the Act provides for rules of court to permit designated persons to apply on behalf of victims for either non-molestation orders or occupation orders. This provision is inspired by legislation in various Australian states, where the power is either confined to the police, or, where conferred more broadly, tends nevertheless to be exercised by the police. However, at the time of writing, no rules for third party applications have been made under section 60 – a review of the issue is ongoing.

---

[88] Thorpe LJ in *Chalmers* v. *Johns* [1999] 1 FLR 392, at 397; Kaganas, '*B* v. *B (Occupation order)* and *Chalmers* v. *Johns*: Occupation orders under the Family Law Act 1996' (1999) 11 *Child and Family Law Quarterly* 193.

[89] Edwards, 'Civil Law Remedies', Policing and Reducing Crime Unit, *op. cit.* n. 55.

[90] *Ibid.*

[91] *Wilson* v. *Webster* [1998] 1 FLR 1097.

[92] Edwards, 'Civil law remedies', Policing and Reducing Crime Unit, *op. cit.* n. 55.

[93] Family Law Act 1996, section 42(2)(b).

In any case, concern has been expressed that the effectiveness of these and other measures may be undermined by the modern emphasis on mediation rather than adjudication for the resolution of private law disputes between separating partners, which buries the problem of domestic violence even deeper into the private world of the family. The prevailing pro-mediation atmosphere may lead some victims to feel that refusal to participate in mediation, particularly in-court schemes, may prejudice the outcome of any court proceedings.[94] The no-fault, forward-looking emphasis may lead to a sidelining of the parties' past conduct towards each other. The violence may thus never be addressed at all, and victims may agree to arrangements, in particular in relation to child contact, which jeopardise their own safety.[95] Despite screening of cases for domestic violence before they are accepted for mediation to prevent the domination of mediation by abusive partners, detecting whether a relationship suffers an imbalance of power derived from abuse can be extremely difficult.[96] The very privacy of private law disputes therefore renders invisible the same violence which advocates of pro-active public intervention are endeavouring to expose to public attention.

4 The problem of victim autonomy and justifying state action against victim wishes

These recent developments in the criminal and civil justice systems raise questions about the proper role of the state in responding to domestic violence. Inspired by feminist critiques of previous law and practice and their promotion of public responses to the problem, the new policies envisage a more active role for the state, fully exploiting its traditional powers in relation to criminal behaviour, and introducing new powers for the state to protect victims under the civil law. That said, the conversion of policy into practice appears to be problematic. However, before any attempt is made to invigorate their implementation as the new Home Office circular requires, or, in the case of section 60, to implement them at all, potential implications of the new policies for victims should be examined.

---

[94] Hester and Radford, *op. cit.*, n. 64 at p. 30.

[95] See texts on child-related issues in the further reading section.

[96] Kaganas and Piper, 'Domestic Violence and divorce mediation' (1994) 16 *Journal of Social Welfare Law* 265; Piper and Kaganas, 'The Family Law Act 1996 section 1(d) – how will "they" know there is a risk of violence?' (1997) 9 *Child and Family Law Quarterly* 267; Greatbatch and Dingwall, 'The Marginalisation of Domestic Violence in Divorce Mediation' (1999) 13 *International Journal of Law Policy and the Family* 174.

The problem of victim autonomy – the goal of victim empowerment

Domestic violence can be conceptualised as the erosion of victims' autonomy by dominant actors in the private sphere, traditionally aided and abetted by the state's failure to intervene on the grounds of protecting family privacy.[97] A central feminist goal is for women to enjoy the maximum possible autonomy, free from pressures exerted by abusive partners and by social factors which discriminate against women in the home and workplace. It is partly the dynamics of a violent relationship which reduce the victim's autonomy which have led to calls, ostensibly on behalf of victims, for the criminalisation of abusers: the victim oppressed by abuse is unlikely to be able to protect herself, so external help is needed. However, pro-arrest and 'no-drop' prosecution policies, designed to subject the problem to state control within the criminal law, and state-initiated applications for civil orders, designed to protect apparently vulnerable victims who are failing to protect themselves, potentially expose those victims who do not wish to participate in legal proceedings to a further form of domination, this time by public agents.[98]

There is a danger that the malevolent control exerted over the victim by the abuser will be replaced, or merely supplemented, by the paternalistic control of law enforcement officers. Hoyle has criticised those who assume that criminalisation will meet victims' needs (by implication assessed according to what victims would want if free to make a proper judgement on the matter) without inquiring whether that was or would be what individual victims actually wanted.[99] The goal of empowering women may be undermined, or at least further postponed, by pursuing interventionist policies in the face of victim opposition. And may even do so without making any gains in terms of ending the violence.[100]

On the other hand, it may be equally unwise to act in accordance with victims' wishes expressed at a time of crisis. As Hoyle and Sanders argue, a victim's decision not to take or support legal action may be rational *given the context in which she has to make that choice*.[101] But, they suggest, many victims may with external help assess their best interests differently, and decide to take steps towards freeing themselves from the violence. So before victims' 'true' wishes are discerned, especially if those wishes are

---

[97] Schneider, *op. cit.* n. 25, pp. 43–4, citing Minow, 'Words and the Door to the Land of Change: law, language and family violence' (1990) 43 *Vanderbilt Law Review* 1665–99, at pp. 1671–2.

[98] Stanko, 'Missing the mark? Policing Battering', in Hanmer, Radford and Stanko (eds), *Women, Policing and Male Violence* (1989, Routledge) at pp. 65, 67; Law Commission Report 207, *Domestic Violence and Occupation of the Family Home* (1992), para. 5.22.

[99] Hoyle, *op. cit.* n. 33, ch. 7, at p. 205.

[100] Hoyle and Sanders, 'Police Response to Domestic Violence: from victim choice to victim empowerment?' (2000) 40 *British Journal of Criminology* 14.

[101] *Ibid.*, at p. 21.

going to dictate others' responses to the violence, the context in which victims make their decisions must be as conducive as possible to their making a choice free from adverse influences – victim empowerment should become the goal. To identify the forms of support required to achieve that, it is necessary first to identify factors which researchers report to be deterring victims from calling the police, pursuing a prosecution, applying for civil law remedies or seeking any other outside help.[102]

The British Crime Survey reveals that only 17 per cent of domestic violence victims recognise themselves as crime victims; a large proportion regard violence as 'just something that happens', and not wrong at all.[103] So it is unsurprising that the police are called out to so few incidents – 12 per cent, according to the survey. Many victims seem to be unaware that harassment is now criminal.[104] Related problems (whether viewed as cause or effect of the abuse – see Part 2) are victims' low self-esteem, self-blame and shame about the abuse, exacerbated by feelings of isolation caused by the apparent uniqueness of their problem, and *actual* social isolation imposed by many abusers as part of their controlling behaviour. These combine to leave victims without access to any support network. Police practices intended to test victims' commitment to legal action, discussed above, leave many victims feeling responsible for the fate of their abuser, a responsibility that they often do not want, not least for fear of reprisals. Victims sometimes wish to protect the abuser, again for fear of reprisals if the police are called, but also because of excuses found to account for the abuse, in the light of which they judge calling the police to be 'unfair'. Victims may also fear that official notification of the abuse may arouse the interest of social services, with the resulting risk of their children being removed.[105] As a result of these perceptions, and being cut off from their normal sources of emotional and social support, victims often resort to private 'coping strategies', altering their own behaviour to try to prevent recurrence of the violence. Yet these same strategies often appear objectively to be contrary to their interests and may decrease the likelihood of their seeking more effective help.

If more cases are to be brought before the courts either by victims themselves or by the state *with* victims' consent, these problems must be addressed. In the experience of one victim support and advocacy

---

[102] The following discussion is derived largely from Hoff, *op. cit.*; Kelly *et al*, *op. cit.*; Hoyle and Sanders, *op. cit.*

[103] Mirlees-Black, *op. cit.* n. 2, ch. 7; male victims are particularly reluctant to classify their experiences as criminal or wrong.

[104] Harris, *op. cit.* n. 34, at p. 19.

[105] Parkinson and Humphries, 'Children who witness domestic violence: implications for child protection' (1998) 10 *Child and Family Law Quarterly* 147 at p. 158; see also Maynard, *op. cit.* n. 30 on victims' experience of social workers.

project,[106] past efforts to support victims had often presumed that they shared their putative allies' 'common sense' appreciation of their status as crime victims and of the action necessary to deal with this. The support offered was thus 'frequently inappropriate and experienced as patronising, judgemental or irrelevant'. Attempts to encourage a victim 'to participate in a prosecution when she is minimising the violence or blaming herself are unlikely to be effective'. Making such efforts where she is not ready to take the action being urged upon her can 'reinforce [her] sense of responsibility' for the situation.[107] This project learnt that if victims are to take any effective action to protect themselves from abuse (whether or not through legal proceedings), they must first be helped to acknowledge that they are crime victims, that they are not to blame, that they have been adapting and limiting their behaviour in an attempt to avoid the abuse, that this strategy is not working, and to reassess the value of their relationship with the abusers.[108] The insight acquired through this kind of support may indicate to a victim that she needs to act to protect herself. But she needs to be confident that she will receive protection when she takes steps to leave the relationship or otherwise end the violence. And before she can be persuaded to participate in criminal proceedings against her abuser, various disincentives to victim compliance in that system (many of which deter crime victims generally, and not just victims of domestic violence) may need to be addressed.

Many victims perceive the police and criminal courts to be unable (or unwilling) to provide effective protection; indeed, violence is often *aggravated* by police involvement. Unless the criminal justice system acknowledges and responds to the dangers faced by victims who participate in its processes, victims remain unlikely to cooperate. Measures to overcome perceived inadequacies in the policing and prosecution of domestic violence have been discussed above in Part 3. In particular, several commentators observe that bail conditions could be used and policed more effectively, to prevent offenders from contacting and abusing victims to deter them from testifying.

Many victims are also fearful of the criminal trial itself, which can be experienced as a 'secondary victimisation'. The ordeal of attending court and giving evidence may in part be improved by new powers introduced by the Youth Justice and Criminal Evidence Act 1999. This Act permits the use of screens, cleared courts, TV links and pre-recorded video evidence and cross-examination for the protection of certain categories of 'vulnerable and intimidated' witnesses, and allows certain defendants to

---

[106] 'Domestic Violence Matters', a civilian unit attached to two police divisions: Kelly *et al*, *op. cit*. n. 33.

[107] *Ibid.*, p. 38.

[108] *Ibid.*, ch. 3.

be barred from cross-examining witnesses in person.[109] Pilot projects are also assessing various schemes for improving the provision to victims of information concerning the progress of their case, and the use by sentencing courts of statements from the victim which describe the impact of the offence on her.[110] These measures may not in fact increase the number of cases where victims have to testify; simply getting the victim as far as the court door may induce a guilty plea.

However, the discussion thus far assumes that victims empowered to make free choices about their situation would want their abusers to be dealt with under the criminal law at all, at least given its current punitive focus. Some victims might be more supportive of criminal proceedings which, instead of punitive sanctions, offered perpetrator programmes designed to help abusers confront and reform their attitudes and behaviour. Such remedies could be available to the courts on sentencing, or be used as a formal diversion of offenders from prosecution, the latter option again avoiding the need for the victim to appear in court.[111] However, more investigation of these programmes is required. Their effectiveness remains unproven, their appropriate design controversial; in particular, some programmes are premised on a micro-level under-standing of domestic violence, focusing on the psychological problems of abusers, while others adopt a pro-feminist stance.[112] The Protection from Harassment Act 1997 has provided a sentencing innovation which is particularly suitable for domestic violence, especially ex-partner abuse. The criminal courts are empowered to dispose of convicted harassers by issuing restraining orders designed to protect the victim from further conduct amounting to harassment or which causes fear of violence; breach of such orders constitutes a serious offence.[113] These orders can prohibit offenders from contacting the victim or her family, and require them to keep away from her home, place of work and surrounding area. Unlike bail conditions, they provide protection after conviction. But like bail conditions, they can only be effective if their terms are suitably framed, if

---

[109] Part II, Chapter I, especially ss. 17–20, 23–28; sections 36–7; note also witness intimidation offences: Criminal Justice and Public Order Act 1994, section 51.

[110] Fenwick, 'Rights of Victims in the Criminal Justice System' [1995] *Criminal Law Review* 843; Hoyle, Morgan and Sanders, *The Victim's Charter: an evaluation of pilot projects*, Home Office Research Findings 107 (2000, Home Office). See generally JUSTICE, *Victims in Criminal Justice* (1998, Justice).

[111] Hoyle and Sanders, *op. cit.* n. 98.

[112] See Mullender and Burton, 'Perpetrator Programmes', Policing and Reducing Crime Unit, *op. cit.* n. 55; Morley and Mullender, *op. cit.* n. 13; Buzawa and Buzawa, *op. cit.* n. 7, ch. 17; Dobash and Dobash, *op. cit.* n. 5, at pp. 241–50.

[113] Protection from Harassment Act 1997, section 5; see Lawson-Cruttenden and Addison, *Blackstone's Guide to the Protection from Harassment Act 1997* (1997, Blackstone), ch. 5. The tough penalties for breach of restraining orders set them apart from similar criminal law remedies, such as bind-overs: 'a completely new concept in the criminal law', *ibid.*

victims are made aware of their existence and terms, and if the policing and prosecution of breaches of the orders is robust.[114]

As for disincentives to victims' use of civil justice, there is evidence that some solicitors are advising their clients not to initiate *any* civil proceedings because of the likelihood that the abuser, spurred into action by the victim's applications for injunctions, may seek orders relating to any children. There is concern that some courts tend to order contact between children and the abusing parent in the name of the children's best interests, despite evidence that contact meetings frequently lead to further abuse of the mother and that children suffer emotionally from witnessing such abuse.[115] If victims are to be encouraged to seek protection from the civil courts, these criticisms require careful scrutiny. Indeed, the Court of Appeal has responded to research findings about the adverse effects of domestic violence on children and their carers by encouraging a more circumspect approach to the assessment of contact applications made by alleged abusers.[116]

In any event, both criminal and civil justice systems have limited functions – they cannot themselves cater for the wider needs of victims of domestic violence. Nor may they be effective alone in ending violence. It may often be the case that only ending the relationship will ultimately cause the abuse to cease, never mind improve the chances of the victim agreeing to participate in legal proceedings to that end.[117] However, without basic physical and material security, many victims will feel unable to end the relationship, especially if they lack alternative accommodation, even only pending the ousting of the abuser from the home. Fear of the socio-economic consequences of the relationship ending – or of the breadwinning abuser being imprisoned – inhibits many victims from reporting or otherwise pursuing domestic violence cases.

The police are not able to deal with these key issues. However, as Domestic Violence Units and other projects have shown, they can form one focal point in a co-ordinated multi-agency response to domestic violence, referring victims to the appropriate statutory and voluntary bodies which *are* able to cater for these wider needs.[118] But some commentators caution that access to material support should not be presented as part of a 'contract' with prosecutors, in return for which victims *must*

---

[114] Harris, *op. cit.* n. 33; Harris identified some difference of opinion between police and prosecutors regarding the suitability of the criminal offences for domestic cases, the latter preferring victims to take the civil route.

[115] Morley and Mullender, *op. cit.* n. 8, at p. 30. See texts on child-related matters in the suggested further reading section.

[116] *Re L, Re V, Re M, Re H (Contact: domestic violence)* [2000] 2 FLR 334; for commentary, see Kaganas, 'Contact and Domestic Violence' (2000) 12 *Child and Family Law Quarterly* 311.

[117] Hoyle and Sanders' research supports this view: *op. cit.* n. 98.

[118] Multi-agency Guidance on addressing Domestic Violence (2000, Home Office).

participate in the criminal process.[119] Such a precondition might operate disproportionately against poor and ethnic minority women, whose lives may already be marked by repeated, unhappy exposure to the criminal justice system and who may accordingly be more reluctant to seek police assistance. Victim autonomy should not be the preserve of the wealthy. All should be afforded the same degree of support to enable them deal with the consequences of their abuse.[120] Any additional support offered to those participating in legal proceedings should address only the specific burdens of such involvement.

When, if at all, ought the state to act in the face of victim opposition?

However, while many victims given such support may be keen to bring or take part in legal action against the abuser, others may remain reluctant. Some victims will want the abuse to end, but also want their relationship with the abuser, whether as partner or as father of their children, to continue. Others may wish to end the relationship, but regard legal proceedings as unnecessary and irrelevant to that goal, feeling – as it seems do some criminal justice agents – that the criminal justice system is ill-equipped to offer them the constructive assistance required to achieve their objectives.[121] Others still may simply be too fearful to act. The question therefore remains: how best to reconcile the conception of domestic violence as a public problem with respect for victim autonomy. On what basis, if at all, can the prosecution of domestic violence be justified where the victim herself does not want that course to be taken? And in the civil sphere, ought it be possible for the state to bring protective proceedings without the victim's consent?

There are several ways in which a legal system could answer these questions, depending upon the view taken of the following: the proper characterisation of offences against the person generally (and domestic violence in particular); the purpose of the legal system in responding to these offences and the civil law issues arising therefrom; and so the proper roles of and relationship between victim and state in this context. Various commentators have suggested differing approaches to this problem, and these are outlined below: the victim complaint model, the offence against society model and the victim protection model. Although it may be helpful for the sake of clarity to present the models here as free-standing theories,

---

[119] Morley and Mullender, *op. cit.* n. 13. The operation of the Criminal Injuries Compensation scheme is important in this regard: see Hayes and Williams, *op. cit.* n. 68, pp. 413–4; see generally Zedner, 'Victims', in Maguire, Morgan and Reiner, *Oxford Handbook of Criminology*, 2nd ed. (1997, Clarendon Press), at pp. 603–605.

[120] This view is endorsed in HOC 19/2000 paras. 7 and 10 (n. 41).

[121] See Cretney and Davis, *op. cit.* n. 33; Hoyle, *op. cit.* n. 33; Hoyle and Sanders, *op. cit.* n. 98.

it will be clear from the discussion that it is unlikely to be desirable in practice to pursue any one of these normative models to the exclusion of influences from the others.[122] The question will thus be one of the relative weight to be ascribed by the legal system to the factors highlighted by each model; and here views will clearly differ.

The victim complaint model[123]

This model is described first in order to outline the case for deferring to victims' wishes, before exploring reasons against doing so. The victim complaint model characterises personal violence generally (and especially where it occurs in private) as an invasion of the rights of the victim, a private wrong. Given that characterisation, and since the victim is best placed to identify her own needs, she should be entitled to determine what action if any should be taken and what remedy should be sought, and the onus is on her to initiate and continue any legal proceedings. Indeed, since the adult victim is presumed to be competent, her privacy and autonomy would *prima facie* be violated if the state were to intervene on the basis of its assessment of her best interests.[124] And the presumption that competent adult decision-makers are best placed to assess their own interests is all the stronger where the individual in question has been given maximum support and opportunity to reach an autonomous decision, as discussed above. While paternalistic state intervention may be proper for child abuse victims, who generally do not to possess sufficient understanding and maturity to assess and act on their own best interests, it is not appropriate in the case of adults.

This model accords most obviously with conventional understandings of civil justice, whereby (by contrast with traditional views of its criminal counterpart, discussed in relation to the offence against society model) that system is viewed as a private rather than a public jurisdiction, vindicating private rather than public interests. The state provides a judge and a set of rules and procedures whereby parties may have their disputes resolved and remedies granted, and it will provide a mechanism for enforcement of its judgments, but that is all. However, criminal justice may also be dispensed pursuant to victim complaints, allowing the victim to determine whether her abuser is arrested, charged and prosecuted, and

---

[122] As Zedner says, pluralism may be preferable in practice to intellectual elegance, 'Reparation and Retribution: are they reconcilable?' (1994) 57 *Modern Law Review* 228, at p. 229.

[123] Cretney and Davis, *op. cit.* nn. 33 and 54. See also Cretney, Davis, Clarkson and Shepherd, 'Criminalizing Assault: the failure of the "offence against society" model', (1994) 34 *British Journal of Criminal Law* 15; Hoyle, *op. cit.* n. 33.

[124] For discussion of competence, see the victim protection model below.

possibly to influence the manner of disposal on conviction.[125] The now-repealed provisions which largely confined the summary prosecution of common assault to victims and those acting with their consent provide an example of the criminal courts being deployed to remedy an essentially private wrong.[126] Influence over disposal, via some form of victim statement to the court, would be important in a system where sentencing was based on principles of restorative rather than retributive justice, and which focused on compensation for victims and mediation. If the victim did not wish to receive compensation or to confront her abuser in mediation, there would be no point in restorative terms in making such provision.[127]

The offence against society model[128]

However, the victim complaint model may be felt to offer an incomplete characterisation of crimes against the person generally, domestic violence included, and to invite practical objections. Not least, legal action cannot be dependent upon victim complaint in homicide cases, and there will not always be relatives who could properly be regarded as secondary victims. But at a theoretical level, characterising violent crime, domestic or otherwise, simply as a private wrong may be inappropriate. The offence against society model offers an alternative characterisation, which has come to dominate the criminal justice system.

On this model, inter-personal violence, like any other conduct proscribed by the criminal law, violates not just the private rights of the victim, but also society' norms, causing collective harm to the public at large. In the case of domestic violence against women, that collective harm

---

[125] Subject to the state retaining the power to guard against deployment of the criminal justice system in a manner unduly burdensome to the defendant; see powers to discontinue private prosecutions, Prosecution of Offences Act 1985, section 6(2), or to reduce charges, section 23.

[126] Offences Against the Person Act 1861, sections 42–43 and 46, repealed by the Criminal Justice Act 1988; sections 44–5 of the 1861 Act, which provide that a defendant privately prosecuted by his victim may not be sued by the victim in the civil courts in respect of the same complaint, are still in force. See Lidstone, Hogg and Sutcliff *et al.*, *Prosecution by private individuals and non-police agencies*, Royal Commission on Criminal Procedure Research Study 10 (1980, HMSO), ch. 5.

[127] Cavadino and Dignan, 'Reparation, Retribution and Rights' (1997) 4 *International Review of Victimology* 233, extracted in von Hirsch and Ashworth (eds.), *Principled Sentencing: readings on theory and practice*, 2nd ed. (1998, Hart), at p. 352; Ashworth, 'Victim Impact Statements and Sentencing' [1993] *Criminal Law Review* 498. See generally the texts extracted in von Hirsch and Ashworth, *op. cit.*, ch. 7 on reparative justice, which need not be victim-oriented; Pollard, 'Victims and the Criminal Justice System: a new vision' [2000] *Criminal Law Review* 5.

[128] Ashworth, 'Punishment and Compensation: victims, offenders and the state' (1986) 6 *Oxford Journal of Legal Studies* 86, discussing the criminal justice system.

might be thought to include the damaging cultural implications of the abuse, each incident reasserting an unequal view of gender relations. Criminal behaviour has the capacity to cause widespread fear, which in turn threatens vigilantist disorder if action is not taken to bring offenders to account. Moreover, offenders left unchecked may go on to abuse other victims, whether future partners or individuals in the current home, such as children of the family. Given these considerations, the task of pro-secuting offenders necessarily falls on the state whose duty it is to protect society from such behaviour, and the sentence prescribed should reflect the public nature of the wrongdoing rather than seek simply to give reparation to the victim. Whilst it may be entirely proper for the state to have regard to the private interests of the victim in pursuing such cases, it cannot be left to the individual who happened to be the object of the particular assault to decide whether to prosecute. If she chose not to complain, the opportunity to express public disapproval of the offender's conduct and to protect other individuals at risk, and society generally, from wrongdoing would be lost. Indeed, not only may the state be entitled to act against the abuser, but victims – as any other citizens – may be said *prima facie* to have a duty to society and to potential future victims to participate in any such proceedings. This model accordingly supports pro-arrest policies and the compulsion of witnesses, necessarily, but on this view justifiably, involving state interference in 'private' life.

The offence against society model has less obvious application to the types of remedy dispensed by the civil courts, which seek not to vindicate any interest of the state, but to satisfy the *private* needs of victims – securing their occupation of the family home and their right not to be molested. The state's interest in civil proceedings may be thought to consist largely of a paternalistic concern for the victim's well-being, discussed below under the 'victim protection model'. But that is not to say that there are no distinct interests which the state could pursue in civil applications. For example, the cost of public rehousing of victims gives the state an economic interest in the question of who should occupy the family home.[129] Under current housing law, the victim is far more likely than the abuser to qualify for the maximum entitlement if she presents herself to the local authority as homeless. So the state clearly has a crude interest in victims acquiring occupation orders. But it is not clear that this alone can justify giving it standing to apply for such orders; the state may be similarly interested in any civil dispute, domestic violence or not, the result of which could leave one of the parties reliant on state support. Nor would it be appropriate, given the lower standard of proof applicable to civil proceedings, for the remedies currently dispensed only by the civil

---

[129] On the costs of domestic violence, see Crisp and Stanko, 'Monitoring costs and evaluating needs', Policing and Reducing Crime Unit, *op. cit.* n. 55.

courts to be regarded as sanctions available to the state. If the state wishes to exclude offenders from their homes as a punishment for wrongdoing, criminal sanctions should be tailored accordingly. However, there may be some justification for state involvement in civil disputes, as in the criminal sphere, in safeguarding the interests of other individuals actually or potentially affected by the violence. Such individuals, not least any children of the family, may be protected by exclusion of the abuser from the home, and it may accordingly be appropriate for the state to be empowered to seek civil remedies on their behalf.

The victim protection model[130]

Another arguable deficiency of the victim complaint model is its presupposition that the decisions of victims concerning the arrest and prosecution of offenders and the pursuit of civil remedies are sufficiently free and informed that they should be acted upon. Although factors discouraging victims' participation in legal proceedings may to some extent be countered by more comprehensive victim support, there will still be cases where victims remain inhibited from making a true choice. As the Law Commission has pointed out, pursuing a strict victim complaint model in the civil courts may paradoxically mean that those most in need of protection, having been so terrorised that they dare not or cannot take any steps to try to protect themselves, are by default denied it.[131] Failure to compel victims to testify in criminal proceedings or to prosecute on the basis of evidence other than victim testimony, may be similarly damaging. This model, whilst concurring with the view that private rights are at stake, accordingly permits the state to prosecute or bring protective civil proceedings on the basis of victims' best interests, objectively assessed, even where their currently stated wishes point the other way.

Paternalistic intervention of this sort needs careful justification, since acting against victims' wishes further undermines their autonomy and (in that sense) damages their interests. Some protective cases will actually be victim complaints in disguise where victims are willing for the state to act on their behalf, provided that the responsibility for doing so is not theirs. In other cases where the victim opposes proceedings, intervention could be permitted on the simple paternalistic ground that the victim's health, or even life, were at risk. The law relating to consent to violence may, as Ashworth suggests, offer an analogy here. Since a victim's consent to violence does not provide a defence in substantive criminal law (in part for reasons of victim protection), why should a victim's refusal to consent to

---

[130] This is inspired by remarks of Lord Edmund-Davies' in *Hoskyns* v. *Metropolitan Police Commissioner* [1979] AC 474 at 501; also Buzawa and Buzawa, *op. cit.* n. 7, ch. 7; Hoyle, *op. cit.* n. 33, ch. 8.

[131] Law Commission Report 207, *Domestic Violence and Occupation of the Family Home* (1992, HMSO), para. 5.22.

prosecution of that violence afford a procedural 'defence'?[132] A threshold test of 'significant harm', similar to that used in cases of child protection,[133] might be adopted here, so that the possibility of such intervention would arise only once the harm had reached a certain level. But this on its own may be thought insufficient justification for proceeding against the wishes of a competent adult.[134]

This raises the controversial question of whether some victims of domestic violence might as a result of the abuse be legally incapable of protecting themselves. Such a finding, combined with satisfaction of a threshold test, would more readily justify paternalistic intervention. Cases setting out tests for determining capacity to consent to or refuse medical treatment may provide an analogy, requiring understanding, retention and belief of relevant information, and the weighing of that information to make a choice.[135] In cases involving pregnant women's refusal of caesarean sections, the acute emotional stress and physical pain experienced by the woman at the time a decision is needed may lead to the conclusion that she is unable to weigh up the information, and so is incompetent to make the decision.[136] By analogy, some of those characteristics associated with 'battered woman's syndrome', such as feelings of helplessness and despair, might be so powerful as to deprive some victims of their capacity to believe that they can be freed from the violence and so to make a decision about whether to initiate legal proceedings. But the circumstances of these cases are far less acute than those in the medical cases, so the analogy is not exact. Alternatively or additionally, some otherwise competent victims' refusal to consent to legal action might be regarded as vitiated by the circumstances in which their refusal is made, the fear to which they are subject or the adverse influence of the abuser preventing them from making their own decision.[137]

But permitting state intervention on the grounds of incapacity or duress would be highly problematic. Experience in the medical context is instructive about the difficulty of defining and assessing capacity, and for the danger of judgments about capacity being infected by decision-

---

[132] Ashworth *op. cit.* n. 126, at p. 113; *R* v. *Brown* [1994] 1 AC 212.

[133] Children Act 1989, s. 31(2).

[134] Some victims may have a mental disorder (unrelated to the violence) as a result of which they are incapable of making a decision on the matter; for an outline of existing powers to protect mentally disordered and other vulnerable adults from neglect and abuse, see Law Commission Consultation Paper 119 and Law Commission Report 231, *Mental Incapacity* (1995, HMSO), Part IX: recommendations for reform of public law protection of vulnerable adults.

[135] *Re C (Refusal of medical treatment)* [1994] 1 WLR 290.

[136] *Re MB (Medical Treatment)* [1997] 2 FLR 426; compare *St George's NHS Healthcare Trust* v. *S* [1999] Fam 26.

[137] Again, medical cases may be analogous: *Re T (Adult: refusal of treatment)* [1993] Fam 95.

makers' understandable paternalistic imperatives.[138] Victims' beliefs that nothing can be done to help them may be rationally based on past experience of ineffective official intervention, rather than the product of internally generated, unwarranted despair, in which case they ought not to be treated as incompetent. And given such experience, the state must be sure of its own capacity to provide effective protection before intervening on these grounds if it is to justify its intervention. Moreover, the ideological implications of singling out domestic violence victims for such 'special' treatment and labelling them as 'incompetent' are significant, raising again those criticisms discussed in Part 2 of theories of domestic violence which focus on the victim's psychology. Use of battered woman's syndrome in other contexts has been similarly controversial.[139]

Proceeding against victims' wishes may in some cases also be impractical; it may be futile to obtain an ouster order against the wishes of a victim who will simply let the abuser back into the house.[140] So it may be appropriate wherever action against victims' wishes is contemplated at least to *consult* them before acting. Indeed, further efforts to empower victims without depriving them of the right to make decisions about legal proceedings may generally be preferred. But in extreme cases protective action might still be thought desirable. Depending on the level at which any threshold test for protective intervention were set, criminal proceedings on offence against society grounds might be warranted in such cases anyway, incidentally protecting the victim. But the option of state-led civil proceedings with their lower standard of proof may offer a useful alternative to prosecution.

A new framework for reconciling these competing claims: the Human Rights Act

Given support to maximise their autonomy, many victims who would otherwise oppose legal proceedings might support prosecution or apply to the civil court. Where this occurs, the public interests in the condemnation of violence, protection of the public and children and of victims' interests and autonomy are all satisfied. But where victims oppose legal proceedings, conflicts between these interests become clear, and must now be resolved within the framework of the ECHR.

---

[138] See Bartlett and Sandland, *Mental Health Law, Policy and Practice* (2000, Blackstone), at pp. 355–6 and texts cited therein; Bridgman and Millns, *Feminist Perspectives on Law: the law's engagement with the female body* (1998, Sweet and Maxwell), at pp. 352–79. The author is grateful to Peter Bartlett for discussion of this issue.

[139] See Nicholson and Sanghvi, 'Battered Women and Provocation: the implications of *R* v. *Ahluwalia*' [1993] *Criminal Law Review* 728; Dobash and Dobash, *op. cit.*, at pp. 228–35.

[140] Law Com. 207, para. 5.22; see below for the effect on these decisions of children's interests, text to note 170.

As seen already, police, prosecutors, judges and other 'public authorities' operating in this area have to act compatibly with rights protected under the European Convention on Human Rights.[141] The starting point in those cases where the victim opposes a particular intervention by the state is Article 8:

Article 8

1 Everyone has the right to respect for his private and family life, his home and his correspondence.

2 There shall be no interference by a public authority with the exercise of this right except such as is in accordance with the law and is necessary in a democratic society in the interests of national security, public safety or the economic well-being of the country, for the prevention of disorder or crime, for the protection of health or morals, or for the protection of the rights and freedoms of others.

Any state interference with the right must therefore be shown to be (i) in accordance with law; (ii) directed towards the pursuit of one of the aims specified in Article 8.2; and (iii) 'necessary in a democratic society', i.e. it must correspond to a pressing social need and the interference with the right must be proportionate, given the aim pursued.

Both criminal and civil action against the abuser *prima facie* interfere with *his* rights under Argicle 8 (and other Convention provisions); but certainly where the victim consents to the action, the interference may be readily justifiable under Article 8.2.[142] However, arrest, prosecution, and state applications to have abusers ejected from the home against *victims'* wishes, arguably interfere with victims' rights to respect for their family and private life, as championed by the victim complaint model, and these interferences too need justification.

It is likely that the action could readily be found to fall within the scope of one or more of the aims specified in Article 8.2, which include several of those factors considered in relation to the victim protection and offence against society models: the interests of public safety, the prevention of disorder or crime, the protection of health (including that of the victim herself),[143] and the protection of the rights and freedoms of others (for example, any children affected by the violence).[144] Assuming therefore

[141] Human Rights Act 1998, sections 6–9.

[142] For potential arguments of alleged abusers under various Convention Articles, see Swindells *et al, Family Law and the Human Rights Act 1998* (1999, Family Law), ch. 13.

[143] See cases involving children: *Andersson (M and R)* v. *Sweden* (1992) A 226–A. See also *Laskey et al.* v. *UK.* [1997] 24 EHRR 39, where criminalisation of consensual violence was justified in part on the basis of protecting the competent adult participants' health.

[144] See generally Starmer, *op. cit.* n. 60, esp. para. 4.56–4.66.

that the action in question has its basis in law, it will be for the state to justify the manner and extent of any interference with the victim's right as being necessary and proportionate. There seems to be no Convention case law directly bearing on the issues raised here. It is possible to infer by analogy with child protection cases that the state would at least be under an obligation to consult the victim and consider her wishes before taking any action which interfered with her rights under Article 8.[145] But in those cases, the intervention is made for the benefit of a child, not a presumptively competent and objecting adult, and so it might be argued that something more than mere protection of the victim is required before intervention can be justified in these cases. How readily intervention will be permitted in individual cases will depend on the courts' evaluation of the state's arguments under Article 8.2.

Moreover, in determining the extent of interference with the right permitted under Article 8.2, the courts will need to ensure that extent of intervention *permitted* under Article 8.2 at least corresponds with that *required* of the state under Articles 2, 3 and 8 itself. As seen already, those Articles impose positive obligations on the state to protect the victim's and others' rights to life and freedom from inhuman and degrading treatment, and Article 8 itself imposes some obligation to protect victims from violence within the home. However, whilst the rights protected by Articles 2 and 3 are absolute, the scope of the state's positive obligations there-under remain uncertain. It is not clear, in particular, whether the state might sometimes be obliged to protect individuals from such treatment even if they object to protection offered. If that were the case, the state could find itself walking a legal tightrope. For example, if a victim claimed that her opposition to legal action against earlier violence was the product of duress, might she argue that the state had failed to take reasonable steps to assess her state of mind and so to determine whether paternalistic protection were warranted, and so failed to fulfil its positive obligation under Articles 3 and 8?[146] We must wait to see how, if at all, the arrival of the Human Rights Act makes any difference to the resolution of those conflicts.

5 Current practice and future directions

In this final section, current law and practice in cases involving reluctant victims are examined in order to identify where the balance between the interests outlined above is currently being struck and how that balance

---

[145] For example, *R* v. *UK* [1988] 2 FLR 445.
[146] The author is grateful to Ivan Hare for the suggestion of this argument. Child victims' objections would presumably be discounted, so why not those of the incapacitated adult? And, given *Laskey* v. *UK* (n. 140), what of the competent?

might be altered in future to enhance the effectiveness of the law in helping to end domestic violence. Note that some of the problems discussed here in relation to criminal justice are not unique to domestic violence, but are part of a wider debate about that system generally.

The criminal justice system

The criminal justice system's approach to unwilling victims, as set out in the relevant police and prosecution policy documents,[147] appears to pursue both offence against society and victim protection concerns. It encourages support of victims to maximise prospects of their participation, but fully contemplates arresting regardless of victim wishes and prosecuting despite victim withdrawal, compelling victims' testimony if necessary and practicable. In making decisions about its handling of a case, the Crown Prosecution Service considers the victim's interests. The reference to the 'interests' rather than 'wishes' of victims implies that the prosecutor's assessment of a victim's needs might be preferred to her own. In some cases where the victim wishes to withdraw her complaint – where the violence seems genuinely to have been a relatively minor, one-off event and the parties are reconciled – it may be in the public interest not to prosecute in order to keep the family together.[148] Looked at another way, the victim's right to respect for her family and private life is not found to be outweighed by any countervailing public interest concerns. The full criminal justice response is not warranted for every minor assault. But whatever the outcome, although account is taken of victims' wishes, decisions about arrest, charge and prosecution are clearly assigned to state agents, not victims. And as the first edition of the Victim's Charter made abundantly clear, even the victims' interests might sometimes have to be sacrificed to greater public interests.[149]

However, as has been seen already, these policies have yet to result in significantly increased arrest and prosecution rates. Research by Cretney and Davis and by Hoyle suggests that this apparent 'failure' of the new policies can be attributed not to the enduring influence of an ideology which trivialises domestics and ignores victims' wishes, but to a tendency on the part of police and prosecutors in many cases to comply with victims' wishes – and many victims do not want their abusers to be

---

[147] *Op. cit.* n. 41.

[148] CPS, *op. cit.* n. 41, para. 5, identifies various factors to be considered in deciding whether it is in the public interest to prosecute; cf. Burton *op. cit.* n. 33, at p. 185.

[149] Home Office, *The Victims Charter: a Statement of the Rights of Victims of Crime* (1990, HMSO). The stern passages indicating the inferior status of victims' interests have no counterpart in the second edition of the Charter, which simply refers repeatedly to victims' interests being 'taken into account', without suggesting what weight might be attached to them.

arrested or prosecuted.[150] Despite the policy guidance, the current default position in practice often appears, at least during the crucial pre-trial stages of arrest, charge and decision to prosecute, to reflect a victim complaint model. The system depends on victims volunteering to report violence for cases to be brought to its attention at all, and thereafter often depends on victims' evidence. Hence police requests for victims to 'make a complaint' before the matter is taken any further. Likewise, prosecutors' failure to compel testimony or proceed without it might be thought to support the view that the complaint 'belongs' to the victim, and that her wishes should accordingly determine the outcome. Certainly, more pragmatic considerations militate against compelling victims' evidence or otherwise proceeding without her cooperation: compelled witnesses often give poor evidence, thereby reducing the chances of conviction; pursuing a prosecution against the victim's wishes, whether compelling her evidence or not, may be ineffective in terms of ending the violence, and may be damaging to her (and her children's) welfare; victims generally may be reluctant to report violence if faced with the prospect of compulsion or an unwanted prosecution.

It seems clear that some victims want their partners to be arrested not to trigger the full criminal justice response, but simply to issue a short sharp shock, or to obtain immediate respite by temporary removal of the abuser. Ford has observed that some use threats of prosecution as a power resource to secure an end to the abuse, or to extract advantageous terms on separation, for example, in relation to occupation of the home or child care. Police powers may therefore be being used by victims as a resource to achieve ends other than the channelling of suspects into court.[151] Seen in this light, victim withdrawal is not necessarily a failure, but may indicate the successful completion of the victim's strategy for controlling the abuser's behaviour.[152]

But there is concern that officials may sometimes defer to victims' wishes without adequately examining their reasons for opposing arrest or prosecution, and without ensuring that those wishes are formed under conditions likely to allow maximum autonomy. Checks to see whether victim withdrawals are the product of intimidation, even where abusers have contacted victims in breach of bail conditions, vary in their rigour.

---

[150] Cretney and Davis, *op. cit.* nn. 33 and 54; Hoyle, *op. cit.* n. 33. Hoyle identifies a complex web of variables affecting the police and prosecution response, including not only victims' wishes, but also offence seriousness, perception of future risk to the victim and the demeanour of both offender and victim.

[151] Ford, 'Prosecution as a Victim Power Resource: a note on empowering women in violent conjugal relationships' (1991) 25 *Law and Society Review* 313. As Hoyle and Sanders observe, not all victims will be sufficiently empowered to be able to play that sort of power game, *op. cit.* n. 98, p. 30.

[152] Cretney and Davis, *op. cit.* n. 37, p. 173.

Whilst some victims are forced to make their withdrawal statements in court, a practice which may protect the police's position and arguably safeguard the victim against intimidation, other cases are investigated far less formally, if at all.[153] At worst, respect for victims' apparent wishes could be used as a cover for inaction in cases where the official is, not necessarily for appropriate reasons, reluctant to intervene. Victim protection concerns, and the possible demands of the positive obligations to which the state is subject under the ECHR, would demand more careful scrutiny of these cases, as would concern for the needs of children in the household. Research suggests that the needs of children, whilst determining police response in many cases, did not sway prosecutors, who would invariably accede to victim wishes in the belief that attempting to prosecute such cases would be futile.[154]

By contrast, as Cretney and Davis demonstrate, if the victim does cooperate, then by the time a criminal case comes to trial, whether domestic violence or not, the offence against society model largely takes over and the victim loses any influence hitherto enjoyed. The victim, whose cooperation has in practice if not in theory been vital to the case's progress to trial, is relegated to the status of mere witness in a prosecution brought in the name of the state, and used to serve the needs of the system, needs which may not coincide with her own.[155] The victim's wishes, interests and 'story' can be addressed at trial only to the extent that they are 'relevant' given the prosecution's construction of the case and the public, 'offence against society' basis for the proceedings, which may leave her feeling alienated from the exercise. Her role and recognition at sentencing is limited. Whilst she may be permitted to make a statement via the prosecutor describing the impact of the offence on her, her personal views as to appropriate outcome are irrelevant.[156] Although the sentence imposed may incidentally fulfil the victim's need to feel vindicated, and although criminal courts may now order compensation for the victim as the sole means of disposal in priority to any fines, her interests and wishes are in practice often secondary to public objectives.[157] This failure of the

---

[153] *Ibid.*, p. 168; Kelly *et al*, *op. cit.* n. 33, p. 50.

[154] Burton, *op. cit.* n. 53.

[155] *Op. cit.* n. 33, ch. 7; much of the following is derived from this source.

[156] *R* v. *Nunn* [1996] Crim LR 210. Many of those that do make a statement are dissatisfied, perhaps because of unrealistic expectations about what the process is intended to achieve: see Hoyle, Morgan and Sanders, *op. cit.* n. 108, who describe further problems in implementing the victim statement scheme. For discussion of systems giving victims greater say, see Ashworth, *The Criminal Process: an evaluation study* (1998, OUP), pp. 33–7.

[157] A court with power to make a compensation order must give reasons if it declines to do so: see Criminal Justice Act 1982, section 67; Criminal Justice Act 1988, section 104. See Ashworth *op. cit.* n. 126, pp. 108–11; Cretney and Davis *op. cit.* n. 33. The victim may qualify for criminal injuries compensation from the state, even without a prosecution: see Hayes and Williams, *op. cit.* n. 68, pp. 413–14 and Ashworth, *op. cit.*

trial and its outcome to address their needs may contribute to the decision of many victims to withdraw.

As Cretney and Davis suggest, finding an appropriate cure for this disjunction between the two phases of the criminal process is not easy.[158] One option would be to improve victims' status within the system in order to encourage greater levels of victim cooperation, for example, by giving them the right to express an opinion about appropriate sentencing or even empowering them to veto prosecution. But such measures risk increasing what for some victims are *unwanted* feelings of responsibility for their abusers' fate.[159] And such reforms, whilst enhancing victim autonomy, would be open to the objection that they undermine conventional under-standings of the public purposes and functions of the criminal justice system, threaten inconsistent treatment of identical offences and neglect the interests of other potential or actual victims, such as the children.

An alternative would be to bring the pre-trial phase into line with the offence against society model, by further encouraging or even requiring police to arrest abusers against victims' wishes and urging prosecutors more regularly to compel victim testimony or to proceed without it. These steps would need careful justification under Article 8 and careful imple-mentation if they were to be at all effective. Wider use and enforcement of the witness compulsion provisions, to the point of imprisoning re-calcitrant victims, would necessarily reduce victim autonomy, even project an image of the criminal courts and the law as a 'patriarchal force' dealing with 'weak' women.[160] Limiting victims' power to determine the course of criminal proceedings would reduce its effectiveness as a bargaining tool for those victims who use it to achieve their own objectives. From the perspective of an offence against society model, such private manipu-lation of the criminal justice system may be thought improper. But as Ford suggests, victims should not need to manipulate a system to achieve ends which would result in any case if the system functioned in their interests.[161] Removing victims' influence over proceedings, whether for their sake or that of their children, may simply have the effect of further dissuading victims from calling the police at all for fear of starting a process over which they will have no control and which they regard as potentially damaging.[162]

However, as Ashworth has argued, even if the principal aim of the criminal justice system is generally public condemnation of abusers, it is possible consistently with that focus to improve all victims' experience as witnesses and to design sentencing options (such as perpetrator

[158] *Op. cit.* n. 33, ch.8.
[159] See Edwards, *op. cit.* n. 33, pp. 211–12.
[160] Cretney and Davis, *op. cit.* n. 54, p. 81.
[161] *Op. cit.* n. 148, pp. 330–1.
[162] Hoyle, *op. cit.* n. 33, p. 218; Buzawa and Buzawa, *op. cit.* n. 7, ch. 13.

programmes) which appear more relevant to victims' objective to end the violence, rather than simply to punish.[163] The new harassment restraining orders illustrate how state-initiated action within the *criminal* courts can be directed at victims' needs, albeit only after satisfying the criminal standard of proof. Such measures, if made available for disposal of other offences, might encourage more victims to support the system's public objectives, or at least mitigate the effects of denying the victim control over the proceedings. The pragmatic considerations identified above which discourage prosecutors from proceeding without victim cooperation pose significant problems which must also be addressed. But prosecutions might be more successful, both in securing convictions and an end to the violence, if victims were offered more extensive support and protection from the system; and the facility of admitting written evidence in lieu of oral testimony could be used to greater effect to overcome the problem of the fearful witness. Indeed, any pro-arrest or pro-prosecution policy would have to be accompanied by improvements in victim support and protection to succeed in its aim. If it is going to demand victim cooperation, or even proceed without it, the system must demonstrate that it can play an effective part in helping to end the violence in victims' lives, and not merely worsen their situation. And such victim-focused measures, even if they did not allow victims the power of decision, would also provide a reminder that domestic violence and all violent crime, whatever its public significance, essentially involves harm to an individual.[164]

The civil justice system

Until the Family Law Act, the civil system's response to domestic violence clearly pursued the victim complaint model – civil proceedings to combat adult abuse were to be initiated by the victim or not at all. Indeed, that remains the predominant approach. The notion that the state should be able to pursue what might be termed its *own* interests by application to the civil courts finds no place in the current system. Indeed, central government guidance directs housing authorities not to put pressure on victims to seek civil remedies to secure occupation of the family home rather than to apply for re-housing.[165] And victims' access to public housing has in some cases militated *against* the court awarding them occupation of the family home, thereby increasing pressure on public resources.[166] In any

---

[163] Ashworth, *op. cit.* n. 126.

[164] *Ibid.*; Cretney and Davis, *op. cit.* n. 33, p. 167–8.

[165] Department of Environment/Department of Health, *Code of Guidance on the Housing Act 1996 Parts VI and VII* (as revised March 1997), at para. 13.10. Victims' experience of housing authorities have often been at odds with this guidance – see texts in suggested further reading.

[166] See Hayes and Williams, *op. cit.* n. 68, at pp. 432–3.

event, occupation orders are often intended to provide only short-term relief rather than a long-term housing solution, so any order made in favour of the victim may simply postpone an inevitable application by her to the local authority.[167] The focus within the balance of harm test on the respondent's conduct rather than the general needs of the victim may be thought to import into the civil process an element of punishment for fault, usually the preserve of criminal justice.[168] But while victims control the instigation of proceedings, they control the state's opportunity to apply the cheap, temporary 'sanction' of ousting the abuser from his home.

However, the novel measures introduced by the Family Law Act – the courts' own motion powers and third party applications – imply that there is room for victim protection concerns to operate against the wishes of victims. The Law Commission justified the introduction of powers for courts in family proceedings to make non-molestation orders on victim protection grounds. They would be useful in cases where the victim was subject to threats or intimidation, or was for some other reason reluctant to apply for an order herself; and such orders would not significantly prejudice respondents' interests, in many (though by no means all) cases simply requiring him to abstain from conduct that was in any case unlawful.[169] The Act leaves the courts to decide whether and in what terms any order should be made in such cases, and what significance should be given to the fact that the victim has not applied for the order.

Perhaps more threatening to victim autonomy is the possibility of third party applications for non-molestation and occupation orders that might be permitted by any rules made under section 60. Section 60 does not explicitly direct that rules should require the third party either to consult or obtain the consent of the victim before making an application; it is left to the rule-maker to determine what, if any, conditions must be satisfied before an application is made, and what considerations should be taken into account by a court hearing such an application.[170]

These provisions appear to permit victim protection-based rules, applications and orders to be made without regard to victims' wishes.[171] However, the Human Rights Act requires any section 60 rule-maker and public authority applicants, and courts hearing such applications and exercising their own-motion powers to make non-molestation orders, to

---

[167] See n. 81 for duration of orders under the Act.

[168] On the relevance of conduct to applications for occupation orders, see Hayes and Williams, *op. cit.* n. 68, pp. 436–44.

[169] Law Com. Rep. 207, para. 5.2.

[170] cf. Law Commission recommendations: *ibid.*, para. 5.23.

[171] See various witnesses to the proceedings of the Special Public Bill Committee, which considered the ill-fated precursor to the Family Law Act, who opposed section 60: *Family Homes and Domestic Violence Bill: Proceedings of the Special Public Bill Committee* HL 55 (1994–1995): Oral evidence: Lord Mackay LC para. 5; HHJ Fricker QC, paras. 71–80.

act compatibly with Convention rights.[172] Since applying against a victim's wishes to remove her partner from the home or making an unsolicited non-molestation order may *prima facie* interfere with her (and his) right to respect for family and private life, the state would have to justify such action under Article 8 of the ECHR. As has been seen, whilst the requirements of the Convention here are not clear, it is fair to suppose that a scheme which at least required victims to be consulted and their wishes considered would more readily satisfy the Convention than one that did not.[173] No consideration appears to have been given to the question of whether intervention against a victim's wishes can be justified without a finding as to her competence or without passing a threshold test.

Where there are children involved, *their* rights may readily justify intervention against the victim's wishes under Article 8 to prevent *them* from suffering significant harm, action which may indirectly protect the adult victim. The courts now enjoy powers under Parts IV and V of the Children Act 1989, whether on application or of their own motion, to exclude an individual from a child's home where that would avoid the need to remove the child, as an adjunct to an emergency protection or interim care order.[174] Inclusion of an exclusion requirement in the order must be consented to by a remaining adult whom the court finds is willing and able to give adequate care to the child.[175] Given the alternative of the child's removal from the home, reluctant victims may come under pressure to consent to removal of the abuser, whether via an exclusion requirement or section 60 occupation order. These cases, like those involving childless victims who could only be protected via a section 60 application, require sensitive handling if the implementation of such remedies is not to be experienced by victims simply as a further attack on their autonomy.

Furthermore, the appropriate identity and qualifications of the third party are debatable. Police may be ill-equipped to assess victims' interests. The task may better suit the skills and experience of social workers. But social work intervention may be perceived as stigmatising, and its association with the removal of children may act as a potent disincentive to victims reporting. Social workers have hitherto confined their attention to child protection issues, and been criticised for failing to pay regard to

---

[172] The broad terms of section 60 FLA appear not to require Convention-incompatible rules or orders to be made, so section 6(1) Human Rights Act 1998 applies (cf. sections 3 and 6(2) HRA); likewise, section 42(2)(b) FLA leaves room for courts making non-molestation orders of their own motion to act compatibly with the Convention, and so section 6(1) HRA requires them to do so.

[173] See text to note 145. For potential arguments of *respondents* against civil orders see Swindells *et al*, *Family Law and the Human Rights Act 1998* (1999, Family Law), ch. 13.

[174] Children Act 1989, sections 38–38B, 44–44B; Law Com. Rep. 207, para. 6.17.

[175] Sections 38A(2)(b) and 44A(2)(b); see Law Com. Rep. 207, para. 6.20.

the interests of adult victims in their own right, rather than simply as mothers.[176] Non-governmental support group applicants may be less threatening to victims, but regulation of such groups may be necessary to guard against victims' interests being hijacked by maverick well-wishers. Again, the manner in which the courts' discretion in awarding and framing orders may provide a safeguard here.

Most fundamentally, some commentators are concerned that opening up the civil jurisdiction to state applicants may at a theoretical, and practical, level encourage a re-privatisation of the problem, not least by the police themselves, reversing the recent preference for criminalisation.[177] If the police have civil orders at their disposal, they may be less inclined to treat the matter as criminal.

However, although sharing many of the concerns expressed above, Humphries and Kaye identify several potential advantages of third party applications, some of which mirror those hoped for from pro-arrest and compulsion powers in the criminal justice system.[178] The onus of applying is removed from the victim at a time of crisis when she may fear reprisals if she initiates the action, thereby ensuring that the interests of both victim and any children are protected where she is unable to act herself. The fate of the action need not be dependent on the victim's own entitlement to Community Legal Service funding or private funds, so civil justice can be dispensed on the basis of need rather than ability to pay. Involvement of the state, in particular the police, from the outset may encourage compliance with the order, on the basis that their initial involvement makes enforcement of the order more likely (though victim-sought orders are equally deserving of full enforcement). Perhaps most importantly, state involvement in a civil action, rather than encouraging re-privatisation of the problem, may challenge the traditional association of civil orders with the idea that abuse is something private to the parties, and a matter in which the state has no substantial interest.

Concluding thoughts

The dichotomy between 'public' and 'private', traditionally translated in legal system terms into criminal and civil, state and individual, can be misleading; a continuum from public to private may be a more helpful

---

[176] Maynard, *op. cit.* n. 30.

[177] Special Public Bill Committee, *op. cit.*: Oral evidence: Lord Mackay LC, para. 5; AC Johnston, para. 42; Written evidence: Refuge, para. 68. Compare the views of the Society of Labour Lawyers, Written evidence: para. 77.

[178] 'Third party applications for protective orders: opportunities, ambiguities and traps' (1997) 19 *Journal of Social Welfare and Family Law* 403.

[179] Schneider, *op. cit.* n. 25, at p. 38.

image.[179] While it is important to protect individuals' private lives from unnecessary state intervention, there are clearly aspects of family, traditionally 'private', life where the state *should* be involved to some degree – not least, to eradicate violence within the family. Indeed, the state may breach its obligations under the European Convention on Human Rights if it fails to involve itself in some family problems, particularly where the individuals in need have repeatedly applied to it for assistance.[180] The state may also be justified in taking legal action in both criminal and civil courts to protect at least some of those victims who have not sought help or apparently oppose it, as it does in cases of child protection. However, in its enthusiasm to atone for past neglect of the problem, the state should not ignore the wishes of those individuals most immediately affected by the violence and the consequent requirements of their rights to respect for their family and private life. But finding the appropriate balance between autonomy, protection and public interests is not an easy task.

From a practical perspective, a sharp distinction between 'public' and 'private' discourages flexible solutions to domestic violence, whereby the criminal and civil courts are seen as offering alternative or complementary remedies to be deployed in response to an individual case. In order to ensure that the most effective use of all available remedies is made in individual cases, some co-ordination of criminal and civil justice agents is required.[181] Enabling the state to bring proceedings in both jurisdictions may be helpful to that end. But direct legal remedies are just a part of the solution to cases of domestic violence and in many cases do not provide a lasting solution. All victims, whether or not they agree to participate in legal proceedings, require material and emotional support. Such support is needed to enable victims to enjoy maximum autonomy, thereby increasing the chances of preventing repeat victimisation, *whether or not* via legal proceedings, and so of improving the long-term prospects of victims. A state which in pursuit of its public concern to eradicate domestic violence recognises and is sensitive to victims' wishes may respond more effectively to the complexities of individual cases than one which does not. But on a larger scale, both legal remedies and the provision of material and emotional support to individual victims will not themselves eradicate domestic violence. That may only be achieved by removing the problematic social structures and ideologies which are said to lie at the root of the problem.

---

[180] See note 60.
[181] See JUSTICE, *op. cit.* n. 108, at pp. 54–5.

Further reading

Criminal justice

Cretney and Davis, 'Prosecuting "Domestic" Assault' [1996] *Criminal Law Review* 162.

Grace, *Policing Domestic Violence in the 1990s*, Home Office Research Study 139 (1995, Home Office).

Morley and Mullender, 'Hype or hope? The importance of pro-arrest policies and batterers' programmes from North America to Britain as key measures for preventing violence to women in the home' (1992) 6 *International Journal of Law and the Family* 265.

Civil justice and mediation

Law Commission Report 207, *Domestic Violence and Occupation of the Family Home* (1992, HMSO).

Kaganas and Piper, 'Domestic violence and divorce mediation' (1994) 16 *Journal of Social Welfare Law* 265.

Housing and welfare benefits

Douglas, 'The Family, Gender and Social Security', in Harris (ed.), *Social Security Law in Context* (Hart, 2000).

Hoff, *Battered Women as Survivors*, ch. 10 (1990, Routledge).

Pascall and Morley, 'Women and homelessness: proposals from the Department of the Environment. II: Domestic violence' (1996) 18 *Journal of Social Welfare and Family Law* 327 (*note that the reforms enacted in the Housing Act 1996 differ in some respects from the proposals criticised here; for brief discussion of the current law, see Lowe and Douglas, op. cit. note 24, at pp. 218–224*).

Child-related issues

Burton, 'Prosecution decisions in cases of domestic violence involving children' (2000) 22 *Journal of Social Welfare and Family Law* 175.

Hester and Radford, *Domestic Violence and Child Contact Arrangements in England and Denmark* (1996, The Policy Press).

Lord Chancellor's Advisory Board on Family Law Matters, *Report to the Lord Chancellor on the question of parental contact in cases where there is domestic violence* (2000, LCD website – http//www.open.gov.uk/lcd/family/family.htm).

Parkinson and Humphreys, 'Children who witness domestic violence: implications for child protection' (1998) 10 *Child and Family Law Quarterly* 147.

Abuse of the elderly and disabled

Law Commission Report 231, *Mental Incapacity* (1995, HMSO, Part IX): 'Public Law Protection for Vulnerable People at Risk'.

4

Parents and children

Jonathan Herring

This chapter will discuss some of the key issues relating to the private law governing children and parents. This topic is dominated by the Children Act 1989, which is now at the heart of English and Welsh child law. This chapter will look at the different understandings of 'a parent' and how the law seeks to recognise (or not to recognise) them. It will then consider the way the law attempts to protect and balance the interests or rights of parents, children and the state in private law disputes.

Different understandings of 'parent'

The term 'parent' may seem straightforward and its meaning obvious. However, it is by no means uncontroversial. The definition of who is the parent of a child has changed from society to society and from generation to generation. Esther Goody, investigating the notion of families around the world, has noted that there are various aspects of parenthood: bearing and begetting children; endowing children with civil and kinship status; nurturing; and the training and sponsorship of children into adulthood.[1] Different people in different cultures carry out these roles. Often it is the child's genetic parents but the functions are also performed by a variety of other people.

Amongst lawyers the following different understandings of parent have been the most commonly discussed:

---

[1] Goody, *Parenthood and Social Responsibility* (1982, Cambridge University Press).

(a) *The biological or genetic parent*

The nature of 'biological parenthood' is not straightforward. Martin Johnson[2] has distinguished four different kinds of biological parenthood: the genetic component (the man whose sperm or the woman whose egg leads to the creation of the child); the coital component (the mating between the man and women leading to the creation of the child); the gestational component (in humans, this is performed by the mother providing a uterus and physical support to the child during pregnancy); and the post-natal component (the caring for the child after birth). In legal materials when commentators write about the biological parent they are normally referring to the genetic component, but this, as Martin Johnson has shown, is only one aspect of biological parenthood. To avoid any confusion, this chapter will avoid talking about biological parenthood and instead refer to the genetic parent.

(b) *The social parent*

In defining parenthood it is common to distinguish between 'genetic' parents and 'social' parents. Social parents are those who carry out the jobs of parenting: feeding, cleaning, washing, and clothing the child, for example. Of course, often the genetic parent and social parent will be the same person, but they need not be. For example, if a wife becomes pregnant by her husband, but during the pregnancy divorces her husband and a new partner moves in, the new partner may become the social parent of the child, while the husband remains the genetic parent. The mother will be both the genetic and social parent.

Even the notion of 'social parent' is complex. In particular, it might be argued that the concept of a social parent reflects gendered expectations of how mothers and fathers behave. A 'good father' may traditionally be perceived as a man who leaves his workplace in time to come home to read to his child before the child goes to bed, and makes sure that he spends 'quality time' with the child during the weekend; while a 'good mother' is required to spend the majority of her time caring for the child. A mother who goes out to work and leaves daytime child care to others may be seen by some as a 'bad mother'. Therefore, the kind of conduct which constitutes social parenthood may depend on what is expected of a mother or father.[3] These traditional images of the ideal mother and father are under challenge with the advent of the 'new man' who seeks to play a full

---

[2] Johnson, 'A Biomedical Perspective on Parenthood' in Bainham, Day Sclater and Richards (eds), *What is a Parent?* (1999, Hart).

[3] It might be that what is regarded as proper parenting for girls would not be proper parenting for boys (Day Sclater, *Families* [2000, Hodder & Stoughton], chapter 7).

role in parenting, and with increasing social acceptance of the 'working mother'.[4]

Placing emphasis on the practical role of parents reflects what is often regarded as the key role of parenthood: the socialisation of children. This involves teaching children the social skills and moral values that are necessary if the child is to become a valued member of society.[5] Some argue that this aspect of parenthood is far more important than the provision of genetic material.

(c) *The psychological parent*

This concept is closely connected with the notion of the social parent. At its heart is attachment theory. John Bowlby[6] argues that children from an early age form an attachment to a single primary unchanging caregiver. This bond is of crucial importance to the child's psychological well-being. This theory in more recent times has been brought to particular prominence for lawyers by the hugely influential work of Goldstein, Freud and Solnit.[7] They developed the idea of the 'psychological parent' who provides the child's 'emotional demands for affection, companionship and stimulating intimacy.'[8] This person may be a blood relation of a child, but need not be. There are two important consequences of their argument. First, a child should only be taken into care by the state and be removed from a psychological parent where there are very strong grounds for doing so. Secondly, on divorce or separation, the child should remain with the psychological parent, and contact with anyone else should not be at a level which undermines the child's bond with the psychological parent.

(d) *The licensed parent*

Licensed parents are people who are appointed by or approved by the state to be parents of a child. Perhaps the best known example in English and Welsh law is adoptive parents. We could have a legal system where only those approved by the state as suitable could act as parents of children. Under such a system on the birth of a child *anyone* could apply to care for and raise the child; the applicants would be assessed and the child

---

[4] The common perception that the mother who spends all day caring for a child is *not* 'working' reflects the lack of value our society places on the care of children.

[5] Although there are those who criticise the role parents play in raising children. For example, it has been claimed that parenting encourages mutual dependence between parents and children, which enables abuse to take place and discourages children from participating in community activities: Cooper, *The Death of the Family* (1971, Allen Lane).

[6] Bowlby, *Child Care and the Growth of Love* (1965, Penguin).

[7] Goldstein, Freud, Solnit, *Beyond the Best Interests of the Child* (1973, Free Press).

[8] At p. 18.

handed over to the best qualified. There would be no presumption that the woman who gave birth to the child would carry out the mothering role, or that the man whose sperm led to the child would have any role in being the father. To many people such a scheme would be the kind of policy adopted only by the most barbaric totalitarian regime and could not be a part of a liberal democracy. That said, if parents are unable to care for children then often licensed parenting is relied upon in the United Kingdom in the form of fostering or adoption.[9]

(e) *The intentional parent*

Chris Barton and Gillian Douglas[10] have argued that the present law relies primarily on the intention to be a parent as key to the notion of parenthood. That is, that the people who have acted in a way which reveals that they have voluntarily undertaken the obligations and status of parenthood are regarded as the parents of a child. This is based on the principle that the law is reluctant to impose legal obligation on people unless these obligations are voluntarily undertaken. For example, a person is only bound by a contract if it can be shown that he or she has voluntarily accepted the contractual obligation. Indeed, as criminal lawyers are keen to point out, if you come across a person drowning in a pond and you simply walk past you will suffer no legal punishment, unless you had undertaken some special duty towards the person. In the same way, it could be argued, a person should not be held responsible for a child unless he or she has explicitly or implicitly undertaken the responsibilities of a parent. Although the genetic parents can normally be said to have undertaken the responsibility of their child, it could also be that others could assume responsibility for a child, for example couples who use assisted reproductive techniques.

(f) *Parental responsibility*

In England and Wales the legal rights and responsibilities of parenthood are captured in the notion of parental responsibility. The law treats the questions 'who is a parent?' and 'who acquires the legal rights and responsibility of parents?' as two separate questions. The law accepts that people who are not parents can receive the legal rights and responsibilities that normally attach to parenthood and, indeed that some people who are parents should not acquire parental responsibility.

---

[9] Adoption is discussed in chapter 6 in this book.
[10] Barton and Douglas, *Law and Parenthood* (1995, Butterworth).

The law and the different kinds of parent

So what weight does the law give to these different understandings of being a parent? As shall be seen, the law does not take a consistent approach in its definition of who is a parent. The law struggles to reconcile the competing claims of the genetic and social (or psychological) parent.

Who is the child's mother?

The law recognises that the woman who gives birth to a child is the mother of the child. But why is this? Is the law recognising the genetic link of the mother to the child, or is the law emphasising the mother's care for the child throughout the pregnancy (i.e. her social parenting during pregnancy)? The answer is that it is the gestational care of the mother and not the genetic link which is crucial. This is revealed by section 27 Human Fertilisation and Embryology Act 1990, which states that if a woman becomes pregnant as a result of licensed assisted reproductive techniques using a donated egg it is the gestational mother who is the legal mother and not the woman who donated the egg. If the treatment is not licensed then it appears the position would be the same under the common law following *The Ampthill Peerage* case.[11] This indicates that as far as the legal definition of mothers is concerned genetic parentage is not significant in relation to parenthood. It is the social parenthood in caring for the child during pregnancy that is crucial.

Who is the child's father?

In the law, it is generally accepted that the legal father is the man who is the genetic father of the child. There are special exceptions to this, namely where the child is born as a result of assisted reproductive techniques at a licensed clinic, in which cases the Human Embryology and Fertilisation Act 1990 provides a special set of rules. Under the Act a person can be a legal father even though he is not the genetic father. For example, where a married woman gives birth following insemination with donated sperm her husband may be regarded as the legal father.[12] Indeed, a genetic father may not necessarily be the legal father. For example, a sperm donor will not normally be regarded as the father of a child born using his sperm.[13] But these are exceptional cases, and if there are no specific statutory provisions to the contrary the 'default' position is that the genetic father is the legal father of the child.

[11] [1977] AC 547, at p. 577.
[12] Human Fertilisation and Embryology Act 1990, s. 28(2).
[13] Human Fertilisation and Embryology Act 1990, s. 28(6).

However, the position is perhaps not quite so straightforward. Complexity results from the fact that the law does not look very deeply into the issue of genetic paternity and relies on various presumptions about who is the genetic father. The law will assume that if a married woman gives birth to a child her husband is the genetic father and he is the father of the child.[14] Similarly if a man is registered at the child's birth as the father of the child it is also presumed that he is the genetic father.[15] It may be that the law relies on these presumptions because until relatively recently it was not possible to carry out scientific tests to find out whether a man was the father of a child. It was therefore not surprising that the courts were willing to accept, for example, that a husband was the father of a child as that would be a reasonable guess as to the genetic paternity. Now that we have the ability to find out the genetic truth these presumptions are not essential. Nevertheless the law still relies upon them. The question is, why? Does the fact that the law is still willing to rely on the presumptions indicate that in fact it is not *actually* genetic parenthood that is the law's concern Rather, the presumptions enable the appropriate social parent (e.g. the husband of the mother) to be named as the father? Or are the presumptions still relied upon because carrying out genetic tests on every child born would be too costly and may infringe personal liberty?

The issue comes to a head when an attempt is made by a man claiming to be the father of a child to rebut the presumptions. If the presumptions exist as part of a genuine attempt to ascertain genetic parentage then we can assume that the courts would order biological tests if the presumptions were challenged. If, however, the presumptions are in reality a way of ensuring that the social father is deemed the father we might expect the courts to be reluctant about ordering tests. In fact the courts in such cases have demonstrated an ambivalent attitude. There are some cases which suggest that the courts are unwilling to order tests for fear that the child's social parenting will be disturbed. Take the facts of *Re F (A Minor)(Blood Tests: Parents Rights)*.[16] The mother was married, but had a brief affair. The affair came to an end; the wife was reconciled with her husband; and subsequently gave birth to a child. The problem was that it was unclear whether the genetic father of the child was the wife's husband or her former lover. The husband and wife had put the affair behind them and did not want biological tests to be carried out for fear that they might reveal that the former lover was the father. If this happened there was a concern that this would destabilise their marriage. The Court of Appeal decided not to order blood tests because it would not be in the child's

---

[14] This is sometimes known as the 'pater est' presumption. It is discussed in Bainham, *Children – The Modern Law* (1998, Jordans) at p. 107.

[15] Births and Deaths Registration Act 1953, s. 34(2).

[16] [1993] 1 FLR 598, [1998] 1 FCR 932.

interests to destabilise her present family. As the biological tests were not carried out the presumption that the husband was the father applied. From this case it could be argued that the law is more concerned about preserving the status of the social parent than discovering the truth of genetic parentage.[17] On the other hand, in other cases the courts have referred to the right of a child to know the truth about their genetic parentage and have been willing to require biological tests to be carried out, despite the objections of the social parents.[18] So then, although the definition of fatherhood is centred around genetic parentage the reluctance of the law sometimes to order biological tests to ascertain genetic parentage indicates that even in relation to the legal definition of a father social parenthood has some significance.

The position of a genetic parent who is not a legal parent

Given that there is not an exact correlation between genetic parentage and legal parenthood the issue arises whether those who are genetic parents, but do not have legal parentage, are given any legal status. For example, even though a man donating sperm to a licensed clinic may not be the father of any child born using that sperm,[19] does he have any rights in relation to those children or does a child have any rights to discover his father's identity? Does it really matter which man provided the relevant sperm?

The law provides no special legal rights to the person who is the genetic but not legal parent. He or she will be in the same position in relation to the child as any other adult in legal terms. However, there is limited recognition of a child's right to knowledge about her or his genetic parentage. Children born as a result of assisted reproduction have rights to discover limited information about their genetic parents;[20] further, adopted children are entitled to obtain a copy of their birth certificate, which may provide the names of their genetic parents. However, both of these are dependent on the child being aware that they have been born using donated genetic material or that they have been adopted. And there is no legal right to be told of either of these facts.[21]

Increasingly there have been calls for the law to recognise clearly that children have a right to be informed of their genetic parentage. There are

---

[17] See recently *Re K (Specific Issue Order)* [1999] 2 FLR 280 which preferred the importance of preserving the emotional health of the mother over any 'right to know' of the child in deciding not to order the mother to tell her child who his father was.

[18] *Re H (Paternity)(Blood Tests)* [1996] 2 FLR 65, [1996] 3 FCR 201.

[19] Human Fertilisation and Embryology Act 1990, s. 28(6).

[20] For example, a child born as a result of assisted reproduction who is intending to marry can discover whether he or she is related to the person he or she is intending to marry.

[21] *Re K (Specific Issue Order)* [1999] 2 FLR 280.

some concrete reasons why a child might want to know his or her genetic parentage. For example, some medical conditions can have hereditary links and so knowledge of genetic parentage may be significant for that reason. If a person's family history is known and it is shown that they are at risk of suffering from, for example, heart disease, then it may be possible to take preventative steps to avoid the disease developing. It has also been argued that knowledge of genetic parentage is essential to a person's sense of personal identity.[22] It is generally agreed that adopted children should be told from as young an age as possible that they are adopted for fear of causing them distress if they are told in their teens that the people they thought were their parents are not in fact their genetic parents. John Eekelaar[23] has asked whether any person would wish to be brought up having been deceived as to their genetic origins. He suggests not. There are therefore some strong arguments that it would benefit a person to know some information about their genetic parents. Against such arguments must be weighed the interests of the genetic parents, who may claim that they have a right to remain anonymous as an aspect of their rights to private life, and the interests of the social parents, who may claim their rights to family life would be disrupted if the genetic truth were revealed.[24]

Parental responsibility: the legal rights and responsibilities of parenthood

The law in England and Wales draws a sharp distinction between being a parent and having the rights and responsibilities of parenthood. Just because you are a parent does not mean that you have parental responsibility. All mothers acquire parental responsibility automatically.[25] Fathers who are married to the child's mother do too.[26] Fathers who are not married to the mother can only acquire parental responsibility by lodging at the court a parental responsibility agreement signed by them and the mother[27] or by persuading the court to make a parental responsibility order under section 4 Children Act 1989.

---

[22] O'Donnovan (1988), 'A Right to Know One's Parentage' (1988) 2 *International Journal of Law Policy and the Family* 27.

[23] Eekelaar, 'The Interests of the Child and the Child's Wishes: The Role of Dynamic Self-Determinism' (1994) 8 *International Journal of Law and the Family* 42.

[24] Article 8 of the European Convention on Human Rights requires the state to respect private and family life.

[25] Children Act 1989, section 2(1), (2).

[26] Children Act 1989, s. 2(1).

[27] Children Act 1989, s. 2(2).

Section 3 Children Act 1989 defines parental responsibility as:

all the rights, duties, powers, responsibilities and authority which by law a parent of a child has in relation to the child and his property.

However, it would be misleading to state that parental responsibility is the source of all the legal consequences of parenthood. First, it should be stressed that just because a father does not have parental responsibility does not mean that he does not have any of the rights and obligations of parenthood. For example, a father may be liable to pay child support under the Child Support Act 1991, even though he does not have parental responsibility. Secondly, as Ros Pickford's research reveals, many people (particularly unmarried fathers) are acting day-to-day as parents towards children, even though they do not have parental responsibility.[28] For example, an unmarried father may bathe, clothe and feed a child (all core elements of parental care of children) without having parental responsibility. Further, it is quite possible to have parental responsibility without carrying out any of the social roles of a parent. A husband who leaves his wife before the birth of their child and never even sees the child could still have parental responsibility, even though he would never have acted in a parental way towards the child. Thirdly, there are a few situations where being a legal parent with parental responsibility gives greater rights than being a non-parent with parental responsibility.[29]

One difficulty for the law is that parental responsibility does not have a consistent meaning. Courts and commentators have struggled to explain the term. The following are some of the most popular interpretations of parental responsibilities:

(a) Parental responsibility may indicate that parents, rather than anyone else, are to have responsibility for making decisions about children. In other words the key role of the concept of parental responsibility is to stress that the state should not normally interfere with the decisions made by parents about children.[30]

[28] Pickford, 'Unmarried Fathers and the Law' in Bainham, Day Sclater and Richards, *What is a Parent?* (1999, Hart).

[29] For example, the consent of a non-parent with parental responsibility is not required before an adoption order can be made, but a parent with parental responsibility needs to consent or have her consent dispensed with under the Adoption Act 1976. The differences between being a parent with parental responsibility and a non-parent with parental responsibility are outlined in Bainham, 'Parentage, Parenthood and Parental Responsibility: Subtle, Elusive Yet Important Distinctions' in A. Bainham, M. Richards and S. Day Sclater, *What is a Parent?* (1999, Hart).

[30] Eekelaar, 'Parental Responsibility: State of Nature or Nature of the State?' (1991) 13 *Journal of Social Welfare and Family Law* 37.

(b) Parental responsibility may emphasise that any rights parents have are to be exercised 'responsibly'. That is for the benefit of the child and not for the benefit of the parents themselves.[31]

(c) Parental responsibility may give the parent a 'stamp of approval' whereby the law recognises that the parent or carer of a child deserves the label of having parental responsibility as it reflects his or her commitment to the child. In other words, its role is symbolic, rather than being of particular legal effect.[32]

(d) Parental responsibility enables parents to give legal authority to third parties to act in certain ways towards children. For example, the law has developed so that a doctor can treat a child if he or she has the consent of a person with parental responsibility. A person without parental responsibility cannot give the doctor a legally effective consent.[33]

Cases and academic opinions could be cited to support all of these visions of parental responsibility and there is much debate over which of these should be seen to be at the heart of parental responsibility. The question is of particular significance when it comes to deciding who should have parental responsibility. The greater the rights that attach to parental responsibility the more restrictive the law may be over who should have parental responsibility; but the fewer the legal rights that attach to parental responsibility the more generous the law could be in the allocation of it. For example, in cases where the courts have taken the view that parental responsibility is simply a status which reflects the commitment that a parent has shown towards a child, the courts have been very willing to grant parental responsibility to an unmarried father who applies for it. In *Re S (A Minor)(Parental Responsibility)*[34] a father who had a conviction for possession of paedophilic literature and had failed to pay child main-tenance was granted parental responsibility on the basis that he was the natural father and so should have parental responsibility to reflect the status 'for which nature has already ordained that he must bear the responsibility'.[35] This case seems to perceive parental responsibility as little more than a confirmation that the man is the father of a child. The approach in *Re S* could be contrasted with *M* v. *M*[36] where a father suffered from a learning difficulty and so was not granted parental responsibility

---

[31] *Ibid.*

[32] Eekelaar, (1998) 'Do Parents Have a Duty to Consult?' (1998) 114 *Law Quarterly Review* 337.

[33] *Re W (A Minor)(Medical Treatment)* [1993] Fam 64.

[34] [1995] 2 FLR 648, discussed in Kaganas, 'Responsible or feckless fathers? – *Re S (Parental Responsibility)*' (1996) 6 *Child and Family Law Quarterly* 165.

[35] At p. 657.

[36] *M* v. *M (Parental Responsibility)* [1999] 2 FLR 737.

on the ground that he would be unable effectively to exercise the rights of parenthood. This decision seems to place greater weight on the idea that parental responsibility gives parents important legal powers to make decisions about children and that the law must ensure that those to whom the powers are given will exercise those powers properly. The father in *M v. M* would certainly appear to have shown as much commitment to the child, if not more, as the father in *Re S*.

The law on the allocation of parental responsibility is highly controversial. In particular, the fact that the law distinguishes between fathers who are and are not married to the mother. One way of justifying the way the law allocates parental responsibility is as follows: in deciding who is to have parental responsibility the law requires a parent to have shown commitment to the child in such a way that she or he deserves to be awarded the rights and responsibilities of parenthood.[37] A mother shows this commitment by caring for the child through the pregnancy. Hence all mothers automatically are granted parental responsibility. A father who has married the mother can be presumed to be supporting his wife (and therefore the unborn child) during the pregnancy and through marriage has shown commitment to the mother and child. The unmarried father has not shown the commitment to his partner and the child through marriage and so is not awarded parental responsibility automatically. In the words of the European Court of Human Rights,[38] 'the relationship between unmarried fathers and their children varies from ignorance and indifference to a stable relationship indistinguishable from the conventional family based unit.' However if the unmarried father has persuaded the mother[39] or the court[40] that he deserves parental responsibility he can be awarded it.

The difficulty for the law in allocating parental responsibility is this: it is clear that there are many unmarried fathers who are committed to their children and play an important role in their children (as much so as many married fathers). But there are also many unmarried fathers who are utterly disinterested in their children. The question is whether it is better to grant all unmarried fathers parental responsibility, but then have a procedure whereby mothers (or others) can apply to the court to have the parental responsibility removed; *or* not to grant unmarried fathers parental responsibility automatically and to place the burden on *them* to apply to the court to acquire parental responsibility if they want it. As already indicated, the strength of the arguments very much depends on

[37] It would therefore be possible to see parental responsibility as a form of licensed parenthood.

[38] In *B v. UK* [2000] 1 FCR 289, at p. 294.

[39] Through lodging a parental responsibility agreement order with the court (s. 4(1), Children Act 1989).

[40] Children Act 1989, s. 4(1).

the meaning of parental responsibility. If it is nothing more than a 'stamp of approval' then there is a strong argument that all fathers should be encouraged to play a full role (whether married or not) and by granting them parental responsibility the law is sending the message that they must bear the responsibilities of being a parent. Similarly, if parental responsibility is seen as just formalising in legal terms the practical care a parent is giving a child, then as the majority of unmarried fathers are playing some role in their child's life, granting them parental responsibility would match the legal position with reality. However, if parental responsibility is about giving a father the rights to make decisions about the child, particularly if it means he can make the decisions without needing the mother's agreement, then the law needs to be more careful in its allocation of parental responsibility. A stronger argument could then be made to support the present allocation of parental responsibility.

A further issue concerns proof of whether a man has parental responsibility. Under the present law a father can produce a document to demonstrate that he should have parental responsibility: a marriage certificate; a parental responsibility agreement; or a court order. However if all unmarried fathers were given parental responsibility automatically then the only way of finding out whether a man did or did not have parental responsibility would be by carrying out blood tests.[41] Again the importance of this issue turns on the extent to which parental responsibility actually give a parent rights of any practical significance.

Concluding thoughts on the law's definitions of parenthood

Andrew Bainham[42] argues that there are three kinds of parent recognised by the law: parentage, parenthood and parental responsibility. He suggests 'parentage' represents the significance that the law attaches to genetic parentage; 'parenthood' describes those who are classified as parents within the law; and 'parental responsibility' represents the legal rights and responsibilities that attach to being a parent. It is quite possible for different people to have parentage, parenthood and parental responsibility. Imagine this: a woman and her partner receive assisted reproductive treatment together, using the sperm of a donor, as a result of which the woman becomes pregnant. She and her partner later separate; the woman marries another man and her husband was granted parental

---

[41] Notably this concern would not work against the suggestion that men registered on the birth certificate would automatically acquire parental responsibility in the Lord Chancellor's Department's consultation paper (*The Law on Parental Responsibility for Unmarried Fathers* [1999, HMSO]).

[42] Bainham, *op. cit.* n. 25.

responsibility.[43] In such a case the sperm donor would have parentage; the mother's original partner would be regarded as the father of the child[44] and therefore have parenthood; and her current husband would have parental responsibility. Bainham suggests that by distinguishing parentage, parenthood, and parental responsibility the law is given greater flexibility. For example, the law can attach some rights or responsibilities to parenthood and a different set of rights or responsibilities to those with parental responsibility. Consider a case where the parents of a child are unable to look after a child, and so the grandmother takes care of the child. To call the grandmother a parent might confuse the child and be regarded as artificial. However, to be able to give her the legal rights and responsibilities that are attached to being a parent (parental responsibility) without calling her a parent seems to be an ideal solution. Further if a genetic father has never played a role in the life of his child, the law can choose to recognise that he is the father and can give him some limited rights without giving him the right to make decisions on day-to-day issues relating to the child (parental responsibility).

Bainham clearly regards this flexibility as a benefit and encourages the law to recognise the different rights that may flow from parentage, parenthood and parental responsibility. However, it is important to notice that in practice (although not in theory) his argument is a gendered one. It is far more likely that different men will have parentage, parenthood and parental responsibility than women.[45] This is because on the breakdown of a relationship children tend on average to remain with their mother. It is therefore more likely that a man who is not a genetic father will be playing the role of the social father, than that a woman is performing the role of a mother. Therefore recognising the differing ways of being a parent means, in reality, recognising a variety of ways of being a father. Giving rights to a variety of different men who, in various ways, are the child's father means a mother may face potential challenges to her care of the child from a wider range of men than if a more straightforward notion of being a father was adopted. So, recognising the different forms of parents can in fact weaken the position of mothers. This is not to say the law's approach as outlined by Bainham should necessarily be rejected, but rather that it should be treated with caution to ensure that it is not used to the disadvantage of mothers.

Although the law is happy to accept that more than two people may have parental responsibility for a child, the law has held tight to the principle that a child can only have two parents, one mother and one

[43] The only way this could be done would be if he were granted a residence order under s. 8 Children Act 1989.

[44] Children Act 1989, s. 28(3).

[45] Egg donation would be one of the very rare cases where genetic and gestational parenthood would be divided for women.

father.[46] The principle is slightly weakened in the Human Fertilisation and Embryology Act 1980 which has accepted that a child can have no father.[47] However, there are no circumstances under which a child can have more than one father or more than one mother. As biological technology develops it may become possible for more than two people to be genetically related to a child, or that an artificial womb will be created, meaning that the gestational element of parenthood could be carried out by machines. These developments could blow open the presumption that a child should have one father and one mother. This leads back to the question of what should be seen as being the key element of parenthood.

As mentioned above, Chris Barton and Gillian Douglas have argued that the primary test for parentage is who has an intention to be a parent. Is this an accurate description of the law? It is clear that in cases involving assisted reproduction and adoption those that the law classifies as parents have certainly demonstrated an intention to be a parent. However, can it be said in the most common kind of parenthood, namely following sexual intercourse, that the parents have manifested an intention to be a parent? The mother could be said to have done so because she goes through the pregnancy and does not have an abortion.[48] In relation to fathers, Barton and Douglas emphasise the methods used to presume or prove that a man is a father all indicate an intention to be a parent: by marrying the mother; by being registered as the father; or applying for blood tests to be carried out. Critics would argue that this is to emphasise the methods for proving parentage with the basis of parentage itself, which is genetic parentage. If scientific tests show that a man is the genetic father it is no defence for him to show that he did not intend the mother to become pregnant. It could be argued that by engaging in sexual intercourse the man has accepted the possibility of a child being born (even if the mother told him she was using contraception) and thus he has manifested an intent to be a parent. However, this 'deemed intention' seems far from 'acceptance of the social role of parenthood' which Barton and Douglas see as the heart of parenthood. The truth is that the law on allocation of parenthood is an uneasy mixture of genetic, social and intentional aspects, recognising the complexity of the circumstances in which people become parents and perform parental roles in modern society.

---

[46] The law has, however, been willing to grant more than one person parental responsibility (s. 2(5) Children Act 1989). Indeed there is no limit to the number of people who can have parental responsibility.

[47] Where a single woman receives treatment using a donor's sperm, for example.

[48] Although her decision not to abort may be based on religious beliefs rather than indicating an intention to be a parent.

Children's rights

This section will consider the ways in which the law does or might recognise that children have rights. Before examining this question directly it is necessary to first examine the way in which children are regarded as a special group within society.

Social constructions of childhood

It might be thought that the concept of childhood is straightforward: a child is a person under the age of eighteen. However, what childhood means is far more complex. In a way our society assumes that child-like characteristics are bad. To call someone infantile, naive or gullible is widely regarded as insulting. But are an adult's approaches to life always better than children's?[49] Society's perception of children is complex: although their characteristics are seen as undesirable, children are also often seen as innocent and incapable of evil. This may explain the sense of shock that surrounded the Jamie Bulger murder.[50]

It is common to assume that children need care and support, and to be taken care of by adults. Clearly this is largely true, but it is important to appreciate that children can have a significant effect on their parents. The parent-child relationship is not all about what the parent does to the child; the child can affect the parent. Children are not just passive recipients of parental care, but also interact with their family. It can even be argued that parenting is a negotiated enterprise: parents and children cooperating together in their family life.[51] It is also important to appreciate that there is not a simple division between adults and children. An adolescent may in some ways be like a child and some ways like an adult. It is not surprising that the law has developed a flexible approach, treating adolescents as adults for some purposes and as children for others.

Children's rights

Before considering whether children have rights it is necessary ask, 'what is a right?' The exact definition of a right has been a topic of great debate amongst those interested in jurisprudence, and so cannot be discussed in detail here. One widely respected definition is that of Joseph Raz who has suggested,

---

[49] See Hill and Tisdall, *Children and Society* (1997, Addison Wesley Longman), for a useful discussion of the position of children within our society.
[50] Jamie Bulger, a toddler, was murdered by two children aged ten, causing a 'panic' about the nation's children. This is discussed in depth in A. Young, *Imaging Crime* (1996, Sage).
[51] James and Prout (eds), *Constructing and Reconstructing Childhood* (1990, Falmer).

a law creates a right if it is based on and expresses the view that someone has an interest which is sufficient ground for holding another to be subject to a duty... His right is a legal right if it is recognised by law, that is if the law holds his interest to be sufficient ground to hold another to be subject to a duty.[52]

A crucial point to note is that where one person has a right another person is under a duty to give effect to his or her interest. In relation to children's rights there are two main questions: (1) should children be given all the rights that adults have? (2) should children be given extra rights over and above those given to adults?

In considering whether children should have the same rights as adults, at one extreme child liberationists claim that children should have the same rights as adults.[53] They argue that children are people and should be treated as equal citizens and should have the same protection under the law as adults. This means giving children all the rights that adults have. Such a view might seem absurd; surely we cannot give children the same rights to drive cars or drink alcohol as adults. However, a more moderate child liberationist viewpoint cannot be so easily dismissed.[54] Moderate child liberationists would accept that most children should not be permitted to drive cars, but this would be because they lack the ability necessary to drive and not because they are children. They would argue that while it is permissible to restrict activities on the basis of lack of capacity it is not permissible to do so on the basis of age. Certainly, it could be argued that there are some twelve-year-olds who would exercise the right to vote in a more responsible way than some adults, for example. Despite its attractions there are four particular problems with the moderate child liberationist viewpoint.

The first is that it might prove hard to work in practice. Taking the example of alcohol, the child liberationist viewpoint would reject a rule that alcohol cannot be served to under 18s and may suggest that alcohol could be served to those who are capable of understanding the potential consequences of abuse of alcohol and have the capacity to decide whether they wish to drink it. This would certainly make the bartender's job more difficult. Is he or she to question everyone who asks for a pint of beer to see if they have sufficient capacity to make the order? (If they did many adults may fail the test!) It is certainly easier for a bartender to have a strict rule that those under a certain age are not permitted to purchase alcohol. A child liberationist may reply that to deny a child a right on the ground of administrative convenience is unacceptable.

---

[52] Raz, 'Legal Rights' (1984) 4 *Oxford Journal of Legal Studies* 1, 13-14.

[53] Holt, *Escape from Childhood: The Needs and Rights of Children* (1974, Penguin).

[54] Franklin (ed.) *The Handbook of Children's Rights* (1995, Routledge) which discusses a variety of topics from a children's rights perspective.

A second, and perhaps stronger, objection to the moderate child liberationist approach is a little more complex. Imagine a six-year-old who does not want to go to school. Many child liberationists have argued that children should not be made to go to school because we do not require adults to attend continuing education classes.[55] We should respect the child's wishes, even at such a young age. The difficulty with this relates to the concept of the right of autonomy. The traditional liberal view is that people should be allowed to develop and live out their lives as they wish, as long as that lifestyle does not harm other people. It is sometimes said that the key to the notion of autonomy is that every person should be encouraged to pursue their version of the 'good life'. So, if an adult wishes to spend his or her life as a train-spotter or in bed this is permissible, assuming it does not harm anyone else. Indeed, our society benefits from the fact that different people pursue different kinds of hobbies, interests, and jobs: this makes for a more diverse and culturally rich society. The difficulty arises in applying this to children. Going back to the six-year-old who does not want to go to school we may indeed be respecting her autonomy and allow her to live her vision of the good life at age six by letting her skip school. However, doing so may mean that once she reaches sixteen, say, the range of options open to her of how to live her life will be severely curtailed if she has no educational qualifications. It may therefore be acceptable to restrict the child's autonomy at a young age so as to maximise her autonomy later on in life.[56]

A third objection to the child liberationist approach is that if now as adults we look back at our childhood and consider how we would we have wanted adults to treat us during our childhood we are probably glad that the adults did not give way to our every whim.[57] We may accept in retrospect that it was right for our freedoms to be curtailed. This may then be used as an argument for not giving children all the rights that an adult has.

A fourth objection is that rather than liberating children the child liberationist approach may in fact lead to the oppression of children. This is because children may be open to manipulation by adults who could persuade children to exercise their rights in a way which benefits adults rather than children.

Despite these criticisms the child liberationists' arguments have been influential and certainly nowadays much of the discussion about children is based on the assumption that the burden is on those who seek to deny a particular adult right to a child, rather than on those who wish to grant

---

[55] Holt, *op. cit.* n. 52.

[56] Eekelaar, 'The Interests of the Child and the Child's Wishes: The Role of Dynamic Self-Determinism' (1994) 8 *International Journal of Law and the Family* 42.

[57] Eekelaar, *op. cit.* n. 56

children an adult's right. However, to many commentators the criticisms outlined above carry weight, in particular over the extent to which children should be allowed to make decisions for themselves. Several academic commentators have attempted to develop a theory of children's rights which acknowledge that children have rights, but do not go as far as the child liberationists. One of the most popular theories has been developed by John Eekelaar. He has proposed an approach to children's rights which requires the law to protect three different interests of a child:

(a) *Basic interests.* These are interests that are central to a child's well-being. They would include the feeding, housing, and clothing of a child. The duty falls on parents or, failing them, the state.

(b) *Developmental interests.* These are the interests that a child has to enable him or her to develop as a person. They might include rights to education and socialisation. Eekelaar suggests that to a large extent these are not legally enforceable and fall upon the wider community.

(c) *Autonomy interests.* These are the interests children have in being able to make decisions for themselves.

Eekelaar suggests that where there is a clash between any of these three interests then the basic and developmental interests would trump the autonomy interest. In other words children should be able to make decisions about their lives unless such a decision would infringe their basic or developmental interests. Using this approach it may be that if a child wanted to have a nose ring she would be allowed to unless it could be shown that this infringed her basic interests (e.g. if it harmed her health) or her developmental interests (e.g. if it would lead to her suspension from school). However, if a child did not want to go to school this choice could readily be overruled on the basis that it would infringe her basic or developmental interests. Eekelaar reaches this theory by requiring one to 'make some kind of imaginative leap and guess what a child might retrospectively have wanted once it reaches a position of maturity.' He suggests that most people would not want to have had their way on every single issue and would agree with his ranking of interests.

It is notable that Eekelaar describes his approach in terms of interests, rather than rights. This is because although he is confident that children have these interests, whether they are respected as rights depends on whether there is a general acceptance they should be protected by the law. Nevertheless he suggests that at least the state should *treat* children as if they had these rights. Other commentators have developed alternative theories and have been less reluctant to refer to rights. For example,

Michael Freeman[58] suggests that we need to protect children's welfare rights; protective rights; rights grounded on social justice and autonomy rights. In a similar vein to Eekelaar he accepts that the autonomy rights should not be exercised in a way that might infringe the other rights.

Objections to children having rights

There are those who object to children having rights. The main objections are as follows:

(a) The first objection is of a jurisprudential nature. There are two main theories about the fundamental nature of rights. The *will theory* argues that rights can only be exercised if the right-holder has the choice of whether to act in a particular way. Those who hold this view would not accept that young children have rights, as they are unable to exercise that choice. However, the approach is rejected by those who prefer the *interest theory* of rights.[59] This theory argues that rights exist for the purpose of protecting a person's interests and are not dependent upon the right-holder being able to exercise a choice. The interest theory would therefore be quite happy with the notion that children have rights.[60]

(b) Some argue that it would be wrong to give children rights because children have 'the right to be children'.[61] It will be noted that this objection is not an objection to children having the right to life, etc., but is specifically a concern about children being expected to make decisions about their lives. For example, there is some evidence from psychologists considering children whose parents are divorcing which suggests that although children do wish to be listened to by their parents and the courts, they do not wish to be required to choose between their parents.[62] This may be one example of a wider argument that children need to be protected from the stresses and strains of the adult world.

(c) There are concerns that stressing the rights of children is overly individualistic. The argument is that rights concentrate on the child in isolation and what he or she can claim, rather than being willing

---

[58] Freeman, *The Rights and Wrongs of Children* (1983, Frances Pinter).

[59] Eekelaar's theory of children's rights is clearly based on the interest theory.

[60] Lucy, 'Controversy About Children's Rights' in Freestone (ed.) *Children and the Law* (1990, Hull University Press).

[61] Campbell, 'The Rights of the Minor' in Alston, Parker and Seymour (eds), *Children, Rights and the Law* (1992, Clarendon Press).

[62] Trowell and Miles, 'Moral Agendas for Psychoanalytic Practice with Children and Families' in King (ed.), *Moral Agendas for Children's Welfare* (1999, Routledge).

to consider the fact that the child lives in a family, in a set of relationships with her parents and siblings. So that any claim made by a child must be seen in the light of the effect of that claim on other members of the family. There is much to be said in favour of this objection. However, the use of rights can still be supported if only on the basis that stressing rights will sound a warning bell that a serious wrong is being done to a child, and we need to ensure that the relationships within which a wrong is done are not abusive ones. The objection is weakened if an approach to rights can be developed in a way that recognises the importance of relationships, rather than adopting one of the many versions of rights which seem to focus exclusively on individual rights.[63]

(d) There are some who criticise children's rights on the basis that they cannot readily be enforced. The child may well be too young to enforce the right him or herself. Although parents are practically in a position to enforce rights on children's behalf this may be of little use where the child is claiming that her parents have infringed her rights. This argument is not so much an argument that children should not have rights, but more an argument that we should realise that rights are of limited effectiveness.

(e) Onora O'Neill has argued that the law would benefit from focussing on the obligations of parents rather than the rights of children.[64] This is because enforcement of obligations would be more effective than children's rights. The disadvantage of her argument is its lack of empowerment for children, especially older children. By giving older children rights which they can seek to enforce themselves, their status as human beings is recognised and they are enabled to take up their roles as citizens. The strength of her argument is that if the focus is on obligations then the state or other interested third parties can more readily enforce the obligation than if the claim is put in terms of rights.

Children's duties

Although much has been written about children's rights, less has been written about children's duties. If we are to impose obligations upon parents to care and raise children and we are to give children rights they can enforce against their parents, should not the law impose some cor-

---

[63] Herring, 'The Welfare Principle and the Rights of Parents' in Bainham, Richards, Day Sclater (eds), *What is a Parent?* (1999, Hart).

[64] O'Neill, 'Children's Rights and Children's Lives' in Alston, Parker and Seymour (eds), *Children, Rights and the Law* (1998, Clarendon Press).

responding duties upon children? Bainham suggests that there might be a duty on children to attend school, corresponding to the right a child may have to education.[65] In theory this appears an attractive argument, but the difficulties lie in the fact that the breach of a duty carries with it moral blame. It would not necessarily be inconsistent for the law to permit a child to make a decision for him or herself, but not attach blame if the child makes the wrong decision.

Do parents have rights?

Having considered the position of children's rights, what about parents' rights? There is much confusion surrounding the notion of parents' rights and it is necessary to distinguish three different forms of 'parents' rights':

(a) *Parents' human rights*. These are the rights parents have as human beings. For example, the parent has a right to life, a right to free speech, etc. These rights would include those protected by the Human Rights Act 1998.

(b) *Parents' child-centred rights*. These are the rights that are given to parents in order to carry out their parental obligations. For example, a parent has a right to clothe, feed and house the child in order to fulfil his or her responsibilities as the parent to care for the child.

(c) *Parents' parent-centred rights*. Alexander McCall Smith has explained that parent-centred rights are given to parents, not specifically to further the welfare of a child but to reflect the interests that parents have in bringing up their children in the way they wish.[66] An example of this may be religious upbringing. Here, it might be impossible to prove that one particular form of religious upbringing promotes a child's welfare better than any other form of religious upbringing, or indeed no form of religious upbringing at all. The right of a parent to involve their child in religious practices therefore does not necessarily reflect the welfare of a child, but rather promotes the interests of the parent to raise the child in accordance with the parent's religious beliefs. These parent-centred rights could also be said to further society's interests as well in that children are brought up to have different beliefs, interests and lifestyles. The rights enable the state to avoid courting controversy

[65] Bainham, 'Honour Thy Father and Thy Mother: Children's Rights and Children's Duties', in Douglas and Sebba (eds), *Children's Rights and Traditional Values* (1998, Dartmouth).
[66] McCall Smith, 'Is Anything Left of Parental Rights?', in Sutherland and McCall Smith (eds), *Family Rights: Family Law and Medical Ethics* (1990, Edinburgh University Press).

by promoting any particular parenting style, and produce a culturally diverse and rich society.

The fact that parents have human rights is, of course, uncontroversial, but why should parents have the other categories of rights? Why is it assumed that children are best brought up by their natural parents rather than anyone else?[67] Roman law has suggested that parents' rights come from the fact that the child is property of parents. The parents created the child from their sperm and egg and therefore acquire rights over children. This now sounds outdated and quite wrong: parents' relationships with their children are not analogous with their relationship to their televisions. It is true that parents do talk of children as 'theirs' and if 'their child' was snatched from hospital after birth they would be entitled to have the child returned to them. However, the fact that there is one similarity between parental rights and ownership rights does not mean they are directly analogous. After all, those who do not produce children can be regarded as parents, for example adoptive parents. Further, the owner of a piece of property can treat it as they wish, including even destroying the property. By contrast parents under English and Welsh law cannot exercise parental rights for their own ends; the parental rights must be exercised for the child's benefit, or, at least, not be contrary to the child's interests.

An alternative model which would be more acceptable than an analogy to ownership would be to argue that parents hold the rights of their child on trust.[68] A trustee has powers to care for trust property, but these powers cannot be exercised for the trustee's own benefit, they must be exercised for the benefit of the beneficiary. In the same way, a parent holds the rights of a child on trust and these rights cannot be exercised for the benefit of a parent, but for the benefit of a child. There are two main versions of this argument. First, that the parents hold the rights of the child on trust for the child. Second, that the rights of the child are held on a purpose trust: the purpose being to promote the welfare of the child. There are concerns about the trust model. It could be seen as too readily able to justify state intervention to ensure that the trustees are acting properly. Trustees are normally subject to fairly strict duties and it may be that although we require the highest standards from trustees, we may only require 'good enough' parenting from parents. That would certainly be true for child-centred rights. For parent-centred rights the state permit parents to make choices about children unless it could be shown that their choice positively harmed the child. So, in relation to religious issues the courts are

---

[67] Given that the law has sometimes been less than enthusiastic in ensuring that the state knows who is a child's father it is surprising that in determining the welfare principle there is much weight placed on the so-called natural parent presumption.

[68] Beck, Glavis, Glover, Barnes Jenkins and Nardi, 'The Rights of Children: A Trust Model' (1978) 46 *Fordham Law Review* 669.

nowadays likely to take the view that parents can raise their child in whatever religion they choose unless it could be shown that a religious practice damages the child.[69]

Parents' duties

Closely related to the question of why parents should have rights is the question of why parents should have obligations towards their children. Why do parents owe moral obligations to their children? John Eekelaar suggests, surprisingly, that there is no straightforward answer to this question. He argues that there are two elements that make up the duty.[70] First, there is a general moral obligation imposed on all people to those who are in need. So anyone who comes across an abandoned child would be obliged to ensure that the child was handed over to the relevant authorities to receive suitable protection. Second, he suggests that as children are vulnerable they have a right to be cared for by someone. However, he stresses that upon whom the duty is imposed is a matter of choice for our society. As our society has accepted that parents should carry that duty the obligation to care for children lies on them. Barton and Douglas have criticised his approach. They have argued that Eekelaar's view would seem to suggest that a society where children were removed from their parents at birth and cared for in state-run institutions would not be immoral. They suggest that the key basis of the moral obligation is the 'acceptance of the social role of parenthood.'[71] As discussed above there are problems with this explanation too. It is perhaps surprising that although it is widely accepted that parents should care for their children it has proved so difficult to find a clear explanation of why this is so.

Children's and parents' rights and duties in law

The court's supervision of parents

It is interesting to contrast the law's approach to day-care centres and child minders with its approach towards parents. Day-care centres must be registered with a local authority and are subject to detailed regulations

---

[69] *Re P (Section 91(14) Guidelines)(Residence and Religious Heritage)* [1999] 2 FLR 573. Following the Human Rights Act it is unlawful to discriminate against a parent on the basis of their religion unless it could be shown that a particular religious practice harmed the child: *Hoffman* v. *Austria* (1994) EHRR 293.

[70] Eekelaar, 'Are Parents Morally Obliged to Care for Their Children?' (1991) 11 *Oxford Journal of Legal Studies* 51.

[71] Barton and Douglas, *op. cit.* n. 10, at p. 29.

and regular inspections to ensure that children's interests are protected.[72] By contrast, there is no direct supervision of parents to ensure that they are caring for their children appropriately. That said, there is some indirect 'policing' of parents.[73] For example, midwives, health visitors and teachers can keep an eye on standards of parenting and if there are concerns then they can inform the local authority who will then investigate fully.[74] However, in general, day-care centres are seen as a suitable areas for legal regulation due to their public nature, whereas parenting is a private activity upon which the state should not intrude unless absolutely necessary. The distinction could be challenged. If the protection of children cared for in day-care centres justifies the state in ensuring that children are protected from various dangers (e.g. that there are adequate fire extinguishers and fire escapes in the centre), why are children raised by parents at home not deserving of the same protection?

The law's regulation of parenting is dependent on someone bringing an issue before the court.[75] The most common cases are those where there are disputes between parents over how a child should be raised. However, the mere fact there is a parent–parent dispute does not necessarily indicate that there is a need for the law to intervene to protect the child's welfare, but rather simply reveals that there is a need to resolve a dispute between adults. If the adults are happy to pursue a form of parenting which harms the child (e.g., by making no effort to encourage the child to participate in any form of physical exercise and feeding the child unhealthy foods) then the law directly does little to intervene, unless the child is suffering significant harm, justifying state intervention. Of course, schools and government education in the media may seek to influence parenting practices, but they are not enforced directly by legal regulation. Indeed the courts have suggested that legal procedures should not be used to resolve day-to-day issues relating to children.[76] All of this means that the direct regulation of parents in private cases involving children is limited.[77]

There may be good reasons for the state not to intervene and to leave parents to raise children as they think fit unless there is clear evidence that children are suffering or may suffer significant levels of harm. The arguments for non-intervention may include the following:

---

[72] Children Act 1989, Part X and Sch. 9; Department of Health, *The Children Act Guidance and Regulations, Volume 2* (1991, HMSO).

[73] Donzelot, *The Policing of Families* (1980, Hutchinson).

[74] Local authority investigations are considered in Chapter 5 of this book.

[75] Herring, 'The Welfare Principle and the Rights of Parents' in Bainham, Richards, Day Sclater (eds), *What is a Parent?* (1999, Hart).

[76] *Re P (A Minor)(Parental Responsibility Order)* [1994] 1 FLR 578.

[77] M. Freeman, 'The Best Interests of the Child? Is the Best Interests of the Child in the Best Interests of Children?' (1997) *International Journal of Law, Policy and Family* 36.

(a) Allowing parents the liberty to raise children as they wish produces a culturally diverse society. A state where the government sets down precisely how children should be raised may produce 'identikit citizens', which would lead to a far less satisfactory society than one where parents are allowed to encourage their children to adopt a variety of hobbies and religious beliefs, for example.

(b) History supports the view that parents are better at raising children than the state. This is at least so in the United Kingdom where the last few decades have seen report after report outlining the abuse children have suffered in state-run care. This is not to say that in some cases where parents are causing their children significant harm they should not be removed and state care provided; but the state should not be over-confident in its abilities to provide high-level care for children.

(c) An argument of a more political nature is that the family is an area of privacy where the state should intervene unless there is public harm.[78] Following the Human Rights Act 1998 the state is specifically required not to infringe the right to respect for family and private life, unless to do so is necessary in order to protect the interests of children.

(d) A similar claim is that parents have a right to raise their child free from state intervention. If parents are to undertake the sacrifice involved in caring for children, then they are entitled to the benefits of a right of protection from state intrusion as corresponding to the duties imposed by the state upon them.

Notably, arguments (a) and (b) recognise that the state has a legitimate interest in what happens with the raising of children, but argue that the state interest is best promoted by non-intervention. Arguments (c) and (d), by contrast, maintain that the state has no place in interfering in family life unless absolutely necessary. This is part of a larger debate over whether it is appropriate to distinguish public and private areas of life.[79]

So far this section has considered how the law only weakly regulates the parenting of children through court orders. However, the law does restrict the way parents act in other ways. First, a parent under some circumstances is required to consult with the other parent. Second, children under some circumstances are able to make decisions for themselves, despite the opposition of their parents.

---

[78] Article 8, European Convention on Human Rights.
[79] See the Introduction to this book.

Requiring co-operative parenting

If parents have separated then in the majority of cases the child will live with one parent (the residential parent) but may have regular contact with another (the non-residential parent). The issue is how decisions should be made about the child. In particular, is there a need for the parents to consult each other on issues relating to the child? Clearly it would not be possible to require parental consultation on every issue. Requiring the residential parent to telephone the non-residential parent to ensure he or she approves what food is being offered for tea would clearly be impracticable. But what about significant issues – should the law require the parents to consult on all important issues, or can each parent make decisions on their own? Or should the law state that the residential parent can make all important decisions?

A case which demonstrates the main issues is *Re J (Specific Issue Orders: Child's Religious Upbringing and Circumcision)*[80] where a child's parents had separated, but disagreed on two related issues. The first was whether the boy should be circumcised, and the second was whether the child should be brought up a Muslim (the mother was a non-practising Christian; the father a non-practising Muslim). The Court of Appeal treated these as two separate questions. It distinguished 'irreversible and important' decisions over which parents should co-operate,[81] and 'day-to-day issues' which should be decided by the parent with whom the child is living (here the mother). Therefore the circumcision required the consent of both parents, while over the issue of religious upbringing this could be decided by the mother, although when the child was having contact with the father he was permitted to teach the child about Islam.[82] The decision is controversial because it appears incompatible with section 2(7) Children Act 1989 which states that each parent could exercise his or her parental responsibility independently without the need to consult with the other parent, except in certain exceptions specifically mentioned in the statute.[83]

The question of when the agreement of both parents should be required involves a dispute between two schools of thought.[84] On the one hand some argue that both parents should fulfil their roles as parents to the greatest extent possible. It is commonly stated that the fact that the parents

---

[80] [2000] 1 FLR 571, [2000] 1 FCR 307.
[81] The Children Act in section 13 sets out certain issues which require the consent of both parents with parental responsibility.
[82] The decision that a circumcision is more important than religious upbringing might be regarded as surprising.
[83] e.g. s. 13 Children Act 1989 which states (in essence) that if a residence order is in force in respect of a child then the child's name and country of residence cannot be changed without the consent of all those with parental responsibility or the leave of the court.
[84] The arguments are discussed in Bainham, 'The Privatisation of the Public Interest in Children' (1990) 53 *Modern Law Review* 206.

have separated should not affect their roles as parents. Therefore before making any important decisions the parents should be required to consult. Without a requirement of consent the non-residential parent could in effect be excluded from playing an important role in the child's life. On the other hand it is argued that granting the non-residential parent a veto over important decisions creates an unjustifiable infringement of the private life of the residential parent and the child. It has been argued that the parent with whom the child lives is the parent who knows the child the best and so is in the ideal position to make decisions in respect of a child. Some fear that a non-residential parent might abuse the power and withhold consent over important decisions in order to exercise control over the residential parent. These arguments are well balanced. The truth is whether there is effective co-operation between the parents and whether the non-residential parent is excluded from the life of the child will depend more on the character of the parties and the relationship between them than on the requirements of the law.

Children restricting parental decision-making

There are two main ways that children can restrict the rights of parents to make decisions for them. First, children can bring applications to the court to seek an order in respect of a particular issue. Secondly, the law has accepted that in relation to third parties who are dealing with children (e.g. doctors or schools) the third party is entitled to follow the views of the child, if the child is sufficiently competent.

Let us consider first applications to courts brought by children. Children may, under the Family Proceedings Rules,[85] bring an application for a section 8 order, but will need leave to do so. However, in the light of *Re C (A minor)(Leave to Seek Section 8 Orders)*[86] it will be rare for leave to be granted. In that case the court refused to give leave to a fourteen-year-old girl who sought a court order to give her permission to go on holiday to Bulgaria with her friend and to move in with her friend's family. The court regarded the issue over the holiday to be too trivial an issue to be resolved by the court and so refused to grant leave. This suggests that many of the issues that children may wish to bring before the court will be regarded as too trivial. The court suggested that the dispute over where the child should live was better resolved by discussion between the family members and was not appropriate for court intervention. A further concern that the courts have expressed is that children being heard in court can be open to misuse by adults persuading children to bring proceedings before court to pursue the adult's interests. As a result of these decisions

---

[85] Family Proceedings Rules, r. 9.2.
[86] [1994] 1 FLR 26, [1994] 1 FCR 837.

any prediction that children will be applying to courts in large numbers for orders that they do not have to eat broccoli is clearly unrealistic. Only if the issue is of sufficient importance, and not one that is best resolved by the family members themselves, is the court likely to give leave to the child to bring an application.

What if a third party such as a doctor has to deal with a child and her parent with competing views? The position the cases[87] have reached is that a doctor can carry out medical treatment on a child if he or she has the consent of either of the parents with parental responsibility; if the child is aged sixteen or seventeen; or under sixteen but sufficiently competent to be able to make the decision;[88] or if the court has given its approval. The case law has been heavily criticised.[89] Although the law recognises the right of a competent child to give consent to treatment, the law does not recognise the right of a competent child to refuse treatment. If the child objects to the treatment, but the parent consents, then the doctor may perform the operation if he or she believes the treatment to be in the child's interests. [90] From a children's rights perspective the law is illogical. This is because the law is not respecting the more important right (the right to refuse treatment), but *is* protecting the less important right (the right to have the treatment requested). It is a greater infringement of someone's liberty to carry out an operation on them against their wishes and a lesser infringement to deny them the treatment they seek. The law is, however, readily explicable on the basis that it is seeking to ensure that a child receives any necessary medical treatment. Once the doctor has decided that the treatment will promote the child's well-being the doctor can provide it if either the parent, the competent child, or the court give consent. The law has therefore maximised the chance that someone can give the requisite consent and that the treatment be provided. The law thus is clearly explicable under the principle of promotion of the child's welfare, even though it is not logical from the perspective of promoting the autonomy rights of the child.

How the court resolves disputes over children before the court

Under section 1 Children Act 1989:

> When a court determines any question with respect to –
>   (a) the upbringing of a child; or

---

[87] *Re W (A Minor)(Medical Treatment)* [1993] 1 FLR 1, [1992] 2 FCR 785.

[88] Commonly known as a *Gillick* competent child.

[89] e.g. Brazier and Bridge, 'Coercion or caring: analysing adolescent autonomy' (1996) 16 *Legal Studies* 84.

[90] Unless there is a court order in force.

(b) the administration of a child's property or the application of any income arising from it,

the child's welfare shall be the court's paramount consideration.

This does not mean that every case involving children requires the court to treat the child's welfare as paramount. The principle does not apply if the case is brought under legislation which sets out alternative grounds governing the court's discretion (e.g. Adoption Act 1976); nor does the principle apply to cases which do not involve the upbringing of the child.[91] The interpretation of section one gives rise to two particular difficulties. The first is the definition of 'welfare'. The second is, what does 'paramount' mean?

The meaning of welfare

It is estimated that 28 per cent of children of married couples will have experienced parental divorce by the time they are sixteen.[92] Given that unmarried couples are even more likely to separate[93] the proportion of children of unmarried couples who will experience parental separation is likely to be even higher. It appears that children whose parents separate are more likely to be disadvantaged as compared with children whose parents do not separate in, for example, the following ways:[94]

(a) *Economics.* Separated families tend to have lower incomes and poorer households than families which have not separated.

(b) *Anti-social behaviour.* Aggression and delinquency are more common among children whose parents have separated.

(c) *Health.* Children whose parents have separated are more likely to suffer health problems and be admitted to hospital.

(d) *Relationships.* Those whose parents have separated are likely to become sexually active at a younger age; become pregnant and give birth outside marriage; and experience divorce in their own marriages.

(e) *Depression.* There are higher rates of depression, smoking and drug abuse among those whose parents have separated.

---

[91] Lowe, 'The House of Lords and the Welfare Principle' in Bridge (ed.), *Family Law Towards the Millennium* (1997, Butterworth).

[92] Rodgers and Pryor, *Divorce and Separation. The Outcomes for Children* (1998, Joseph Rowntree) provides a thorough review of the research to date.

[93] The evidence for this is outlined in a rather polemical way in Morgan, *Farewell to the Family?* (1999, IEA).

[94] Rodgers and Pryor, *op. cit.* n. 90.

It is crucial to appreciate the limited significance of these findings. First, they do *not* show that all children whose parents separated suffer in these ways. In fact the majority of those children whose parents separate do not suffer in these ways. But it seems on average that children whose parents are separated are twice as likely to suffer than those whose parents do not separate. Secondly, it is not possible to say that divorce causes these consequences. It might be, for example, that some of these adverse consequences are linked to poverty following divorce and not caused by the divorce itself. Most importantly, the research does not suggest that children would not suffer in these ways if the parents had stayed together. In fact there is some evidence that children who live with warring parents who stay together may suffer even more than children whose parents separate. Thirdly, there is no evidence that the age of children affects the level of harm, nor does the sex of a child.[95]

The crucial issue for the law is why children suffer in these ways, and whether there is anything that the law can do to lessen the adverse effects. One finding of interest is that children whose parents die do suffer from some of the disadvantages mentioned above, but not in such a severe way. So, what can we do to improve the well-being of children after divorce? Rodgers and Pryor set out the following significant points:[96]

(a) The fact that bereaved children do not suffer as badly as separated children suggests that it is not the loss of a parent figure which is the most significant factor in the adverse consequences for children.

(b) Economic disadvantage may play an influential role in educational achievements but does not explain some of the other consequences.

(c) Conflict between the parents, especially if witnessed by the children, clearly causes distress to the child. In particular it is linked to behavioural problems. This may be particularly significant when considering the law on domestic violence.

(d) Parental distress is linked to various harms to the child. This suggests that counselling for parents undergoing separation is important.

(e) Children are especially distressed by experiencing multiple breakdowns of parental relationships.

(f) Contact with the non-residential parent may assist the child. However, it is the quality of the contact which is important.

---

[95] *Ibid.*
[96] *Ibid.*

The meaning of paramountcy

Section 1, Children Act 1989 has been interpreted by some to mean that the interests of children are to be the sole consideration. As the Court of Appeal explained in *Re P (Contact: Supervision)*,[97] 'the court is concerned with the interests of the mother and father only in so far as they bear on the welfare of the child.' Therefore paramountcy means that the interests of parents can never outweigh the interests of children. This is perhaps a surprising interpretation because if Parliament had wanted it to be the sole consideration it could have said so in clear words. It certainly seems unjustifiable to make an order that would require a huge sacrifice of parents for only a marginal increase in the welfare of the child.[98]

The welfare principle in practice

When applying the welfare principle the court will consider the factors listed in section 1(3), which include, for example, the needs and feelings of the child. Each judge then is given a wide discretion to weigh up the different factors to decide what is in the welfare of the child. It can therefore be difficult to predict how the judge might decide a particular case. That said, the case law does suggest that there are certain presumptions, or perhaps better called assumptions, which a court will normally follow. For example, it is generally thought more appropriate for a mother than a father to care for a very young child;[99] if there is a dispute between a natural parent and someone else over who should care for the child there is a strong presumption in favour of the natural parent, which means that only if the natural parent is shown to be clearly unsuitable should anyone else be considered as a primary carer of a child;[100] there is also an assumption that children benefit from contact with their siblings and their parents.[101]

Following the Human Rights Act the courts will have to recognise that parents and children under article 8 have a right to respect for family and private life. This includes the right to contact with each other. So on divorce both parents will have a right of contact with the child.[102] Only where it is necessary in the interests of children to cease contact will it be permissible not to order contact.[103] The Court of Appeal has recently taken the view that the Human Rights Act and the approach taken by the courts

---

[97] [1996] 2 FLR 314, at p. 328.
[98] Herring, *op. cit.*, n. 61.
[99] *Brixley v. Lynas* [1996] 2 FLR 499, [1997] 1 FCR 220.
[100] *Re D (Natural Parent Presumption)* [1999] 2 FCR 118, [1999] 1 FLR 134.
[101] *Re L (A Child)(Contact: Domestic Violence)* [2000] 2 FLR 334, [2000] 2 FCR 404.
[102] *Hokkanen v. Finland* [1996] 1 FLR 289.
[103] *Glaser v. UK* [2000] 3 FCR 193.

to date under the Children Act are indistinguishable in relation to contact.[104] In other words there is no difference between stating that there is a strong presumption that contact will promote the child's welfare, but that the presumption can be rebutted if there is strong evidence to the contrary, and stating there is a right to contact which can be infringed if necessary in the interests of the child. Whether this is so all depends on the meaning of the word 'necessary' in article 8. The use of the word necessary might suggest that if there is evidence that contact is marginally not in the interests of the child then that would not be sufficient to justify an infringement of the parent's right of contact. However, under the Children Act even if the contact is marginally not in the interests of a child the order should not be made.[105]

Applying the welfare principle when there are conflicting interests of different children

How does the law deal with cases that involve two or more children? The court cannot resolve such cases simply by stating that the welfare of the child is paramount because the question is then, which child's welfare is paramount? It might be expected that the law would deal with such cases by simply balancing the interests of all the children involved but, perhaps surprisingly, the law has not taken this straightforward approach.

The leading case is *Birmingham City Council City Council* v. *H (A Minor)*[106] which involved a mother who was herself a minor (being under sixteen) and her baby. The mother and baby had been taken into care, but had been separated by the local authority. The mother applied for contact with her baby. The evidence suggested that it was in the mother's best interest that contact took place but that contact was not necessarily in the baby's interests. It was therefore crucial to determine which child's interest was paramount. The House of Lords took the view, relying on the wording of sub-section 1(1), Children Act 1989 that it was the child who was the subject of the proceedings whose welfare was paramount. It was held that because the mother was applying for contact with the baby, the baby was the 'subject of the proceedings' and so it was the baby's interests which were paramount. Therefore contact was not ordered. There has been some academic criticism of this case in which it was argued that it was wrong that an essentially procedural point should determine the outcome of the case.[107] Which child brings the proceedings and which is the subject of the application could be a matter of chance. So, although the approach of the

---

[104] *Re L (A Child)(Contact: Domestic Violence)* [2000] 2 FLR 334, [2000] 2 FCR 404.
[105] Herring, *op. cit.*, n. 61.
[106] [1994] 2 AC 212.
[107] Douglas, 'In Whose Best Interests?' (1994) 110 *Law Quarterly Review* 379.

House of Lords was correct as a matter of statutory interpretation, there is a strong case for arguing that it could have approached the issues at a more theoretical level, either by saying in such cases that the interests of the two children had to be balanced with each other, or that a minor mother's interests were lower that her baby's.[108] Subsequent cases have accepted that if two children are the 'subject of the proceedings' then the court is permitted to balance the interests of the two children.[109]

There is another set of cases which less obviously involve a clash between the interests of children. These are cases where the law can be seen as putting the interests of children as a group over the interests of the particular child in question. For example, this might explain the law concerning the enforcement of section 8 orders. If a mother, with the benefit of a residence order, refuses to permit her child's father to see the child as required by a contact order, the court must decide how to enforce the order. The Court of Appeal has confirmed that the child's welfare is not the paramount consideration in deciding how to enforce the order.[110] If necessary, this could even involve the imprisonment of the mother. From one perspective, it is most peculiar to enforce an order that has been made for the purpose of promoting the child's welfare in a way (imprisoning the mother) which will almost inevitably harm the child. One explanation is that although imprisonment may not promote the interests of the actual child the punishment will send the message to the general public that if court orders are not obeyed serious consequences will follow. This might ensure that more court orders are followed which will in the long term benefit children generally.

A similar argument could be made about the law on international child abduction whereby an abducted child should be returned to the country of habitual residence unless there are strong reasons against this.[111] Simply proving that the child has settled in her new country of abode and that therefore it would be contrary to her interests to be returned to her country from which she was removed is an insufficient reason. Were the law to be otherwise it might too readily lead the courts to permit the child to stay with the abductor, which might thereby encourage abduction. Again this might be an example of sacrificing the interests of the particular child in order to discourage child abduction generally.

---

[108] *Birmingham CC v. H* was applied in *Re F (Contact: Child in Care)* [1995] 1 FLR 510.

[109] *Re T and E (Proceedings: Conflicting Interests)* [1995] 1 FLR 581, [1995] 3 FCR 260. Cromack and Parry, 'Welfare of the Child – Conflicting Interests and Conflicting Principles: *Re T and E (Proceedings: Conflicting Interests)*' (1996) 8 *Child and Family Law Quarterly* 72.

[110] *A v. N (Committed: Refusal of Contact)* [1997] 1 FLR 533, [1997] 2 FCR 475.

[111] The Hague Convention, discussed in Hayes and Williams, *Family Law* (1999, Butterworth), ch. 5.

Cases where the interests of children and parents conflict

In considering conflicts between the interests of adults and children it might be useful to refer back to the different kinds of rights that parents have.

(a) Parents' human rights clashing with children's rights

As mentioned earlier the courts' interpretation of the welfare principle should mean that orders can be made which infringe the human rights of parents if the welfare of the child is promoted, even slightly. In fact the courts have held back from making orders which do infringe parents' human rights, and they have done so by using a variety of arguments. One is to treat the interests of the parents and children as 'one'. As Butler Sloss LJ stated in *Re T (A Minor) Wardship: Medical Treatment*:[112]

> The mother and this child are one for the purpose of this unusual case and the decision of the court to consent to the operation jointly affects the mother and son and so also affects the father. The welfare of the child depends upon his mother.

This might be criticised for not considering the other side of the coin, namely that the welfare of the parent may be dependent on the welfare of the child. Certainly a child brought up by an unhappy parent is likely to be unhappy herself, but a parent bringing up an unhappy child is likely to be an unhappy parent. The courts have also argued that court orders relating to children should not be used to try to change parents' lifestyle. So, in *Re D (Residence: Imposition of Conditions)*[113] the Court of Appeal allowed an appeal against a condition attached to a residence order which had sought to prevent a mother having her partner live with her because it was feared he would be a bad influence on the child. The Court of Appeal stated that the judge should consider whether or not the mother (given her lifestyle and relationships) should have residence of the child, rather than trying to turn the mother into a 'perfect mother' by the use of court orders. Through these and other methods of reasoning,[114] the courts have been able in effect to protect parents' human rights, while stating that the welfare of the child is the sole consideration. Now that the Human Rights Act is in force the courts will have to be more explicit about recognising that parents do have rights, although it is clear from the European Convention that parents' rights to private and family life can be infringed if this is necessary in order to protect the interests of their children.[115]

---

[112] [1997] 1 FLR 502 at p. 510.

[113] [1996] 2 FLR 281.

[114] For further discussion see Herring, *op. cit.*, 61.

[115] See Herring, 'The Human Rights Act and the Welfare Principle in Family Law – Conflicting or Complementary?' (1999) 11 *Child and Family Law Quarterly* 223.

(b) Parents' child-centred rights clashing with children's rights

It will be recalled that parents' child-centred rights are rights given to parents for the benefit of children. It is therefore not surprising that a court will readily require parents to exercise their child-centred rights in a way that promotes the child's welfare. For example, if the parent refuses to consent to treatment necessary to save a child's life, the court will readily authorise the treatment, despite the parent's objections.[116]

(c) Parents' parent-centred rights clashing with children's rights

Parents' parent-centred rights are designed to protect the parents' interests in raising their children as they wish. They relate to those aspects of a child's upbringing where there is no formal state-approved view, such as religious upbringing. But there are limits to this because parents will not be able to cause the child serious harm in the name of their religion. For example, the courts in several cases have been willing to overrule the objections of Jehovah's Witness parents to blood transfusions needed to save the life of their child. Despite this, concerns have been expressed that doctors are too reluctant to overrule the religious objections of parents to blood transfusions, providing their children with less effective treatment until a blood transfusion is the only option left.[117] To take a less extreme example, if the child suffers from a skin complaint which is irritating but of no long-term detriment to health, and the parents refused to permit the child to receive medical treatment, the law would be unlikely to intervene. Can this be justifiable in terms of the child's rights? Do children have weaker rights because of their parent's beliefs? Or does support for children's rights involve also supporting the religious values of the different groups into which children are born?

Controversial applications of the welfare principle

This section will briefly discuss three issues involving children and parents that have particularly troubled the courts in recent years.

The natural parent presumption

The natural parent presumption is the presumption that it is better for the natural parent than anyone else to raise their child. The leading case in this area is *Re M (Child's Upbringing)*.[118] The Court of Appeal ordered the

---

[116] e.g. *Re E (A Minor)(Wardship: Medical Treatment)* [1993] 1 FLR 386.

[117] Bridge, 'Religion, Culture and Conviction – The Medical Treatment of Young Children' (1999) 11 *Child and Family Law Quarterly* 1.

[118] [1996] 2 FLR 441.

removal of a child from the couple with whom he had been living in England for the past four years, and that he be returned to South Africa to live with his birth parents. Although there was evidence that the child had settled in well with the couple and life in England and that he would be harmed psychologically if he were forced to leave them, this was insufficient to rebut the strong presumption that a child is better brought up by his natural parents than anyone else. Interestingly, at first instance Thorpe J[119] had referred to the 'natural parent' presumption, but had suggested that the couple in England had become the child's psychological parent through their care for the child. However, the Court of Appeal stressed that the presumption in favour of the natural parent is a presumption in favour of the genetic, not social, parent. In more recent cases there have been some suggestions that the attitude of the court may have moved on since *Re M (Child's Upbringing)*. For example, in *Re L (A Child)(Contact: Domestic Violence)*[120] Thorpe LJ suggested that in deciding whether a birth parent should have contact with a child it was the quality of the relationship which was of far more importance than the fact of the blood tie. The approach taken in the European Court in considering the right to respect for family life also seems to regard the strength of the actual relationship of the parent with the child to be of crucial importance.[121] However, neither the Children Act cases nor the cases under the European Convention have gone so far as to say the blood tie is irrelevant.

The psychological evidence that a genetic parent is the best person to care for a child is not clear. For example, there is evidence that adopted children do just as well if not better than children from similar backgrounds brought up by their natural parents.[122] The *Re M* case shows that a child can form so close a bond with a couple that they become for her 'psychological parents' with whom she can bond, and to remove her from these people is to remove her from those who in her eyes are her parents. Indeed in that case, following the court order, the child was returned to South Africa but could not settle and was eventually returned to the couple in England.

So why do the courts place such weight on the 'natural parent presumption'? Two explanations are offered. First, it could be argued that what the courts are enforcing is the right of parents to care for their children, rather than a straightforward application of the welfare principle.[123] Evidence might suggest that a baby born to an unmarried,

---

[119] As he was then.

[120] [2000] 2 FLR 334, [2000] 2 FCR 404.

[121] e.g. *Söderbäck* v. *Sweden* [1999] 1 FLR 250.

[122] Performance and Innovation Unit, *The Prime Minister's Review of Adoption* (2000, Performance and Innovation Unit).

[123] Such a right could be contained within article 8 of the European Convention.

unemployed drug-taking couple would in fact be happier if on birth they were handed over to a middle-class, law-abiding couple. However, to remove the child would be perceived by many to be unwarranted social engineering and therefore unacceptable. For the state to intervene by removing children from those it regards as unsuitable parents requires the strongest of justifications.[124] Secondly, the natural parent presumption may be an acknowledgement by the courts that it is impossible to know who would be the best parent to bring up a particular child. If we cannot be absolutely sure that someone will be better than another at bringing up a child, then respecting the natural parents may be as sensible an approach as any other.

Rights or presumptions of contact

One particularly controversial topic is whether following parental separation there should always be contact between a child and a parent, in particular where there has been domestic violence between the parents or towards the child. At one level it may be thought to be a straightforward matter of deciding on the basis of psychological evidence whether contact would be in the best interests of the child.[125] However, the issue is complicated by the fact that the residential parent is the one who must ensure that the child is available for the contact sessions. Under the Human Rights Act this means that although the non-residential parent will have the right of contact with his or her child, a contact order may be said to interfere with the residential parent's right to respect for private and family life.[126] This is especially so given the evidence that some formerly abusive partners use contact sessions to retain a degree of control over their former partners.[127] In the leading case on whether contact should be ordered following domestic violence, *Re L (A Child)(Contact: Domestic Violence)*,[128] two points of particular interest emerged. First, Thorpe LJ suggested that in disputes over contact which are presently regarded as legal disputes and over which much time is spent in costly court procedures, a more profitable way of dealing with such disputes may be through family therapy or counselling. This is interesting as it represents a move away from seeing contact as involving legal rights or interests which are enforced by the courts towards seeing the difficulty as a psychological problem. The argument against Thorpe LJ's suggestion is

---

[124] Chapter 5 in this book.

[125] This was the approach stressed by the Court of Appeal in *Re L (A Child)(Contact: Domestic Violence)* [2000] 2 FLR 334, [2000] 2 FCR 404.

[126] Article 8, European Convention on Human Rights.

[127] This evidence was considered by the Court of Appeal in *Re L (A Child)(Contact: Domestic Violence)* [2000] 2 FLR 334, [2000] 2 FCR 404.

[128] [2000] 2 FLR 334, [2000] 2 FCR 404.

that without the coercive edge of the law, therapy and counselling may simply enable the stronger party to manipulate the weaker. Further, it is not clear how such an approach is consistent with the evidence that contact can be used as a tool to perpetuate abuse. The second point of interest is that the Court of Appeal accepted that there should not be a right to contact or even (at least according to Thorpe LJ) a presumption in favour of contact. Rather, each case should be treated on its own facts. This means that contact cases cannot now be rapidly resolved by judges stating that unless there are exceptional facts contact should be ordered. It may mean contact cases become lengthier and the courts may be readier to deny direct contact.

Finances

It is a revealing reflection on our society that most children think that more money would make them happier. This raises an important issue of whether children have a claim on their parent's finances. What level of money and material benefits is a child entitled to receive from his or her parents? The issue is particularly significant on the breakdown of a relationship. Imagine a common kind of situation: a mother and father separate and the child is to reside with the mother. The mother has no employment, but the father has a good income. It is generally accepted that the father should pay money to support the child. But what level of support can a child require? Here are some of the possibilities:

(a) The parent is required to provide the child with the amount needed to enable the child to live at a 'minimally decent level'. This sum could be at the level that would be paid by the state through income support to a parent and child.

(b) To provide the child with an 'adequate level' which would cover not only the minimum necessary, but would include some non-essential items. The level could be set at the amount of money paid by a local authority to foster parents, which is more than the minimum, but is not generous.

(c) The parent could be required to pay the amount that the couple spent on the child while they were together. This argument could be justified on the basis that the child's financial position should not be prejudiced by the parents' separation.

(d) The state could fix a percentage of the parents' income, to which a child can be entitled.

The difficulty in selecting between these approaches is this. Generally the state permits parents to decide the amount of money spent on a child. If a well-off couple decide for ideological reasons not to buy their children toys and spend very little money on their child, then as long as the child does not suffer significant harm there would be no legal intervention. There is no doubt that if a child were to apply to the court for a specific issue order that she should be paid more pocket money this would fail.[129] If the parents separate why should this lead to an increase in her entitlement? This might suggest that the most a child could claim would be level (a), above. However, in *T* v. *S*[130] where, following the separation of the parents the father won the national lottery, the court suggested that the child is entitled to be brought up at a level commensurate with their parents' income, an approach closer to principle (c) above.

The Child Support Acts 1991 and 1995 focus on ensuring that the child receives at least level of support (a). However the formula used by the Child Support Agency is not restricted to this level. Although there is a maximum level payable and a smaller percentage of the father's income is required once he has paid the maintenance requirement (which is fixed at approximately [a] above). The new law on child support, which is not yet in force but soon will be, is found in the Child Support, Pensions and Social Security Act 2000. This is closer to principle (d) and moves away from the complex formula found in the Child Support Acts. In the simplest terms the Act requires non-resident parents to pay 15 per cent of his or her income for one child, 20 per cent for two and 25 per cent for three or more. There is no maximum that is payable. This means that children of the ultra-rich can enjoy highly luxurious lifestyles if the Act applies. The core reason for reform is that the Child Support Act formula had proved highly complex, resulting in injustices in some cases and involving the agency in such time-consuming calculations that little time was left for enforcement of the assessments made.[131]

A further area of dispute concerning the financial support of children is whether the obligation should follow genetic parenthood or should rely on social parenthood. If a man fathers a child, leaves the mother and moves in with another woman who has children from a different man, should his primary obligation be towards the children who are living with him or towards his biological children? On the one hand there is evidence that men feel a stronger moral obligation to support children with whom they live, in which case if the law enforced that obligation there may be fewer enforcement problems because the legal obligation would then match the perceived moral obligation.[132] Against this is the argument that from the child's perspective a more stable source of income may be found

---

[129] *Re C (A Minor)(Leave to Seek Section 8 Orders)* [1994] 1 FLR 26, [1994] 1 FCR 837 reveals that the court will not be willing to be willing to consider trivial issues.

[130] [1994] 2 FLR 883, [1994] 1 FCR 743.

[131] Davis, Wikeley and Young, *Child Support in Action* (1998, Hart).

[132] Eekelaar and Maclean, *The Parental Obligation* (1997, Hart).

in enforcing the obligation of his or her birth family, rather than the present partner of his or her resident parent, which may or may not be a stable influence in the child's life. The Child Support Acts and the Children Act all place the burden of financial child support primarily on the birth parents of the child.[133]

When the welfare principle does not apply

As emphasised above the welfare principle does not apply to all cases involving children. It does not apply where the statute specifically states that (for example, in cases under the Adoption Act or Matrimonial Causes Act 1973), or where the case does not directly concern the upbringing of the child (for example, where the mother seeks a non-molestation injunction against the father). One point to stress about these exceptions is that they are *not* cases which are unimportant to children's welfare: whether their parents divorce; whether domestic violence injunctions are granted; and how property is distributed on divorce are of great importance to children. Indeed a cynic might say that these are cases where the parents' interests are particularly important and that is why the welfare principle is not applied.

Criticisms of the welfare principle

There have been many criticisms made of the welfare principle. These will be briefly summarised:

(a) The principle is not practical. If the court were truly to ascertain what is in the interests of the child it would have to hear evidence from a wide variety of sources. The courts lack the time and resources to receive all the evidence required to make a proper assessment of what would promote the interests of the child.

(b) The principle requires the impossible. Even if the court did receive all the evidence, in many cases it would be impossible to predict what would happen in the future and therefore what would be in the best interests of the child.

(c) There is no consensus over what promotes a child's welfare. Even if the court had all the information it needed and could predict the future, it is by no means certain that there would be consensus over what is in the child's best interests. For example, if one parent

---

[133] That said, a step-parent who marries the parent of a child may thereby assume financial responsibility for a child under the Matrimonial Causes Act 1973.

encourages hard work at school and imposes strict discipline, whereas the other parent has a laid back attitude to homework and to disciplinary matters, would there be consensus among the general public that one style of parenting is better than another?

(d) The principle is misused in practice. Some commentators argue that even if the welfare principle is justifiable in theory the way it operates in practice is unacceptable. Some feminist commentators argue that under the guise of promoting the interests of children the courts have infringed the rights of women. For example, Frances Olsen has argued 'legal protection of children can be and has been used as a basis of controlling women'.[134]

(e) The principle encourages litigation. Because of the ambiguity over what welfare means, it can be argued that the vagueness encourages litigation because the parties will seek a court hearing in the hope that the judge might rule in his or her favour.[135]

(f) The welfare principle places insufficient weight on the interests and rights of others and of moral principles that the law should uphold. As has already been noted there is a danger that the welfare principle places insufficient weight on the rights of parents. Helen Reece has considered the use of the welfare principle in cases where the courts have considered whether children should reside with gay parents. These cases[136] have placed weight on the argument that children may be teased if placed with gay parents. She argues that there is a danger in these cases of the welfare principle perpetuating discrimination against gay parents and not promoting equal rights of gay and lesbian people to be parents.[137]

Despite these criticisms the welfare principle has shown surprising durability. The key argument for favouring the interests of the child over the interests of other family members is that the child is the person who has the fewest options. At the end of the day, any of the adults could walk away from the child and ask the local authority to care for the child; a child does not have that option. Further, the welfare principle ensures that the court carefully considers the position of the child, which might not

---

[134] Olsen, 'Children's Rights: Some Feminist Approaches to the United Nations Convention on the Rights of the Child' (1992) *International Journal of Law, Policy and the Family* 192.

[135] Schneider, 'Discretion, Rules, and Law: Child Custody and the UDMA's Best Interest Standard' (1989) *Michigan Law Review* 2215.

[136] e.g. *B v. B (Custody, Care and Control)* [1991] FLR 402, [1991] FCR 1.

[137] Reece, 'The Paramountcy Principle: Consensus or Construct?' (1996) 49 *Current Legal Problems* 267. See also Altman, 'Should Child Custody Rules be Fair?' (1997) 325 *Journal of Family Law* 354.

otherwise be stressed when the courts are dealing with a dispute between two adults.

Alternatives to the welfare principle?

As discussed above, there are objections to the welfare principle and it is therefore useful to consider some of the alternatives to the welfare principle. The following are some guiding principles that could be used to determine the decision of the court if there is a dispute over children:

(a) The primary carer principle

This is based on the argument that on parental separation the law should presume that the person who has undertaken the majority of the child care during the child's minority, should be the person who continues to care for the child after the separation. Further, that in issues of dispute over the upbringing of the child the primary carer should decide what should happen to the child unless there is clear evidence that the child will be significantly harmed by a decision. The approach is based on the evidence, mentioned above, that a child forms a bond with one 'psychological parent' and that he or she will suffer significant harm if that bond is broken. Further, that such a parent will know the child better than anyone else and will therefore be in the best position to make decisions relating to the child. A different argument in favour of the primary carer principle is that a parent's care for a child is not adequately appreciated in society. The primary carer principle may be one way for the law to recognise the work that the parent has done. Carol Smart and Bren Neale have suggested that the law needs to recognise the difference between caring for a child and caring about the child.[138] It is the former (the 'doing' of parenting) that is far more important than the latter, they argue.

Those who oppose the primary carer principle tend to do so on two grounds. First, that it is anti-men. This may be a little unfair, because although it is true that the majority of care is carried out by women, that is often the fathers' choice. That said, others argue that society is structured in such a way as to make it easier for women than men to carry out the child-care role. The second objection is that the primary carer principle might work against the child's interests. It does not follow that the person who undertook the majority of the child care before separation will be the best person to continue the care in the very different circumstances that the parties will face after separation.

---

[138] Smart and Neale (1999), *Family Fragments?* (1999, Polity).

(b) Presumed joint residence

Here the presumption is that the child should split his or her time more or less equally between both parents. Although at one time popular in the United States, it has never gained enormous popularity in England and Wales. The main advantage of a joint residence approach is that both parents are able to play as full a role as possible in the child's life. The fact that the parents have separated should not affect each parent's relationship with the child. The disadvantage of this approach is that the child may feel unsettled in constantly changing her residence. The approach also requires that the parents have a reasonable relationship with each other so that the necessary arrangements can be made when regularly sharing the child. There is a danger that the child will become a battleground and each parent will attempt to make their time with the child more enjoyable.

(c) Co-operative parenting

This approach advocates that each parent should be encouraged to play as full a role as possible in the lives of their children. For example, Martin Richards has suggested that in deciding disputes over where the child will live, the child should be placed with the parent who will do the most to encourage contact with the other parent.

(d) Balancing all the interests of the parties

Others have argued that the flaw in the welfare principle is placing too much weight on the interests of the child. Helen Reece has argued that 'the paramountcy principle must be abandoned and replaced within a framework which recognises that the child is merely one participant in a process in which the interest of all the participants count'. It may be that by recognising that it is in a child's interests to be raised in family relationships which are just and respect the rights of each family member, this could enable the courts to consider the interests of all family members, under the head of considering the interests of children.[139]

Concluding thoughts

This chapter has raised a number of strong tensions running through the law of children and parents. There is a delicate balance between protecting the interests of genetic parents and social parents; between protecting children and recognising that children have rights; between protecting children and permitting parents leeway to raise children as they believe

---

[139] Herring, *op. cit.*, n. 113.

best; between the interests of individual children and children as a group. How the law strikes these balances has changed over time and will, no doubt, change in the future.

Further reading

Bainham, 'The Privatisation of the Public Interest in Children' (1990) 53 *Modern Law Review* 206.

Bainham, 'Honour Thy Father and Thy Mother: Children's Rights and Children's Duties', in Douglas and Sebba (eds) *Children's Rights and Traditional Values* (1998, Dartmouth).

Bainham, *Children – The Modern Law* (1998, Jordans).

Bainham, 'Parentage, Parenthood and Parental Responsibility: Subtle, Elusive Yet Important Distinctions', in A. Bainham, M. Richards and S. Day Sclater, *What is a Parent?* (1999, Hart).

Barton and Douglas, *Law and Parenthood* (1995, Butterworth).

Brazier and Bridge, 'Coercion or Caring: analysing adolescent autonomy' (1996) 16 *Legal Studies* 84.

Eekelaar, 'Are Parents Morally Obliged to Care for Their Children?' (1991) 11 *Oxford Journal of Legal Studies* 51.

Eekelaar, 'The Interests of the Child and the Child's Wishes: The Role of Dynamic Self-Determinism' (1994) 8 *International Journal of Law and the Family* 42.

Eekelaar and Maclean, *The Parental Obligation* (1997, Hart).

Freeman, *The Moral Status of Children* (1997, Martinus Nijhoff).

Goldstein, Freud, Solnit, *Beyond the Best Interests of the Child* (1973, Free Press).

Herring, 'The Welfare Principle and the Rights of Parents' in Bainham, Richards, Day Sclater, *What is a Parent?* (1999, Hart).

Herring, 'The Human Rights Act and the Welfare Principle in Family Law – Conflicting or Complementary?' (1999) 11 *Child and Family Law Quarterly* 223.

Hill and Tisdall, *Children and Society* (1997, Addison Wesley Longman).

McCall Smith, 'Is Anything Left of Parental Rights?' in Sutherland and McCall Smith (eds) *Family Rights: Family Law and Medical Ethics* (1990, Edinburgh University Press).

Pickford, 'Unmarried Fathers and the Law', in Bainham, Day Sclater and Richards, *What is a Parent?* (1999, Hart).

Rodgers and Pryor, *Divorce and Separation. The Outcomes for Children* (1998, Joseph Rowntree).

5

Public law children's cases: whose decision is it anyway?

Bridget Lindley, Jonathan Herring and Nicola Wyld

Introduction

The tragic stories of abuse, injury and death of children, which have received media attention during the last few decades, have placed the protection of children high on the social policy agenda.[1] Simultaneously the importance of encouraging parents to take responsibility for their children's upbringing, and ensuring that children have a sense of who their family is, even if they do not live with them, has received increasing recognition.[2] Indeed, the United Nations Convention on the Rights of the Child states that parents have common responsibility for the upbringing and development of their child (article 18). The role of the state is to provide assistance to support parents in this task, and (only) to intervene when a child is in need of protection from abuse, maltreatment, or neglect (article 19). It has been a challenge for successive governments to achieve the right balance between adopting a hands-off approach to the task of child-rearing, by allowing parents to decide how to care for their children; and a hands-on approach by effectively telling them what is and what is not acceptable parenting, and empowering the state to remove children from their care when they get it wrong. This task is made more challenging by the fact that what is considered good for, and harmful to, children is subject to redefinition by society,[3] according to current thinking and research on children and families[4] (which may, in itself, be subject to different emphasis depending on the context of the debate).[5]

---

[1] Department of Health, *Child Protection: Messages from Research* (1995, HMSO).

[2] e.g. *Re L (A Child)(Contact: Domestic Violence)* [2000] 2 FLR 334.

[3] See, for example, the discussion by the Court of Appeal on whether it is appropriate for parents to be naked in front of their children in *Re W (Minors)(Residence Order)* [1999] 1 FLR 869.

The Children Act 1989 establishes a comprehensive legal framework for the care and protection of children, which is designed to achieve the right balance in law between providing for parental autonomy, whilst also empowering the state to intervene to protect children at risk of harm, according to established 'threshold' criteria.[6] However, its implementation is complex. Not only do parents have responsibility for the care and protection of their children until they are old enough to make decisions for themselves, but also two different state agencies, namely courts and local authorities, are responsible for protecting children at risk of harm and promoting their welfare. Decisions about the care of children may therefore be made by parents, older children or young people, the local authority and the courts, or a combination of any of these. Tensions will inevitably emerge when the views of these different decision-makers conflict. The possibility for any of the decision-makers to impose their views on the others will depend entirely on the status of the child and the legal procedures, if any, which govern the context in which the decision is made.

The implementation of the Human Rights Act 1998 (HRA) has triggered feverish debate amongst lawyers about the extent to which our domestic law complies with the European Convention on Human Rights and Fundamental Freedoms (ECHR). It therefore seems appropriate to explore this web of decision-making in public law cases with the HRA in mind. The aim of this chapter is, therefore, to examine how decisions are made about children who are subject to compulsory intervention by the state; to identify the tensions which exist between the different decision-makers; and to consider how the implementation of the HRA may impact upon these processes in the future.

Who decides about the care of children? The respective roles of parents, children, courts and local authorities

Parents

In general, parents are the main decision-makers about the care and upbringing of children. This reflects the expectations of the United Nations Convention on the Rights of the Child and the ECHR.[7] Most

---

[4] Department of Health, *Child Protection: Messages from Research* (1995, HMSO), at pp. 11–23.

[5] See for example the different approach to policy on children and families between government departments, discussed in Lindley, 'State Intervention and Parental Autonomy in Children's Cases: Have we Got the Balance Right?' in A. Bainham, S. Day Sclater, and M. Richards (eds), *What is a Parent?* (1999, Hart), at pp. 197–198, footnote 4.

[6] S. 31, Children Act 1989.

[7] And indeed the ECHR.

parents, and certain others, have parental responsibility for their children.[8] This is defined in the Children Act as being 'all the rights, duties, powers, responsibilities and authority which by law a parent of a child has in relation to the child and his property.'[9] In effect, this means that parents have responsibility for, and autonomy to decide about, the upbringing of their children. Parents with children in need[10] can expect support from the state to help them in this task of child-rearing because local authorities are under a duty to 'safeguard and promote the welfare of children within their area who are in need ... by providing a range and level of services appropriate to those children's needs'.[11] In law, parental autonomy is therefore unfettered except where it is restricted by court order or statute. This arises, for example, when there is a court order determining the exercise of parental responsibility under section 8,[12] or authorising state intervention under Part IV of the Children Act (discussed below); and/or when a particular course of action is prohibited by statute.[13] In practice, however, parental authority may also be circumscribed when other decision-makers, such as children themselves and local authorities, exert influence which supersedes the parents' exercise of their parental responsibility.

Children

Mature children and young people are also important decision-makers, either because they have a right to make decisions for themselves;[14] or because they may take control of a situation by voting with their feet. The children's rights movement has gained considerable ground in the last 20 years, and the position of older children who wish to influence or

---

[8] Mothers and married fathers automatically have parental responsibility for their children (s. 2(1),(2), Children Act 1989), and for them it is inalienable, unless their child is adopted. Non-married fathers can acquire parental responsibility by agreement or court order (s. 4). Others caring for, or seeking to care for, children can acquire parental responsibility if granted a residence order (s. 8), a guardianship order (s. 5), or an adoption order. Wherever parental responsibility is acquired by means of a residence order, it is revocable (s. 12(2) Children Act 1989) except in the case of unmarried fathers.

[9] S. 3, Children Act 1989.

[10] As defined by s. 17, Children Act 1989.

[11] S. 17, Children Act 1989.

[12] Where there are disputes between parents as to the exercise of parental responsibility, the court has the power to make orders under section 8 of the Children Act 1989 which will determine residence, contact arrangements, specific issues and any steps which the court decides should be prohibited in relation to the exercise of parental responsibility.

[13] For example, the Child Abduction Act 1984, which makes it a criminal offence to remove a child from the jurisdiction for more than one month without the consent of all those with parental responsibility.

[14] Such as the right of those over 16 to consent to medical treatment (s. 8 Family Law Reform Act 1969).

challenge decisions being made about them has been substantially enhanced. The law originates from three main sources.

(1) Gillick *competence*

The first is the case of *Gillick* v. *West Norfolk Health Authority*.[15] Although it concerned the child's right to consent to medical treatment, the case introduced the notion of *Gillick* competence into family law. It effectively set a precedent for children being able to challenge their parents' exercise of parental responsibility when they are old and mature enough to understand the issues being decided. Lord Fraser stated that parental rights 'exist for the benefit of the child and are justified only insofar as they enable a parent to perform his duties towards the child'.[16] Lord Scarman also made it clear that parents' rights exist for the child's benefit and consequently 'yield to the child's right to make his own decisions when he reaches sufficient understanding and intelligence to be capable of making up his mind on the matter'.[17] The principles established in this case have been applied far more broadly than the medical context in which they first arose, both in case law[18] and by statute.[19] Indeed, *Gillick*-competent children are now important players in the decision-making process when there are disputes about their care and welfare, whether it is in a private or a public law context.[20] For example, in private law children now have a statutory basis for challenging their parents' decisions by having the right, albeit limited,[21] to apply for leave to apply for s. 8 orders. In public law *Gillick*-competent children who disagree with the views of the Guardian ad Litem can have their views represented directly to the court by their solicitor in care proceedings.[22]

---

[15]   *Gillick* v. *West Norfolk and Wisbech AHA* [1986] AC 112.

[16]   At p. 170.

[17]   At p. 186.

[18]   e.g. *Re S (A Minor)(Independent Representation)* [1993] 2 FLR 437.

[19]   e.g. s. 43(8) Children Act 1989.

[20]   In *Re B (Change of Surname)* [1996] 1 FLR 791 the Court of Appeal thought it would be rare for a court to override the wishes of teenagers (even though they were willing to do so in that case).

[21]   There have been a number of cases which have considered the criteria for granting leave to a child to apply for a s. 8 order. It is now well established that the criteria in s. 10(9) for granting leave do not apply, but instead the court must consider the child's maturity and understanding of the issues and must have regard to the likelihood of success of the application. It is also clear that such applications are discouraged and should be approached cautiously (*Re C (Residence: Child's Application for Leave)* [1995] 1 FLR 927; *Re C (A Minor)(Leave to Seek s. 8 Orders)* [1994] 1 FLR 26).

[22]   FPC (CA 1989) R. 1991, r. 12 and FPR 1991, r. 4.12; see also *Re H (A Minor)(Care Proceedings: Child's Wishes)* [1991] 1 FLR 440.

(2) Children's advocacy

Secondly, the UN Convention on the Rights of the Child has also fuelled the children's rights movement both in general, and specifically, by raising the profile of the right for children to be heard in the decision-making process. Article 12 requires that:

> 1. States parties shall assure to the child who is capable of forming his or her own views the right to express those views freely in all matters affecting the child, the views of the child being given due weight in accordance with the age and maturity of the child.
>
> 2. For this purpose, the child shall in particular be provided the opportunity to be heard in any judicial and administrative proceedings affecting the child, either directly, or through a representative or an appropriate body, in a manner consistent with the procedural rules of national law.

Although not binding on our domestic law because there is no international court to enforce it, the UK Government ratified this Convention in 1991. It should therefore be complied with, and its articles provide an important benchmark of how children's rights should be guaranteed within our domestic law.[23] Article 12 has received a lot of recent attention and is now being implemented in many aspects of formal decision-making about children, both in an administrative and a judicial context. For example, recent guidance on child protection procedures within local authorities envisages children's participation as an integral part of the process,[24] and indeed its implementation is a current priority for the Department of Health. The need for looked-after children to have access to an independent advocate who can support them in expressing their views within the administrative decision-making process has gained ground in the last decade.[25]

A wide range of advocacy services has been developed by the voluntary sector. These have included local authority children's rights services (the majority of which are now managed by voluntary agencies); the two specialist children's advocacy organisations, Voice for the Child in Care (VCC) and ASC National Youth Advocacy Service (NYAS); and by local projects of the large children's charities. However, in 1999, all the major children's advocacy providers formed the Children's Advocacy Consortium. The aim of the Consortium is that every local authority should have a children's rights and advice service as part of the Quality Protects

---

[23] See C. Lyon, 'Children and the Law – Towards 2000 and Beyond. An Essay in Human Rights, Social Policy and the Law' in C. Bridge (ed.), *Family Law Towards the Millennium* (1997, Butterworth).

[24] See for example paras. 5.43, 5.57–8, 7.8, 7.11–12, and 7.19–22 of Department of Health, *Working Together to Safeguard Children* (2000, Stationery Office).

[25] See Voice for the Child in Care, *Shout to be Heard* (1998, VCC).

Programme (see below) and that every child looked after should have a statutory right to an independent advocate. These services should be provided according to national standards of good practice drafted by the Consortium.[26]

The Government has also begun to recognise the need for children to be heard in the decision-making process when they are looked after.[27] Indeed, although the Government was not willing to legislate during the parliamentary passage of either the Care Standards or the Children (Leaving Care) Acts to provide a statutory entitlement for children to access advocacy support, it has in its response to the Waterhouse Report (yet another report chronicling abuse in care, this time in North Wales)[28] accepted the recommendation that children should have a statutory entitlement to independent advocacy when making a formal complaint under section 26 of the Children Act.

(3) Guardians ad litem

Thirdly, children have a view, either directly or indirectly in court proceedings and are represented by the so-called 'tandem system', embracing both welfare and legal representation. Section 41 of the Children Act requires the court to appoint a guardian ad litem unless it is not necessary to do so to safeguard the child's welfare. It is the guardian's duty to safeguard the child's interests by reference to the welfare checklist in section 1(3) of the Act, amongst other things, to have regard to the wishes and feelings of the child in light of his or her understanding and to convey these wishes to the court. Where there is conflict between the guardian's instructions and those of a child competent to give instructions, the child's solicitor must act on the instructions of the child. Competent children therefore have the right to be fully legally represented in public law proceedings while at the same time the court will be advised of their best interests.[29]

---

[26] Voice for the Child in Care, *How do Young People and Children Get their Voices Heard?* (1998, VCC).

[27] One of the six initial Government priority areas for securing funding in meeting Government objectives for improving outcomes for looked-after children and children in need, is listening to the views and wishes of children, young people and their families. In the second year of the Quality Protects programme this priority was extended to stating that particular attention should be given to the involvement of young people collectively and by the development of children's rights services and independent advocacy.

[28] Department of Health, *Learning the Lessons, The Government's Response to Lost in Care, the Report of the Tribunal of Enquiry into the Abuse of Children in Care in former County Council Areas of Gwynedd and Clwyd since 1974* (2000, Department of Health).

[29] See the Report of the Child Act Subcommittee on the Subject of the Separate Representation of Children in Public and Private Law Proceedings under the Children Act 1989, approved by the Lord Chancellor's Advisory Board on Family Law (1999, LCD), paras. 4.22 and 4.32.

The Criminal Justice and Courts Act 2000 has provided for the establishment of the Children and Families Advisory Support Service (CAFCASS). The creation of the Children and Families Advisory Support Service and the impact of the 1998 Human Rights Act[30] is also likely to enhance the representation of children in private law proceedings. The purpose of this new service is to amalgamate the functions of the family court welfare service, GALRO service and the children's division of the Official Solicitor's office into one agency. The functions of the service are to safeguard and promote the welfare of children before the courts in family proceedings; give advice to courts; make provision for children to be legally represented and to provide information, advice and support to children and their families.

Local authorities

The state has the power, and indeed is under a duty, to intervene in family life to protect children who are at risk of harm.[31] There are three tiers of state intervention: investigation, emergency intervention and long-term care of the children. The local authority has a central role to play in all three, but the extent of it is determined by the degree of judicial control to which it is subject.

The first level of state intervention relates to child protection investigations. Local authorities are under a duty to make enquiries where they have reasonable cause to *suspect* that a child may be suffering from significant harm.[32] Local authorities are obliged to see the child during such enquiries, unless they are satisfied that they already have sufficient information about them.[33] Where they are denied access to the child, they are obliged to apply for an emergency protection order, a child assessment order or a care order, unless they are satisfied that the child's welfare can be satisfactorily safeguarded without doing so.[34] In cases where the local authority decides, as a result of these enquiries, not to apply for any compulsory order, then it is under an obligation to review the case at a later date.[35]

Although the duty to make enquiries is imposed by primary legislation, its implementation occurs within administrative procedures set up by the Area Child Protection Committee, which is established by the local

---

[30] Article 6 of the ECHR (right to a fair hearing). See also *Community Care* 7–13 December 2000, at p. 7.
[31] Again this complies with the expectations of the UN Convention cited above.
[32] S. 47 Children Act 1989.
[33] S. 47(4) Children Act 1989.
[34] S. 45(5) Children Act 1989.
[35] As long as the child's name is placed on the child protection register, s. 47(7) Children Act 1989.

authority. The Department of Health has recently issued new guidance to local authorities in *Working Together* (1999)[36] on how these procedures should be drawn up to provide for inter-agency co-operation. The procedures involve gathering information about the needs of the child, the parents' ability to meet those needs, and the level of risk to a child. They also ensure that co-operative decisions are made about whether the child's name should be placed on the child protection register, whether an application for an order authorising compulsory intervention should be recommended, how plans should be drawn up to ensure the child's future protection and how cases should be reviewed.[37] Although it does not have the full force of statute, this guidance is issued under s. 7 of the Local Authority Social Services Act 1970 and should therefore be followed unless there are exceptional circumstances to justify a variation.[38]

Although the local authority is under a clear duty to initiate protective action for children who are the subject of s. 47 enquiries, it does not acquire parental responsibility during the course of the enquiries. Not surprisingly there is therefore a clear expectation that the local authority will work in partnership with the family throughout the inquiry and subsequent planning process. Indeed, this guidance is far more prescriptive than previous guidance as to how parents, children and other family members should be informed about, and involved in, the process. Both parents and the local authority therefore have a legitimate basis for deciding about plans for the future care of the child concerned (where child protection concerns are substantiated). But within the child protection framework the local authority has no legal basis for imposing a plan on parents, without the making of a court order. Where the case involves an older child, their agreement to future plans is also very important because without it they may frustrate the plan by voting with their feet. Thus, although decisions about registration are taken by the multi-agency conference, any subsequent plans for the child's protection need to be discussed and agreed between parents, older children and local authorities. Otherwise it is almost inevitable that the partnership will break down and that the local authority will apply for a court order to legitimise any further steps they wish to take. At that point, the parents' exercise of their parental responsibility and the views of the older child will almost certainly be overridden.

[36] Department of Health, *Working Together to Safeguard Children A guide to inter-agency working to safeguard and promote the welfare of children* (1999, Stationery Office).
[37] For a much more detailed discussion of the new guidance and its impact on parents' exercise of their parental responsibility, see B. Lindley, 'Working Together 2000: How will Parents Fare Under the New Child Protection Process?' [2000] *Child and Family Law Quarterly* 3 at pp. 213–228.
[38] S. 7 requires local authorities in the exercise of their social services functions to act under the general guidance of the Secretary of State.

The local authority has an important role to play within the second tier of state intervention, which relates to emergency measures, such as emergency protection orders. It is the function of the court to determine whether the statutory grounds have been established, but once the order is made the applicant (which is usually the local authority) has responsibility for looking after the child for the duration of the order. Indeed the emergency protection order authorises the applicant to remove the child to appropriate accommodation, or prevent the removal of the child from accommodation already being provided. The order also operates as a direction to parents to comply with any request to produce the child.[39] However, this is subject to the applicant being under a duty to return the child to the person from whom they were removed[40] or their family, if it appears that it is safe to do so.[41] In practice, this rarely occurs. Once an emergency protection order is made, the child normally remains in the care of the local authority for the duration of the order, and although parents retain their parental responsibility, the local authority can override it and insist upon their plan for the child's protection. Despite the fact that parents have parental responsibility, they cannot prevent these enquiries being carried out once the threshold for intervention has been reached. Indeed the duty on the local authority to see the child during the enquiries means that the parents have to co-operate, otherwise the local authority will have grounds to apply for an emergency protection order.[42] Thus the local authority has overall control for the duration of the emergency protection order, and any parent or child who wishes to challenge the local authority's plans will have to oppose the initial application (if they are given notice of it), or apply to discharge the order after 72 hours.[43]

The local authority has a similar role in the third level of intervention, namely where a long-term care or supervision order is made. Again, the court decides on whether the order should be made, but once made, the local authority acquires parental responsibility and is then under a duty to draw up plans which will promote the child's future safety and welfare.[44] Parents retain their parental responsibility for the duration of the order, and the local authority is expected to work in partnership with them when making and reviewing plans for their child, seeking their agreement and co-operation wherever possible.[45] Indeed there is a specific duty on the local authority to ascertain and give due consideration to the wishes and

---

[39] S. 44(4) Children Act 1989.
[40] Or allow the child to be removed by the person from whom they were removed.
[41] S. 44(10) Children Act 1989.
[42] S. 44(1)(b) Children Act 1989.
[43] S. 45(8), (9) Children Act 1989.
[44] S. 22 Children Act 1989.
[45] Department of Health, *The Children Act Regulations and Guidance*, Volume 3 (1991, HMSO), para. 2.49–2.50.

feelings of children and parents in relation to all decision-making about a child who is under a care order under sub-sections 22(4) and (5). However, where there is no agreement, the authority is under an overriding duty to make plans for the child's care for the rest of their minority, irrespective of the child's and parents' wishes. Indeed, there is an explicit provision in the Act which empowers the local authority to determine the extent to which the parents may exercise their parental authority when necessary.[46] The local authority is therefore clearly in the driving seat, and there is no scope for those who disagree with them to apply to the court to challenge their decisions, unless they can successfully apply to discharge the care order (discussed further below).

Courts

The function of the court differs in emphasis between private and public law cases under the Children Act 1989. Although some believe that the Act is designed in such a way as to involve the court as little as possible in private disputes about children,[47] in public law cases the courts are more interventionist with the court being under a duty to determine whether particular thresholds have been reached to merit compulsory state intervention. In private law cases, parents are encouraged to settle disputes about their children wherever possible, with mediation both inside and outside the court process being promoted as an alternative forum to the court, to settle disputes about children.[48] When cases do end up in court, the court will consider the 'no order principle' in sub-section 1(5) before making an order. Indeed, although the right of children to apply to the court to challenge decisions of their parents is now established, there have been few cases involving child applicants. Where they have been heard the courts have stressed that such disputes are better settled between parents and children themselves, without the intervention of the court.[49]

---

[46] S. 33(3) Children Act 1989. The recent case of *Re P (Children Act 1989 ss. 22 and 26: local authority compliance)* [2000] 2 FLR 91 confirmed that this requirement was directory, not mandatory in the sense that any non-compliance on the part of the local authority would be treated as irregularity rather than rendering the authority's decisions void. It was held that in consulting the parent, the authority was also permitted to override their views and exercise of PR under s. 33(3)(b) of the Act.

[47] See the discussion in Bainham, 'The Privatisation of the Public Interest in Children', (1990) 53 *Modern Law Review* 206.

[48] See, for example, s. 29 of the Family Law Act 1996 which requires all those applying for legal aid (legal help with litigation) in connection with children disputes (amongst other things) to attend an appointment with a mediator before they can proceed with their application.

[49] See footnote 21 above.

In public law cases, the primary task of the court is to hear the evidence and decide whether or not the statutory criteria have been established to merit compulsory state intervention. In the case of emergency protection orders the court must be satisfied that there is reasonable cause to *believe* that the child will suffer significant harm if they are not removed to accommodation provided by the local authority, or if they do not remain in the place where they are already being accommodated, or where the local authority is making enquiries under section 47 and where those enquiries are being frustrated by access to the child being unreasonably refused.[50] In the case of care orders the court may make an order where it is *satisfied* that a child under 17 is suffering, or is likely to suffer, significant harm,[51] and that that harm is attributable to the care given to the child, or likely to be given to them, not being what it would be reasonable to expect a parent to give them, or the child being beyond parental control.[52] A care order will only be made once these threshold criteria are satisfied if such an order will positively promote the child's welfare as determined by the welfare principle and the 'no order' principle in section 1.[53] However, the options open to the court are generally restricted by the fact that it cannot make a conditional order.[54] Although the court will expect the local authority to provide a care plan at the final hearing setting out its proposals for the child's future care and protection,[55] this plan will not be binding because there is no power for the court to make the care order on condition that the care plan is followed.[56] Further the court cannot on its own motion review the case if the care plan presented to the court at the time of the hearing is subsequently abandoned in favour of a radically different plan. This means that the court must either make the care order applied for, make no order, or make a residence order in favour of someone else. Once the care order is made there is no possibility of judicial scrutiny of what the local

---

[50] S. 44, Children Act 1989.

[51] 'Harm' means ill-treatment or the impairment of health or development (s. 31(9)). Where the question of whether the harm suffered by the child is significant turns on the child's health or development, his health or development shall be compared with that which could reasonably be expected of a similar child (s. 31(10)).

[52] S. 31(2) Children Act 1989. When interpreting 'significant harm', the guidance issued in conjunction with the Children Act refers to the dictionary definition of 'significant' as being 'considerable, noteworthy or important': Department of Health, *The Children Act Regulations and Guidance, Vol. 1 Court Orders* (1991, HMSO) (para. 3.19). This received judicial endorsement soon after the Act was implemented (*Humberside County Council v. B* [1993] 1 FLR 257), but there has been little other case law interpretation of what constitutes *significant* harm.

[53] A care order normally lasts until the child is 18, unless it is discharged at an earlier date (s. 33(1) Children Act 1989).

[54] Although an interim care order can be made with certain directions: s. 38(6) Children Act 1989.

[55] *Manchester City Council v. F* [1993] 1 FLR 419, [1993] 1 FCR 1000.

[56] *Re T (A Minor) (Care Order: Conditions)* [1994] 2 FLR 423.

authority does with the care order. Indeed it has been held in one case that delaying a final hearing by making repeated interim orders was inappropriate because it was trying to achieve judicial scrutiny of the local authority's care of the child, a practice which was not permissible under the Children Act.[57] In effect this means that once the order is made, the local authority's power to decide what to do with the order is unfettered unless it acts so unreasonably as to warrant judicial review or revocation of the care order.

The tensions between the different decision-makers

This analysis shows that the power to make decisions may be shared between different people/agencies either concurrently or consecutively. This power-sharing may lead at best to an uneasy relationship, and at worst to outright conflict, between the different decision-makers when they disagree. Normally, where there is outright conflict, parties may litigate to resolve a dispute. However, in public law cases, judicial remedies to settle a dispute are not always available. This can cause considerable tension in relation to the decisions of the local authority which are not appealable or challengeable in an external forum, yet are made in an administrative context in which the courts and the parents/ children have no 'right' to participate. Some examples of this are outlined below:

Coercive accommodation

The duty on the local authority to provide support services for children in need includes the provision of accommodation in particular circumstances, notably where the person caring for the child is 'prevented (whether or not permanently, and for whatever reason) from providing him with suitable accommodation or care.'[58] This service was always intended to be voluntary, and this was underlined by the fact that when the Children Bill was passing through Parliament, a proposed amendment to introduce a notice requirement for a child to be removed from accommodation was specifically rejected because this was considered to undermine the voluntary nature of the arrangement.[59] Since implementation of the Children Act, however, practice has proved to be not quite so

---

[57] *Re L (Sexual Abuse: Standard of Proof)* [1996] 1 FLR 116.
[58] S. 20, Children Act 1989.
[59] See Hansard HL, vol. 502 cols.1337, 1342–4, Children Bill Committee Stage; vol. 503 cols.1411–13 Report Stage, vol. 512 cols. 737–9 Consideration of Commons Amendments.

simple. The practice of children about whom the authority has some 'concerns' (often unspecified) being placed or kept in accommodation under threat of court proceedings if the parents do not agree has been documented, even in cases where the statutory criteria for an emergency protection order or care order have not been established.[60] Parents whose children are voluntarily accommodated have full parental responsibility and the local authority does not acquire it. Yet parents are often too frightened to challenge the local authority by exercising their right to remove their child from accommodation[61] for fear of precipitating an application for a compulsory order under part IV, which, if granted, would give the local authority parental responsibility. In practice, this coercive use of accommodation effectively enables the local authority to override parents' wishes even though there is no legitimate basis for doing so.

Partnership in child protection cases

A similar tension frequently arises in child protection cases. The local authority does not acquire parental responsibility during the course of enquiries, yet the duty to make enquiries when the threshold in section 47 is reached is unequivocal. If the concerns are substantiated, it must also draw up plans to promote the child's future protection and welfare.[62] There is a clear expectation in the new guidance that parents will be provided with appropriate information about the nature and outcome of the enquiries, and that they will be 'partners' in the process.[63] However, the compulsory nature of the enquiries has clear implications for the exercise of the parents' parental responsibility. Not only do the parents have to allow the child to be seen, on request, during the course of the enquiries, but in practice they have to comply with the local authorities' child protection plan, otherwise they risk triggering an application for a compulsory order. The fact that the enquiry process is administrative rather than judicial means that there is very limited scope for parents to challenge decisions and plans drawn up within the process. There is no

---

[60] J. Hunt and A. McLeod, *The Last Resort Child Protection, the Courts and the Children Act,* (HMSO, 1999), at pp. 35–42. The recent case of *R* v. *A Metropolitan Borough Council ex parte J,* reported in (2000) 24 *Adoption and Fostering* 61, confirms that arrangements for placement of a child in accommodation which does not have the parents' agreement is judicially reviewable, but in practice many parents are too fearful of the consequences to seek such a remedy.

[61] S. 20(7) provides that a person with parental responsibility can remove a child from accommodation, and there is no notice requirement for this.

[62] See paras. 5.64–5.82 *Working Together to Safeguard Children* (Stationery Office, 2000).

[63] Department of Health, *Working Together to Safeguard Children* (Stationery Office, 2000), Chapter 7.

'right' under the Children Act for them to have advanced disclosure of evidence being produced at the child protection conference in support of the local authorities proposals; for them to attend the conference itself; or for them to appeal against a decision to place their child's name on the child protection register.[64] Although parents are expected to be part of the core group that has responsibility for drawing up and implementing the detailed child protection plan for every child whose name is placed on the register, their only opportunity to disagree with plans being proposed is within the core group itself. In effect, despite having parental responsibility, they are unable to appeal against any parts of the plan with which they disagree. Indeed, although it is outside the scope of this chapter to discuss it in detail, the goal of partnership, which is the cornerstone of child protection work, may in itself be flawed because of the inherent conflicts within the social worker's role.[65] Once the section 47 threshold has been reached, it is therefore clear that the real power to make decisions about children lies with the local authority, and not those with parental responsibility, unless the parents are willing to risk triggering an application for a compulsory order.

Care plans

The local authority also has considerable power to draw up and implement care plans once a compulsory order is made without necessarily being subject to judicial scrutiny. Whilst there is no suggestion that local authorities act in bad faith, this lack of scrutiny has caused

---

[64] There is still no provision for appeal against registration. In rare cases, parents may be able to challenge a decision to register if they can establish grounds for judicial review, but this will be in exceptional rather than routine cases. In the case of *R v. Hampshire County Council ex parte H* [1999] 2 FLR 359, the Court of Appeal held that a decision regarding registration was void (where there was no evidence to substantiate the concern about a likelihood of significant harm). It held that it was not enough to register children under the category of emotional abuse, merely relying on the fact of a stressful family situation. However, the Court of Appeal added that recourse to judicial review should be rare in child protection. This echoed an earlier case, *R v. East Sussex CC ex parte R* [1991] 2 FLR 358, in which, Sir Stephen Brown said, refusing an application for judicial review regarding registration on the child protection register, that 'recourse to judicial review of decisions which do not involve removal from the parents should be rare and only adopted in exceptional circumstances.' In most cases, parents therefore lack the opportunity to challenge the decisions and recommendations of the conference in a formal forum.

[65] For discussion of this see Lindley, 'Working Together 2000: How Will Parents Fare under the New Child Protection Process?' [2000] *Child and Family Law Quarterly* 1 at pp. 10–13; also Corby, Millar and Young, 'Parental Participation in Child Protection Work: Rethinking the Rhetoric', (1996) 26 *British Journal of Social Work*, 475; and Bell, 'Working in Partnership in Child Protection: The Conflicts', (1999) 29 *British Journal of Social Work* 437.

problems both in courts and outside. In the judicial context, it is now well established that the local authority must provide a care plan,[66] stating their proposals for the child's future care, for scrutiny at the final hearing in care proceedings.[67] There are reported cases and academic discussion[68] which has highlighted the difficulties which emerge when the threshold criteria have been established but the Guardian ad Litem and/or the court disagree with the care plan or wish to oversee implementation of the plan.[69] The pre-Children Act case of *A* v. *Liverpool City Council*[70] established the principle that where Parliament has entrusted the care of children under an order to the local authority it is not for the court to interfere with the local authority's discretion by dictating how it should care for the child. With the exception of contact (which the court does have the power to order even if it conflicts with the local authority's plans for the child),[71] this principle is still upheld today. This means that any attempt by the court to oversee the implementation of the care order has failed. This occurred, for example, in the case of *Kent County Council* v. *C*[72] in which the Justices made a care order with a condition that the Guardian ad Litem continued to be involved in the case. It was held on appeal that they had no power to attach such a condition. There is some suggestion that the *A* v. *Liverpool City Council* principle may need to be reconsidered by Parliament in the foreseeable future so as to give courts the power to review the implementation of care plans, at least in relation to the implementation of plans for adoption.

The autonomy of the local authority to implement the care plan of its choice also causes difficulty for parents and other family members once the court process has been concluded. If a care order has been made on the basis that, for example, a child will be placed with the maternal grandmother under a care order, but this plan is subsequently abandoned in favour of a plan for adoption outside the birth family, there is no current requirement that the local authority should have the new plan approved by the court.[73] It only needs to be approved by an adoption panel, often

---

[66] The Children Act 1989: *Guidance and Regulations, Volume 3, Family Placements*, (HMSO, 1991); Local Authority Circular LAC (99) 29, *Care Plans and Care Proceedings under the Children Act 1989*.

[67] *Manchester City Council* v. *F* [1993] 1 FLR 419; *Re J (Minors) (Care Plan)* [1994] 1 FLR 253 approved in *Re L (Sexual Abuse: Standards of Proof)* [1996] 1 FLR 116.

[68] See for example Hayes, 'The Proper Role of the Courts in Child Care Cases' [1996] *Child and Family Law Quarterly* 201; also Smith, 'Judicial Power and Local Authority Discretion – the Contested Frontier' [1997] *Child and Family Law Quarterly* 243.

[69] See for example the case of *Re G (Minors)(Interim Care Order)* [1993] 2 FLR 839; *Re T (A Minor)(Care Order: Conditions)* [1994] 2 FLR 424.

[70] [1982] AC 363.

[71] *Re B (Minors)(Care: Contact: Local Authority Plans)* [1993] 1 FLR 543.

[72] *Kent County Council* v. *C* [1994] 1 FLR 308.

[73] Although the court will need to make any adoption order.

convened by the local authority itself, before it can be implemented. This has been the subject of some concern within the current review of adoption law, resulting in provisions for a placement order being included in the adoption bill currently before Parliament.[74] Clauses 15–20 of the bill provide for an order which authorises the adoption agency to *place* a child with prospective adopters, and it is envisaged that parental consent will be given or dispensed with at this stage. If enacted, this would mean that placement for adoption, which in practice often becomes an irreversible step in the child's life, would become subject to judicial authority, rather than being an administrative decision as it is at present.

The examples cited above suggest that, despite the role of the court, the emphasis on continuing parental responsibility which pervades the Children Act, and the enhanced status of children to participate in decision-making, it is the local authority which, potentially, has the greatest power to make decisions about children. This is because the decisions which local authorities are empowered to make concern the day-to-day care of, and the need to avoid unnecessary disruptions for, children. Such decisions usually have considerable impact on the child's life and are therefore likely to carry the greatest weight in any subsequent decisions about their welfare. A good example of this arises in current adoption practice. An application for an adoption order can only be heard after the child has had his home with the prospective adopters for at least 13 weeks. This means that judicial consideration of whether or not parents are reasonable in withholding consent under s. 16(2)(b) Adoption Act 1976 has in reality become a paper exercise, the test for reasonableness having in effect become an assessment of the child's welfare.[75]

This overriding power of duty on the local authority to make important decisions in public law cases is of particular significance when the likely impact of the Human Rights Act is considered. Whereas there are clear procedures and court rules which govern the court process to ensure that parties have a fair hearing and that the rules of natural justice are normally applied, there is no equivalent procedural rigour within the administrative processes in which local authority decisions are made. This may mean that whereas court decisions about children are likely to comply with the ECHR, administrative decisions of the local authority may not. To consider this argument further it is necessary to examine in more detail the Human Rights Act and its potential impact on public law cases involving children.

[74] Department of Health, *Adoption of Children Adoption Bill* (2001, Department of Health).
[75] Indeed this has been acknowledged in the recent review of adoption law because the proposed test to dispense with consent in the adoption bill (cited above) is that it should occur 'where the court is satisfied that the welfare of the child requires the consent to be dispensed with' (Clause 44 (2)(b)).

The effect of the Human Rights Act 1998 on the public law relating to children

The Human Rights Act (HRA) incorporates the European Convention for the Protection of Human Rights and Fundamental Freedoms (ECHR) into domestic law. The HRA will therefore increase the scope for parents and children[76] to challenge the care decisions of local authorities. The HRA states that 'so far as is possible to do so, primary and subordinate legislation must be read and given effect to in a way which is compatible with convention rights',[77] and that it is 'unlawful for a public authority to act in a way which is incompatible with a Convention right'.[78] These provisions require some explanation. The definition of public authority includes both courts and local authorities.[79] The 'convention rights' are defined in section 1 HRA as being the rights and freedoms listed in the ECHR (with a few exceptions). The most significant rights for this chapter are the right not to be subject to torture or inhuman or degrading treatment in Article 3; the right to a fair hearing in Article 6; and the right to respect for private and family life in Article 8.[80] The Human Rights Act therefore requires local authorities to act in accordance with these rights, and the courts to interpret the Children Act and other legislation in accordance with these rights, if at all possible. These articles are potentially relevant for four issues that are of particular importance to public law provisions concerning children. First, the articles in some circumstances may compel local authorities to intervene in family life in order to protect a child. Second, the articles restrict the circumstances in which local authorities may interfere in family life. Third, the articles have much to say about how the state should treat a child once he or she has been taken into care. Fourth, the articles set down the minimum standards of procedural fairness when courts or local authorities make decisions relating to the children.

Requiring state intervention (Articles 3 and 8)

Article 3 of the European Convention states:

---

[76] Children can bring claims in their own rights, or parents can bring actions in order to protect the rights of children: *S and G* v. *Italy* [2000] 2 FLR 771; [2000] 3 FCR 430.

[77] S. 3(1) HRA 1998.

[78] S. 6 HRA 1998.

[79] S. 6 HRA 1998.

[80] For a general discussion of the effect of the Human Rights Act in this context see Fortin, 'The HRA's impact on litigation involving children and their families' [1999] *Child and Family Law Quarterly* 239.

No one shall be subjected to torture or to inhuman or degrading treatment or punishment.

In *A* v. *UK*[81] the European Court of Human Rights interpreted this article to mean that not only is the state forbidden to cause torture and inhuman or degrading treatment to its citizens; the state is also required to protect all citizens from such harm, even if caused by another citizen.[82] *A* v. *UK* involved a child who had suffered harsh corporal punishment. It was held the criminal law on corporal punishment in the UK afforded the child inadequate protection from torture or inhuman or degrading treatment. In *Z* v. *UK*[83] the Commission applied the reasoning in *A* v. *UK* to a case which concerned allegations that local authorities had infringed article 3 by not taking into care children who had been neglected by their parents. The Commission stated that:

> the protection of children who by reason of their age and vulnerability are not capable of protecting themselves requires not merely that the criminal law provides protection against art. 3 treatment but that, additionally, this provision will in appropriate circumstances imply a positive obligation on the authorities to take preventive measures to protect a child who is at risk from another individual.[84]

Therefore the local authority's failure to remove children from inadequate parents meant that the state had failed to provide the children with protection from inhuman and degrading treatment and hence breached article 3. The Commission suggested that a positive duty on a local authority arose when there is 'a real and immediate risk of ill-treatment contrary to article 3 of which they knew or ought to know'.[85] What amounts to inhuman or degrading treatment will depend on all the circumstances of the case including the age and sex of the victim, the nature and duration of the treatment, and the effects on the child of the treatment.[86]

Even if the treatment does not constitute inhuman or degrading treatment the state may still be required to intervene by the HRA because a child has a right to respect for his or her private and family life under article 8. The requirement of 'respect' places both positive and negative obligations on public authorities.[87] It is therefore arguable that if the child is suffering abuse or ill-treatment, from which the state offers no pro-

---

[81] *A* v. *UK* [1998] 2 FLR 959.
[82] *A* v. *UK* [1998] 2 FLR 959.
[83] [2000] 2 FCR 245.
[84] At p. 266.
[85] At p. 266.
[86] *A* v. *UK* [1998] 2 FLR 959.
[87] See e.g. *X, Y, and Z* v. *UK* [1997] 2 FLR 892, [1997] 3 FCR 341.

tection, this will constitute an infringement of the child's right to respect for his or her private life under article 8, even though the harm is not sufficiently serious to involve article 3. However, state intervention to protect children may constitute an infringement of the parents' right to respect for *their* family life and so will only be permitted under article 8(2) if the intervention is necessary in the interests of the child. If the harm is less than torture or inhuman or degrading treatment it may be hard to show that intervention in family life is 'necessary'.

These points give rise to three observations. The first is in relation to division between issues which are seen as private and those which are public. The traditional liberal view is that the state may legitimately interfere in public issues, but should not interfere in private matters, such as how parents raise their children. It is now very widely accepted that child abuse, although taking place in the home and in a sense therefore 'private', is legitimately subject to legal intervention. Following the Human Rights Act it is not just permissible for the state to intervene in family life in such cases, but it is positively required. That said, in *X* v. *UK* the Commission limited the state's responsibility to intervene to where it is aware of the ill-treatment of children. Whether the European Courts, or English courts considering the Convention, go further and require local authorities to investigate suspicions of abuse remains to be seen.[88]

Secondly, the articles are relevant to the debate over the balance of power between the courts, local authorities, children and parents in the public law area, discussed earlier in this chapter. Under English and Welsh law a court cannot make a care order if the local authority has refused to apply for one.[89] As a result of the European Court's interpretation of these articles a local authority will be under a duty to take steps to protect a child. It may be that following the HRA, the decision whether to apply for a care order cannot be seen as simply an issue for the local authority's discretion, because the European Convention sometimes requires the state to take steps to protect children. It may therefore be possible for the court to order a local authority to apply for a care or supervision order in order to comply with its obligations under the HRA.

Thirdly, it is arguable that if children are suffering ill-treatment which is at a level which infringes article 3 the state will be required to protect them from harm, even if that harm is not caused by their parents. The House of Lords in *Lancashire CC* v. *A*[90] interpreted the threshold criteria to mean that if it was not clear whether a child was being abused by her parents or another primary carer then a care order could be made. However, it ruled out the possibility of making a care order when it was clear the parents were not responsible for the significant harm. Whether this is justifiable in

---

[88] See ss. 37 and 47 Children Act 1989 for present duties to investigate suspicions of abuse.
[89] *Nottinghamshire CC* v. *P* [1993] 2 FLR 134, [1994] 1 FCR 624.
[90] [2000] 1 FLR 583, [2000] 1 FCR 509.

the light of the child's right to protection from inhuman and degrading treatment under article 3 (whoever causes it) is a matter for debate. That said, if the parents are not responsible for the harm, removing the child from the parents may not protect the child from the harm.[91]

Restricting intervention in family life

Under paragraph 1 of Article 8:

> Everyone has the right to respect for his private and family life, his home and his correspondence.

The right to family life in article 8 includes the right of parents and children to live together without interference from the state.[92] The removal of a child from parents by the state will therefore inevitably constitute an interference with both the parents' and the child's right to respect for family life.[93] Indeed any interference with the domestic arrangements of the family by the state will constitute an infringement of the article 8 right.[94] Hence the making of a care order or supervision order will normally involve an infringement of article 8(1).[95] Such interference will only be consistent with the Convention if the second paragraph of article 8 is satisfied:

> There shall be no interference by a public authority with the exercise of this right except such as is in accordance with the law and is necessary in a democratic society in the interests of national security, public safety or the economic well-being of the country, for the prevention of disorder or crime, for the protection of health or morals, or for the protection of the rights and freedoms of others.

This requires proof that the interference in family life is in accordance with the law;[96] pursues a legitimate aim; is proportionate;[97] and necessary. Each of these requirements will be considered separately.

---

[91] But it would be possible to imagine a situation where it was clear the children were being sexually abused and although it was clear the parents were not abusing the children it was unclear who was. In such a case removal of the children from the parents and the abuse (wherever it came from) might be thought to be appropriate.

[92] *Johansen* v. *Norway* [1996] EHRR 34.

[93] Although if a father does not live with a child and has no contact with her then there may be no family life between the father and child: *B* v. *UK* [2000] 1 FLR 1.

[94] *McMichael* v. *UK* [1995] 20 EHRR 205; *Johansen* v. *Norway* [1996] EHRR 34.

[95] Article 8 has been found to protect links between wider relatives, such as grandparents-grandchildren: *L* v. *Finland* [2000] 2 FLR 118.

[96] *W* v. *UK* (1987) 10 EHRR 29.

[97] Stressed in, for example, *Price* v. *UK* 12402/86 D&R 224.

The requirement that any interference is in accordance with the law essentially requires that the measures were based on national law, and not simply based on the decision of a local authority or social worker, without statutory basis.[98] However, the requirement has been interpreted to mean more than this and includes a requirement that the law relied upon has the necessary quality of law: 'requiring accessibility and forseeability so as to give the individual adequate protection against arbitrary interference.'[99] This is particularly important in relation to procedural fairness which will be discussed further below.

The requirement that the interference pursues an aim which is legitimate is normally readily shown in cases of child protection. A legitimate aim would certainly include protecting a child from abuse or suspected abuse.[100] Abuse here can include protecting children from injury to health, development or morals.

The intervention must be necessary in a democratic society. In deciding whether intervention was necessary the court will consider whether the reasons used to justify the intervention were relevant and sufficient.[101] In deciding whether the intervention is necessary the court may have to consider both the interests of the child in being protected from harm and the right of parents to respect for family life, but the interests of the child are of 'crucial importance.'[102] The 'necessity' requirement suggests that if there is a doubt whether the child is suffering a sufficient level of harm to justify an interference with family life, then the court should not make an order.

The requirement that the interference is proportionate means that the degree of interference into family life must be appropriate given the level of harm feared. This requirement was considered in *Söderbäck* v. *Sweden*.[103] The European Court decided that it was not disproportionate to make an adoption order in favour of the mother and her new husband that brought to an end the parental status of a father. This was because there was only occasional contact between the child and the father, while there were strong reasons in favour of consolidating and formalising the child's relationship with the mother and her new husband. When the case involves removal of a child from his or her parents the proportionality requirement means that the removal must be the only option available to protect the child adequately. In *K and T* v. *Finland*[104] the European Court held that removing a child from her mother at birth was not proportionate

[98] *L* v. *Finland* [2000] 2 FLR 118.
[99] *Anderson* v. *Sweden* (1992) 14 EHRR 615.
[100] *L* v. *Finland* [2000] 2 FLR 118.
[101] *Olsson* v. *Sweden (no 1)* (1988) 11 EHRR 259, at p. 285.
[102] *L* v. *Finland* [2000] 3 FCR 219, at p. 240.
[103] [1999] 1 FLR 250
[104] [2000] 3 FCR 248; [2000] 2 FLR 79.

to the threat faced by the child. The court stressed that the child was with her mother in hospital, which was a safe environment, and so it could not be claimed that removal of the child from the mother was the only option available to ensure the child's safety.[105] In that case it was also stressed that the mother had not been given a chance of even beginning her family life with the child and demonstrating that she could be an adequate mother for the child. This, therefore, required the strongest justification.

The requirements of article 8(2) may well be consistent with the approach taken in the Children Act in that a care order or a supervision order can only be made if the threshold criteria set out in section 31 are satisfied, which include that the child is suffering, or is likely to suffer, significant harm. Further, the court can only make the order once it is established that to do so would promote the child's welfare. The requirement of proportionality could readily be incorporated into the combination of these provisions. That said, it is likely that in future it will be common for those challenging a local authority's application for a care or supervision order to argue that such an order would be disproportionate to the threat facing the child. So when considering applications for care and supervision orders the language of court decisions will change following the HRA, with increased reference being made to proportionality, even if the concept will rarely mean that the decision reached by the court is different from that which would have been reached before the HRA.

Justifying the extent of the intervention

Even if the child is taken into care this does not mean that the parents' right to respect for family life comes to an end. Article 8 requires the state to respect the right of contact between a parent and a child taken into care; indeed the state may be required to enable contact to take place in some circumstances.[106] The approach of the European Court has been summarised as follows in *L* v. *Finland*:

> … taking a child into care should normally be regarded as a temporary measure to be discontinued as soon as circumstances permit, and that any measures of implementation of temporary care should be consistent with the ultimate aim of reuniting the natural parent and the child. … In this regard a fair balance has to be struck between the interests of the child in remaining in public care and those of the parent in being reunited with the child. … In carrying out this balancing exercise the Court will attach particular importance to the best interests of the

---

[105] Although the mother had from time to time suffered from mental illness at the time of the birth she was in good mental health.
[106] *Glaser* v. *UK* [2000] FCR 193.

child, which depending on their nature and seriousness, may override those of the parent. In particular, the parent cannot be entitled under art. 8 of the Convention to have such measures taken as would harm the child's health and development.[107]

As this quotation reveals, the European Court has accepted that although the signatory states may have a wide margin of appreciation in deciding whether a child should be taken into care, a 'stricter scrutiny' is required in judging limitations on contact between a parent and a child in state care.[108] Further, the state intervention should be designed to enable the children and the parents (or other relatives) to retain contact and ultimately to be reunited. [109] Of course, it is permissible for the local authority to decide that reunification of parents and children is not possible, particularly if the parents pose an ongoing risk to the child. Indeed the child's right to respect for her private life or her family life with her foster parents may not permit the state to reunite the parents and children.[110] However, what is clear from the decisions of the European Court is that convincing evidence is required before it is permissible to give up on the possibility of reuniting parents and children taken into care and therefore terminate contact between them. An example of where it would be proportionate to completely sever contact would be where it has been found that the parent sexually abused the child.[111]

Procedural fairness

So far it has been argued that the Human Rights Act will impose new obligations upon the local authority and opens new avenues of legal challenge to local authorities. However, as argued earlier in this chapter, placing responsibilities on local authorities is of little effect unless there are effective procedures which enable the parent or child to challenge the decisions which are made. It is perhaps here that the HRA will have the greatest impact. Procedural fairness in the decision-making of local authorities about children is required by both article 8 and article 6.[112] Article 6(1) states that,

> in the determination of his civil rights and obligations … everyone is entitled to a fair and public hearing within a reasonable time by an independent and impartial tribunal established by law.

---

[107] *L* v. *Finland* [2000] 3 FCR 219, at p. 241.
[108] *S and G* v. *Italy* [2000] 2 FLR 771.
[109] *Scott* v. *UK* [2000] 1 FLR 958.
[110] *L* v. *Finland* [2000] 3 FCR 219, at p. 238–239.
[111] *L* v. *Finland* [2000] 3 FCR 219; [2000] 2 FLR 118.
[112] Emphasised in *W* v. *UK* (1987) 10 EHRR 29.

'Civil rights' are not comprehensively defined in European case law, but broadly speaking they relate to private rather than public law rights.

The case of *R* v. *UK*[113] concerned the internal (pre-Children Act) procedures used by the local authority to assume parental rights over the applicant's children and to terminate her access to them. It also considered the absence of remedies against the local authority's decisions and the length of certain related judicial proceedings. In finding that articles 8 and 6(1) had been violated, the court held that decisions made by local authorities within an administrative process (regarding children in the public care system) must be of a nature which 'ensures that the views and interests of the parents are made known and duly taken into account by the local authority.' The case of *McMichael* v. *UK*[114] extended this principle in a case which concerned the applicant's right to see confidential documents in a 'children's hearing' in the Scottish courts. The European Court confirmed that, although Article 8 contains no explicit procedural requirements, the decision-making process leading to measures of interference must be fair and such as to afford due respect to the interests safeguarded by article 8. This is because, as the European Court in *Kroon* v. *Netherlands*[115] stressed, the key purpose of article 8 is to protect families from arbitrary actions by public authorities. It should be stressed that the procedural protections are not restricted to the actual making of the care order, but cover subsequent decisions about how the child should be treated in care.[116]

Before setting out the particular procedural requirements required by article 6 it should be stated that the European Court in *W* v. *UK*[117] has stressed:

> The Court recognises that, in reaching decisions in so sensitive an area, local authorities are faced with a task that is extremely difficult. To require them to follow on each occasions an inflexible procedure would only add to their problems. They must therefore be allowed a measure of discretion in this respect.

This suggests that although the European Convention sees protection of parental rights through procedural fairness as an important aspect of the Convention in this area, the law must also recognise that this is not an area of the law where legalistic requirements of procedural protection is appropriate. Bearing that in mind, what follows is a list of some of the elements of procedural fairness that may be required by articles 6 and 8. It does not purport to be a complete list.

---

[113] [1987] 10 EHRR 74.
[114] [1995] 20 EHRR 205.
[115] (1994) 19 EHRR 263.
[116] *Olsson* v. *Sweden* (1998) 11 EHRR 259.
[117] *W* v. *UK* (1988) 10 EHRR 29.

(1) Notice

Parents should normally be given notice of any local authority plans to remove their children.[118] However, in an emergency, it would be consistent with the European Convention to remove a child after an *ex parte* application as long as there is an opportunity to challenge the removal within a reasonable length of time.[119]

(2) There must be a means of challenging local authority decisions

Articles 6 and 8 require there to be a procedure by which any decision of a local authority can be challenged. Article 6 specifically states that 'in the determination of his civil rights and obligations ... everyone is entitled to a fair and public hearing'. However in *Elsholz* v. *Germany*[120] the European Court indicated that this does not mean that on every occasion where someone wishes to challenge the decision of a local authority he or she has a right to have access to a public court hearing. Instead the court will consider 'whether the proceedings as a whole ...were fair'. What precisely this will involve will depend on the facts of the particular case. An appeals process may require an oral hearing, especially if there are important issues which cannot be resolved on the written materials.[121] For example, before a child is taken into care an oral hearing will be required before an independent tribunal at which the parents should be able to express their views and cross-examine witnesses,[122] unless the circumstances are exceptional.[123] This is not to say that an oral hearing is required whenever a decision is made about a child in care. In *L* v. *Finland*[124] the European Court found that the fact that there was not an oral hearing when contact with a child in care was restricted was not in breach of article 6. This was because when seen in the light of all the proceedings which related to the child while in care, most of which had involved an oral hearing, it could not be said that the procedures taken as a whole were unfair.

(3) Reasons for decisions

Swindells *et al* have suggested that article 6 includes a requirement that if a court or local authority makes an important decision concerning a child in care it must provide reasons for its decisions.[125] However all that the wording of article 6 requires is that 'judgment shall be

---

[118]   *K and T* v. *Finland* [2000] 3 FCR 248; [2000] 2 FLR 79.

[119]   *Re J (Abduction: Wrongful Removal)* [2000] 1 FLR 78.

[120]   [2000] 2 FLR 486.

[121]   *Elsholz* v. *Germany* [2000] 2 FLR 486.

[122]   *McMichael* v. *UK* (1995) 20 EHRR 205.

[123]   *L* v. *Finland* [2000] 3 FCR 219; [2000] 2 FLR 118.

[124]   [2000] 3 FCR 219; [2000] 2 FLR 118.

[125]   H. Swindells, A. Neaves, M. Kushner and R. Skilbeck, *Family Law and the Human Rights Act 1998* (1999, Jordans), at p. 105.

pronounced publicly'; the wording of the article itself does not explicitly require reasons for the judgment. That said, it is certainly arguable that the phrase 'fair hearing' in article 6 necessarily incorporates the requirement that reasons are given for any judgment.

(4) Access to legal advice

Articles 6 and 8 have been held by Lord Nicholls in *Re L (Police Investigation: Privilege)*[126] to include, in the context of care proceedings at least, the right of access of confidential legal advice.

(5) Attendance at decision-making meetings

Normally parents should be allowed to attend meetings at which decisions are made concerning children in care. However, this is not an absolute right. In *Scott v. UK*,[127] although the mother was not permitted to attend one important meeting held by the local authority which concerned her child, although there were many others where she was allowed to attend. Looking at the procedures used to make decisions relating to the child as a whole there was no breach of her article 6 rights. The court did stress the fact that she had had before the meeting ample opportunity to raise issues, and had been told of the result of the meeting.

(6) Access to documentation

If there is a hearing which a parent is to entitled to attend then parents should be entitled to all relevant reports or documents, unless it would be contrary to the interests of children to reveal the documents to the parents.[128]

(7) Keeping parents informed

S and G v. Italy[129] has recently recognised that the state has a duty to communicate with parents and provide information to them concerning children in their care. In that case the leaders of a children's home had criminal antecedents and there were also concerns that they were affecting the children's attitudes towards their mother. It was held by the European Court that this information should have been passed on to the children's mother.

(8) Delay in decision-making should be avoided

The European Court has made it clear that delay should be avoided when local authorities make decisions over children who are in care or are being taken into care.[130] Speed is particularly important in relation

---

[126] [1996] 1 FLR 731.
[127] [2000] 1 FLR 938.
[128] *L v. UK* [2000] 2 FLR 225.
[129] [2000] 2 FLR 771, at p. 807.
[130] *Scott v. UK* [2000] 1 FLR 958.

to contact issues because if there is a lengthy time during which children do not see their parents, restarting contact may prove difficult and any hope of reunification may be dashed.[131]

Now we shall turn to consider the potential impact of the HRA's requirement for procedural fairness on UK law.

The likely impact of the HRA on decision-making in public law cases

As the European Court has accepted that articles 6 and/or 8 apply to cases involving compulsory state intervention, we suggest that certain local authority decision-making procedures may need to be overhauled in order to guarantee procedural fairness. First, despite the detailed and clear expectations about how the enquiries should be conducted in the new guidance, the lack of procedural *requirements* within the child protection framework means that a fair process is not guaranteed for those who may wish to challenge decisions and plans, such as parents and children. Indeed it could be argued that the only way this could be achieved would be to formalise it with access to an impartial and independent tribunal to review decisions which are challenged. This might mean, for example, that those presenting information to a child protection conference (parents and professionals alike) should not be involved in decision-making, which should be left to the chair or a panel of independent child-care professionals who can hear the evidence and assess the risk; that there should be a specific time limit for the advance disclosure of reports to parents and older children; that the latter should have a *right* to make representations with no possibility of parents being excluded except in very exceptional circumstances (for example, where there were safety issues around attendance); and that there should be a right to appeal against being placed on the child protection register to a judicial body where appropriate. Secondly, long-term or 'permanency' planning for children in care may also need to become a more formalised process where there is a departure from the care plan presented to the court in care proceedings. The suggestion that the courts may need to oversee the implementation of care plans in the current review of adoption law may need to be given serious attention if this problem is to be redressed.

This is particularly important because of the lack of judicial remedies or other opportunities available to challenge such decisions at present. The complaints procedures introduced by Children Act 1989, section 26, were intended as a mechanism for ensuring local authority accountability in this context. However, they fall short of guaranteeing procedural fairness

---

[131] *Glaser* v. *UK* [2000] 3 FCR 193.

because, despite comprising an independent element, they are powerless to force a change of decision on the local authority.[132] The only other avenues open to those wishing to challenge local authority decisions are, applying to discharge the care order under s. 39, or applying for judicial review (JR) where, for example, the authority has acted unreasonably, or is in breach of a statutory duty).[133] However, neither are likely to be very successful. A discharge application may be doomed because the effect would mean that the child would return home, which may not be a realistic or safe alternative to the local authority's plan. A judicial review application may be equally fated for two reasons: firstly, because it has been discouraged as an appropriate remedy in case law, certainly in relation to child protection;[134] and secondly, because it is a discretionary remedy which may not be granted even if grounds are established, because events may have moved on in the child's life by the time of the hearing so as to make any change of decision meaningless. Only an appeal to an independent tribunal or court would ensure protection of the rights under the HRA to procedural fairness and protection of the parents or child's rights not have their family or private life disproportionately interfered with.

Conclusions

The implementation of the HRA provides a very good opportunity to revisit local authority decision-making powers in respect of children in their area. In the analysis in this chapter of the way decisions are made in relation to vulnerable children there has been no suggestion that local authorities act in bad faith, or that children's safety and protection should in any way be compromised in the name of ensuring there has been procedural fairness. However, it is inevitable that there will be disputes from time to time between social workers and family members about what will best safeguard and promote a child's welfare. When such disputes occur in an administrative context, we suggest that articles 6 and 8 implicitly, if not explicitly, at the very least require there to be access to an independent and impartial tribunal which can adjudicate upon the

---

[132] S. 26(7) Children Act 1989 provides that the local authority must have 'due regard' to the findings of the complaints officer/panel, but ultimately it makes the decision about how the matter will proceed. This means that it can in effect ignore the outcome of the complaints process.

[133] See for example the case of *R* v. *A Metropolitan Borough Council ex parte J*, (2000) 24 *Adoption and Fostering* 61.

[134] See for example footnote 29.

dispute where it has not already been subject to judicial scrutiny.[135] No doubt family lawyers will be looking out for cases in the coming months to test the applicability of these articles to public law cases under the HRA. Until then we can only speculate that the general ethos of the ECHR in protecting the individual from unwarranted intrusion by the state should place local authority accountability for its decision-making firmly on the agenda for debate when considering the likely impact of the HRA. This would be most welcome. Improved procedural fairness in this context will not only promote the rights of parents and children, it would improve the quality of the decisions made in respect of children.

Further reading

Department of Health, *Child Protection: Messages from Research* (1995, HMSO).

Department of Health, *Learning the Lessons, The Government's Response to Lost in Care, the Report of the Tribunal of Enquiry into the Abuse of Children in Care in former County Council Areas of Gwynedd and Clwyd since 1974* (2000, Department of Health).

Department of Health, *Working Together to Safeguard Children* (1999, Stationery Office).

Fortin, 'The HRA's impact on litigation involving children and their families' [1999] *Child and Family Law Quarterly* 239.

Hayes, 'The Proper Role of the Courts in Child Care Cases' [1996] *Child and Family Law Quarterly* 201.

Lindley, 'State Intervention and Parental Autonomy in Children's Cases: Have We Got the Balance Right?' in A. Bainham, S. Day Sclater, and M. Richards (eds), *What is a Parent?* (1999, Hart).

Lindley, 'Working Together 2000: How will Parents Fare Under the New Child Protection Process?' [2000] *Child and Family Law Quarterly* 1.

Lyon, 'Children and the Law – Towards 2000 and Beyond. An Essay in Human Rights, Social Policy and the Law' in C. Bridge (ed.) *Family Law Towards the Millennium* (1997, Butterworth).

Smith, 'Judicial Power and Local Authority Discretion – the Contested Frontier' [1997] *Child and Family Law Quarterly* 243.

Voice for the Child in Care, *Shout to be Heard* (1998, VCC).

Voice for the Child in Care, *How do Young People and Children Get their Voices Heard?* (1998, VCC).

---

[135] This occurs in relation to decisions made in other administrative contexts such as immigration and social security, where there is access to the Immigration Appeals Tribunal and Social Security Appeals Tribunal. It is not clear what the rationale is for not having equivalent access to a tribunal when such decisions are made about the care of children, for whom the parents have parental responsibility.

6

Adoption law:
a balance of interests

Caroline Bridge

Introduction

Formal legal adoption is a relatively modern concept. Its roots lie in the changes evident in society after the first world war: numbers of orphaned children needed the permanency and stability that family life supposedly provided and cohabitation, which had become increasingly common, gave rise to the need for secure legal arrangements for both children and birth parents. The first Adoption Act was passed in 1926 with these social purposes in mind.[1] In comparison with the current law that Act was limited. It did not provide for the child's full integration into the adoptive family, it set out only limited grounds for permitting adoption without parental consent, and did not fully address inheritance issues. Adoption was, as Cretney and Masson suggest, a 'private or amateur activity'.[2]

But as the nature of social problems changed so the nature and purpose of adoption also changed. Adoption became a way of dealing with some of the uncomfortable social and human problems that emerged during the 1950s and 60s. Its upsurge during this period was due, primarily, to the increasing numbers of young single mothers unable to care for their illegitimate babies. Social, moral, financial and a variety of practical pressures combined to present adoption as the way out for both mother and child. By having the baby adopted straight after birth the mother was perceived as enabled to resume her life untarnished by the product of past immoral conduct. For the baby, adoption was widely perceived as a lucky escape from the shame of illegitimacy. Illegitimacy still carried a social stigma yet the numbers of such births were high. Sexual liberation had

---

[1] The Adoption of Children Act 1926.
[2] *Principles of Family Law* (1997, Sweet & Maxwell) at p. 877 and Triseliotis (1995) 2 Ad and Fostering 37, at p. 39.

arrived but the contraceptive pill had yet to become widely available and abortion was unlawful./As a result, large numbers of white babies were adopted by childless married couples – those whom Lowe and Douglas describe as seeking to avoid the 'oppressive taint of infertility'.[3] In a secretive process[4] designed to facilitate an irrevocable transfer of all legal rights and powers from birth parents to adoptive parents, such babies became the lawful offspring of their new family, born to them as 'a child of the marriage'.[5] The image thus conjured up is one of a traditional family, more redolent of the 1950s than the twenty-first century, and although it smacks of legislation of earlier times, that is not so.

The Adoption Act 1976, consolidating the recommendations of the Houghton Committee enacted in the Children Act 1975 and the Adoption Acts 1958 to 1964, came into force in 1988. It remains the current law, despite government consultation in 1989,[6] a White Paper in 1993[7] and a draft Bill in 1996.[8] Now adoption has returned to the political agenda. Major research studies have been reported,[9] a new review has been published by the Department of Health,[10] issues about trans-racial adoption, open adoption and adoption by single and homosexual parents are being publicly debated, and the Prime Minister himself announced a series of measures to promote and speed up the adoption process.[11] Further consultation on a range of proposals was launched, a White Paper was published in December 2000[12] and new legislation is promised during 2001. The essence of the prompt for more appropriate regulation lies in the changing use being made of adoption. Adoption today is primarily about older children. As fewer babies are placed for adoption, concern centres on those children who are often emotionally damaged by years in care, sometimes disabled or of mixed race, and perceived as needing a permanent home. Adoption is now an integral part of the child care strategy offered by local authorities and professional adoption agencies.[13]

---

[3] Lowe and Douglas, *Bromley's Family Law* (1998, Butterworth) at p. 616.

[4] The court can make an adoption order without the mother knowing the identity of the adopters.

[5] Adoption Act 1976, s. 39.

[6] Interdepartmental Review of Adoption Law Discussion Papers 1990–1994

[7] *Adoption: the Future* Cm 2288 (1993, HMSO).

[8] *Adoption – a service for children* (1996, HMSO).

[9] A large programme of adoption research was commissioned by the Department of Health with Lowe and Murch *et al*, *Supporting Adoption – reframing the approach* (BAFF) (1999, Department of Health) being part of that larger project.

[10] *Adoption Now – messages from research* (2000), Department of Health, compiled by Emeritus Professor Parker, bringing together the most recent research on adoption and showing a rise of 16 per cent since 1998 in the number of children placed for adoption.

[11] Statement made 7 July 2000, see *The Prime Minister's Review of Adoption* (Performance and Innovation Unit).

[12] *Adoption – a new approach* (29 December 2000).

[13] Lowe and Murch (1999) *op. cit.* n. 9 at p. 9.

However, despite recognition of the many changes, the Adoption Act 1976, albeit amended by the Children Act 1989, still reflects the social, legal and moral attitudes of previous decades.

Conceptual and philosophical tensions within the framework of adoption law and practice abound. Conflict exists, for example, between the fundamental principle of maintaining family relationships as reflected in the Children Act 1989, and the decision to place older children in care with prospective adopters. These children have memories and attachments from the past and although the permanency of adoption may be considered the most desirable outcome in terms of future security and stability, the maintenance of contact with that past may also be fundamental to future emotional well being. Conceptual tensions are inherent in the notion of a complete and irrevocable legal transference of parental responsibility for a child and the existence of a contact agreement or order facilitating contact between the child and birth parents, siblings or wider family. Can adoption as opposed to a residence order ever be entirely appropriate in these circumstances? Or does the legal presumption in favour of the natural parent require ongoing contact in the child's interests in most cases?

Such dilemmas demand a revisiting of the problems inherent in striking a balance between the interests of the three sets of participants in the adoption triangle – those of the child, birth parents, and adoptive parents. The welfare of the child is central to these considerations yet may be tempered by the interests of others. Is the child's interest truly the first concern[14] or does the law's emphasis on the blood tie, with the child being brought up by a natural parent, however imperfect, alter the balance of interests? Where will the balance lie when the natural parent is confronted with stable loving adopters, already attached to the child? Do the interests of the adoptive parents carry any significant weight? They are, after all, indispensable to the process. Fundamental to these issues is the question of the circumstances and grounds that should prevail before a child is moved from the natural parents and placed with an adoptive family. How should the discretion to dispense with the natural parent's agreement to the adoption be exercised? The Human Rights Act 1998 has the potential to shift the balance as between the three sets of interests, given that it will require the courts to protect the rights of adults as well as children[15] although, as Jonathan Herring asserts, the European Court, thus far, has been successful in promoting the welfare of the child despite its emphasis on rights.[16]

---

[14]   Adoption Act 1976, s. 6.

[15]   But a fair balance has to be struck between the interests of the child and those of the parent with the court attaching particular interest to the best interests of the child. See *Johansen* v. *Norway* (1996) 23 EHRR 33.

[16]   'The Human Rights Act and the Welfare Principle in Family Law – conflicting or complementary?' [1999] *Child and Family Law Quarterly* 223.

Ideological tensions abound in the law and practice of adoption. This is particularly so in relation to issues such as ethnicity and racial identity. The placement of mixed race children with white adopters is contentious and, in the interests of a 'same race' matching policy, is avoided entirely by some local authorities. Yet in the context of children lingering ever longer in care, a paucity of suitable black or mixed race adopters, and the Children Act requirement that local authorities give these matters 'due consideration',[17] the issue remains in the forefront of policy and practice debates. If adoption still seeks to replicate the traditional nuclear family, as it attempted to do in earlier decades, further questions about the definition of family today are raised. Recognition of a diverse range of family forms is as important as recognition of cultural and religious diversity, but this prompts a further debate around the concept of status and contract in family law. Is the ideal of permanency in adoption still one of providing life-long membership of the traditional family – the status of family member, of belonging to a unit? Alternatively, could adoption be more aptly considered within the context of a general move from status to contract in family law – a contract for permanent child care? Would this be so in relation to inter-country adoption or is that a service designed to meet the needs of childless couples or single people? Perhaps inter-country adoption is an altruistic response, prompted by humanitarian concerns.

The purpose of this chapter is to explore some of these key issues and analyse the tensions and debates inherent in the law, policy and practice of adoption. The aim is to highlight particular conceptual themes that emerge from the interplay of interests and to consider these within the context of the broader philosophical approaches to family law in England and Wales today. These are the issues with which the local authorities, the courts and the government have to grapple and all too often they pull in different directions.

Modern adoption law

Adoption Act 1976

In order to set the particular issues in their rightful context, it is necessary to give a brief overview of the adoption process and the legal changes brought about by the Children Act 1989. The provision of a new and permanent home for a child and the severance of legal links with the birth family is the primary purpose of adoption law. Simply put, the child is moved, irrevocably, from one family to another. Section 12 (1) of the Adoption Act 1976 provides for the transfer of parental responsibility from

---

[17] Children Act 1989, s. 22(5)(c).

birth parents to the adoptive parents.[18] The adoptive parents thus take on all those attributes of legal parenthood that pertain to the parents of children born within marriage or to the unmarried mother alone [19] and the child is treated for succession and citizenship purposes as a member of the adoptive family.[20] The child must be under 18,[21] the adoptive parents at least 21,[22] and the adoption order made on the application of one person[23] or otherwise by a married couple. Although these legal requirements appear straightforward, the reality is that far more stringent criteria are applied by agencies as the demand for available children to adopt outstrips the supply. However, although this is the case for what are, effectively, stranger adoptions, step-parent and relative adoptions account for more than half the total of all adoptions today.[24] This is so despite being far removed from the traditional notion of adoption and creating a potential for distorting family relationships and severing links with a birth parent after divorce or separation.

Adoption practice is heavily regulated. In terms of process, local authority social services departments play a powerful and central role, investigating, assessing[25] and providing reports to the court.[26] While payment[27] and private placements of children are prohibited[28] placement with prospective adopters is a vital part of the adoption process.[29] It is then

---

[18] Amended by the Children Act 1989, Sch. 10, para. 3.

[19] Children Act 1989, s. 2(1). The unmarried father who acquires parental responsibility by either order or agreement under s. 4 of the Children Act receives a lesser form of responsibility in that it may be removed by court order on the application of the child or mother.

[20] Under s. 39(1) of the Adoption Act 1976, the child gains the right to inherit on the intestacy of his adoptive parents rather than his birth parents and under the British Nationality Act 1981 s. 1(5) he becomes a British citizen if he was not already one, once he is adopted by a British citizen. The prohibited degrees of marriage between the adopted child and his birth family are retained.

[21] S. 12(5). In *Re B (Adoption Order: Nationality)* [1999] 1 FLR 907 the House of Lords ruled that there should be an order in relation to a child of nearly 18 when the process was being used essentially to confer citizenship.

[22] S. 14(1A), although one adoptive parent need only be 18 if their spouse is 21 and either is the mother or father of the child.

[23] This could, for example, be one cohabiting partner with a joint residence order made in favour of both partners.

[24] *Judicial Statistics 1999* (2000, HMSO).

[25] The agency is required to establish a panel which considers all the information obtained about the prospective adopters and the child and recommend a 'match'. The agency then makes the final decision.

[26] Adoption Agencies Regulations 1983 prescribe the duties of voluntary agencies and the Adoption Rules 1984 prescribe the content of the report.

[27] Adoption Act 1976, s. 57.

[28] Adoption Act 1976, s. 11(1).

[29] The agency must review the placement if no application for an adoption order is made within three months.

up to the adopters to apply for the order. Again the statute prescribes certain preconditions. The child placed by an agency or related to the adopters must be at least 19 weeks old and at all times during the 13 weeks preceding the date when the order is due to be made must have made his home with them.[30] The court must be satisfied that all is well between the child and adopters and that sufficient assessment has taken place. The child's wishes must be ascertained and given due consideration.[31]

The order can only be made by a court.[32] This is only right as the consequences are enormous. Not only does the child gain new and permanent parents but the old ones lose their parental responsibility. An adoption or freeing order is the only way in which this major step can be achieved. And the natural parent or guardian must agree, freely, unconditionally and with full understanding, to the making of the order. This agreement[33] must be in relation to specific adopters – although the latter can retain anonymity and thus the secrecy of the adoption – and may be withdrawn at any time before the making of the order. To help eliminate this fear for adopters and the child, the statute provides that a court may make a freeing order thus effectively declaring that a child is free for adoption without further evidence of parental consent.[34] Where parents do not agree to the making of the adoption or freeing order, the court may dispense with agreement but only in accordance with restricted grounds.[35] These provisions have given rise to a considerable amount of case law and section 16(2)(b) and its requirement for reasonableness on the part of the parent has prompted much of the jurisprudence considered later in this chapter. Section 6 of the Adoption Act 1976 is the central core of the court's inquiry. In reaching its decision, the court must seek to safeguard and promote the welfare of the child throughout his childhood and only when this is so will it consider whether to dispense with a parent's agreement. It is immediately noticeable that the welfare of the child is *not* the court's paramount concern as it is in any question relating to upbringing although it clearly outweighs all other considerations. In terms of a balancing of all the interests involved the child's predominates, but the court can, of course, consider other matters.

---

[30] Adoption Act 1976, s. 13(1).
[31] Under the 1996 draft Adoption Bill consent is required where the child is aged 12 or over.
[32] As authorised by s. 62 of the Adoption Act 1976. Most applications are made in the county court although the three tiers of court up to and including the High Court share jurisdiction.
[33] The agreement of those with parental responsibility is required. This does not therefore include the unmarried father unless he has parental responsibility.
[34] Adoption Act 1976, s. 18.

The Children Act and adoption law

It is the fundamental change of legal status at the core of adoption that distinguishes it from proceedings under the Children Act 1989. While that Act brings in a range of measures which address the upbringing of children, the Adoption Act 1976 creates a total and irrevocable legal transplant between one set of parents and another. In the Children Act, the child's welfare is the court's paramount concern while in adoption the child's interests are the first consideration. Where court orders regulating upbringing can be varied, set aside or discharged, adoption is, effectively, for life. This is why, in part, adoption was not incorporated in the reforms brought about by the Children Act, but was intended to be addressed later as part of a 'rolling programme' of family law reform. Nonetheless, some changes were introduced by the Children Act.[36] In particular, adoption proceedings were listed as 'family proceedings'[37] and thus the court hearing an adoption application also acquired the jurisdiction to make a contact, residence or other section 8 order whether or not any such application had been made. The machinery was thus in place to consider alternatives to adoption. In this way the Children Act reform enabled greater openness in adoption and enhanced flexibility in the process regularising a child's position within a family. But whereas residence provides a means of securing a degree of stability for a child in the sense of determining where he or she is to live, it bears no comparison to the life-long change of status brought about by adoption. The choice facing a court between a residence order and an adoption order focuses intensely on the very essence of adoption – its complete legal severance and its permanency. Only where these attributes will promote the child's welfare will they be preferred to the regularised care and retention of parental rights that a residence order offers.[38]

Inter-country adoption

The decline in the number of babies available for adoption – albeit large numbers of older children in care are still awaiting adoptive placements – has created continued interest in adopting a young child or infant from

---

[35] Adoption Act 1976, s. 16.

[36] The minimum age for adopters was amended thus permitting a joint application by a married couple where the parent of the child is at least 18 and the other spouse at least 21. Adoption Act 1976, s. 14(1B).

[37] Children Act 1989, s. 8(4)(d).

[38] In *Re M (Adoption or Residence)* [1998] 1 FLR 570, CA, there was a difference of judicial opinion as to whether adoption or residence would best serve the child's interests. The case was complicated by the prospective adopters' threat to reject the child if an adoption order were not made. In the event a residence order was made with the hope that the adopters would accept the solution.

abroad. Whether prompted by humanitarian concerns such as the sight of abandoned infants in Romanian orphanages, or the desire of a childless couple or single person (who have possibly not received local authority approval in this country) for a baby, the laws and procedures of this country and those of the child's country of domicile have to be met. Attempts have been made to regulate and control inter-country adoption in the interests of children.[39] For example, the Hague Convention on the Protection of Children and Co-operation in Respect of Inter-country Adoption 1993 aims to reinforce a legal standard affecting children and achieve uniformity between states[40] and, more recently, the International (Inter-Country Aspects) Act 1999 attempts to ensure that children adopted from overseas have the same protection as others. Although it is beyond the scope of this chapter to address the particular policy issues in inter-country adoption it should be noted that cases coming before English courts may well highlight some of the major domestic dilemmas – very often in a dramatic way.[41]

Adoption issues

Family forms and family values

The process of adoption is about children finding permanent substitute families. The emphasis is on permanence and families. In this sense adoption enhances the status of the family as an institution. However, the particular family form embraced by adoption law and practice, identified as superior and promulgated by legislative statements of family values generally, is that of the nuclear married family. Support for the institution of marriage and a 'damned by faint praise' attitude towards cohabiting couples is evident in the Family Law Act 1996, for example.[42] The Adoption Act itself uses the language of marriage and wedlock, asserting

---

[39] In *Re R (Inter-country Adoptions: Practice)* [1999] 1 FLR 1042, Bracewell J urged the effective use of The Department of Health Guide to Inter-country Adoption (Practice and Procedure) 1997 in order to safeguard and protect the welfare of children in inter-country adoptions.

[40] See J. Rosenblatt, *International Conventions Affecting Children* (2000, Kluwer Law International) for the full text and discussion of the Hague Convention.

[41] For example *Re C (Adoption: Legality)* [1999] 1 FLR 370 where the child's welfare demanded that the court impose a lower standard of protection for the child than would have been the case in the domestic context; and *Re R (No 1) (Inter-country Adoption)* [1999] 1 FLR 1014, where Romanian parents were deceived into permitting their daughter to visit England with prospective adopters.

[42] The principles in s. 1 are headed by the directive, 'the institution of marriage is to be supported' while s. 41(2) states that cohabitants 'have not given each other the commitment involved in marriage'.

Family Law: issues, debates, policy

that the adopted child be treated as if 'born to the adopter in wedlock'.[43] These family values are reflected in the adoption process. The attitudes permeating the selection of adopters are intensely focused on marriage and a lifestyle which approximates with the social worker's and adoption panel's values and morals. An acceptable model of family life is thus devised and sought amongst prospective adopters, whose initial aim in turn must surely be to second guess the moral and family values of those with the statutory powers. It is, supposedly, this family form which offers stability and security and promotes the long term well-bring of its members. It is portrayed as powerful yet protective, with its members accepted, supported and loved unconditionally.

Whilst this model of family life is unlikely to be realised by many, agencies are undoubtedly intent upon seeking the ideal – stable, non-smoking, fit, active, intelligent, probably white, young happily married couples as prospective adopters. In a recent major study by Lowe and Murch, 91 per cent of adoptive families in the particular research sample comprised two married adults, while just 9 per cent were described as single parent families.[44] Within the same study older children in care and seeking adoption were shown to want a sense of *belonging* with 'parents' who were 'nice', 'kind', 'funny' and 'normal', who would care for them well, love them and bring them up properly.[45] Children wanted to know about their new parents' jobs, hobbies, activities, appearance and some-times their house and garden. These images represent the very model of the nuclear married family, in its own home with other children, extended family and pets. It can thus be argued that adoption law and practice privileges the traditional, male-headed, private, heterosexual, 'normal' married family – that it holds up this one family form as aspirational, powerful and superior. Even the 1993 Government White Paper supports this perception, asserting that adopted children must have the same prospect as other children of a stable and enduring relationship with two parents and therefore 'there must be a strong presumption in favour of adoption by married couples'.[46] The 2000 White Paper, however, makes no such distinction but simply asserts that 'National Standards ... will make it clear that people will not be automatically excluded from adoption on grounds of age, health or other'.[47] But while the power of the existing ideal actively excludes non-traditional couples it might also blind local authorities to seeing that some married couples are not ideal. In other

[43] Adoption Act 1976, s. 39 (1) (a) and (b).
[44] Lowe and Murch *et al, Supporting Adoption – Reframing the Approach* (1999, BAAF) at p. 72, 76.
[45] Thomas and Beckford *Adopted Children Speaking* (1999, BAAF) at p. 38.
[46] *Adoption: The Future,* DOH (1993) at para. 4.37.
[47] *Adoption – a new approach* (December, 2000) at para. 6.22.

words, the focus on an ideal which excludes some suitable adopters may also have the effect of including inappropriate adopters.

Orders in favour of parents and step-parents conform, in general, to the nuclear marital family ideal. It is often the mother and her new husband who seek to adopt the child, severing links with the father and his extended family but legally integrating the child into the new family.[48] Where a natural parent has had virtually no contact with the child, or the child has – with good reason – come to fear the natural father,[49] such adoptions may enhance the child's welfare. But where a valuable relationship is effectively cancelled out the application is likely to be refused.[50] Although a residence order is likely in situations which simply call for the regularisation of the child's position[51] the proportion of step-parent adoptions has risen to the extent that they now comprise 55 per cent of all adoptions. As Barton notes, the most 'fruitful class-free – if not gender-free – route to adoption is through marriage to the mother of someone else's children'.[52] The 2000 White Paper will not alter this position. In contrast, adoptions by relatives are less likely as these run a high risk of distorting family relationships.[53]

However, whilst adoption agencies seek stability and permanence for children within the bosom of the nuclear family, the diverse nature of the family and family forms is beginning to be recognised more widely in English law. Of primary importance in extending the legal definition of the family, albeit within a particular context, is the House of Lords decision in *Fitzpatrick* v. *Sterling Housing Association Ltd.*[54] Here the issue was whether

[48] Following recommendations by the Houghton Committee, which formed the view that such adoptions were inappropriate, the courts were required to make more use of the alternative orders, such as custodianship. However, these reforms failed and were formally repealed by the Children Act 1989.

[49] As in *Re B (Adoption: Father's Objections)* [1999] 2 FLR 215.

[50] *Re P (Minors) (Adoption)* [1989] 1 FLR 1. More recently the Court of Appeal in *Re G (Adoption Order)* [1999] 1 FLR 400 refused to make a step-parent adoption order and gave the natural father's interests greater weight.

[51] *The Review of Adoption Law* (1992) at paras. 19.2–3 considered that step-parent adoptions might still be valuable in some cases but proposed that the birth parent should not have to adopt their own child and proposed a new form of adoption order for step-parents. The 1993 White Paper described this as a Parental Responsibility Agreement or Order, to be entered into by the birth parent and his or her new spouse. In contrast, the 2000 White Paper makes no special provision for step-parent adoptions.

[52] Barton, 'Adoption – The Prime Minister's Review' [2000] *Family Law* 731.

[53] The draft Adoption Bill 1996 makes special provision for relative adoptions. In 'In Whose Best Interests? – post-adoption contact with the birth family' [1998] *Child and Family Law Quarterly* 53, at p. 67–69 Ryburn makes the point that the best placements for children are often found within the 'wider kin network' and urges greater consideration to be given to adoption within the extended family. The focus on speeding up the adoption process, so integral to the proposals in the 2000 White Paper, may well detract from a proper exploration of placement within the extended family.

[54] [1999] 2 FLR 1027 HL.

a homosexual man who had lived with his male partner in a stable and monogamous relationship for 18 years was entitled to succeed to a protected tenancy. In holding, by a majority, that a same-sex partner could be regarded in law as a member of a tenant's family, the House of Lords articulated those attributes of a relationship that helped determine it as familial – the necessary hallmarks of mutual interdependence, a sharing of lives, of caring and love and of commitment and support. Although the speeches in the House of Lords made clear that the judgment was not about the rights of homosexuals as such but about the particular provisions of the Rent Act 1997, the question can be asked – where would such a 'family' stand in relation to adoption criteria?

Certainly the Adoption Act makes no provision for joint applications from other than a married couple. In this, the Act upholds the traditional norm. It does, however, allow an adoption application from a single person[55] whether or not that person cohabits with another or does so in a homosexual or heterosexual relationship. But while there is a world of difference between the legal definition of a prospective adopter and the actual selection criteria used by agencies, the overwhelming majority of applications are from married couples, albeit many are step-parent applications.[56] In the Lowe and Murch study, just 5 per cent of approved adopters across the range of statutory and voluntary agencies were single people living without a partner or spouse and a tiny proportion of that number was homosexual.[57] Given the well-known stringency of agency demands this is not surprising. Nonetheless, the issue of homosexual adopters and thus of alternative family forms has been judicially considered. In *Re W (Adoption: Homosexual Adopter)*[58] a girl was placed (after several previous disrupted placements) with a family comprising two women living together in a lesbian relationship. The matter came before the court as freeing proceedings rather than an adoption application, thus avoiding direct confrontation between the prospective adopter and the natural mother.[59] The latter had objected on the ground that an adoption order in favour of a person living in a homosexual relationship was contrary to public policy. The High Court nonetheless granted the local authority's application stressing that its duty was to promote the welfare of the child, that the child had thrived in the placement and that there were

---

[55] Adoption Act 1976, s. 15.

[56] A married woman may adopt jointly with her partner, unlike a cohabiting woman who must adopt as a single person. Step-parents adopting with a natural parent made up 34 per cent of the total in Murch *et al, Pathways to Adoption* (1993), Table 2.3.

[57] The responding agencies approved 1,932 families, 96 single parents, including 3 homosexual adopters.

[58] [1997] 2 FLR 406.

[59] This procedure had also been used in *Re E (Adoption: Freeing Order)* [1995] 1 FLR 382 where the prospective adopter was lesbian and the natural mother objected.

no public policy grounds excluding a homosexual person from applying to adopt. However, this case did not present a major advance in gay rights[60] given the significance of agency policies in preferring the married family and no government proposal to permit joint adoptions by other than heterosexual married couples.[61]

It remains the case that homosexual adopters are only likely to succeed where the child has already proved difficult to place, either because of extremely disturbed behaviour or special physical or emotional needs. *Re E (Adoption: Freeing Order)*[62] is an example of a natural mother's objections to a single lesbian adopter being overruled in relation to a very difficult-to-place girl from a chaotic background. There the first instance judge concluded that 'it is undesirable that [the child] should have gone to a lesbian … but this case is a special one' – a position endorsed in the Court of Appeal.[63] Although each case will turn on its own facts and the child's welfare must be weighed in the balance alongside the qualities of the prospective adopter, the homosexual family[64] will not be regarded as in the forefront of potential adopters. As the judgment in *Re E* makes clear, homosexual adopters are second-best and only in comparison with a childhood in care will they be perceived as a less detrimental alternative. Adoption law and practice thus introduces a ranking of family forms, with the traditional norm granted an overall superior position.

Currently a single cohabitant might be granted an adoption order with a joint residence order made in favour of both parties[65] – a procedure noted as virtually constituting a backdoor method for cohabiting couples to adopt a child jointly.[66] While statistics might indicate that a number of single people are becoming adoptive parents, it is more likely that the single applicant is part of a cohabiting couple. This was apparent in the Lowe and Murch study where the small percentage of single parent adopters actually consisted of cohabiting couples and divorcees.[67] Given the increasing incidence of stable heterosexual cohabitation and the numbers of older children in care awaiting adoption, it is reasonable to expect that agencies will cast their net more widely in search of adopters

---

[60] R. Bailey-Harris's comment at [1997] *Family Law* 597.
[61] *Adoption – a new approach* (2000) does not address the nature of prospective adopters at all except to assert that people will not be automatically excluded on grounds of 'age, health or other'.
[62] [1995] 1 FLR 382.
[63] *Ibid.* at p. 387.
[64] The issue of homosexuality arose in the context of dispensing with a natural parent's agreement and in *Re D (An Infant) (Adoption: Parent's Consent)* [1977] AC 602 the House of Lords concluded that a homosexual father had withheld his agreement to the adoption of his son unreasonably.
[65] See for example, *Re AB (Adoption: Joint Residence)* [1996] 1 FLR 27.
[66] Lowe and Douglas, *Bromley's Family Law* (1998, Butterworth) at p. 629.
[67] *Op. cit.* at p. 76.

and that a reformed law will enable cohabiting couples to make a joint application. But ideological debate must also broaden for without an acceptance of the diverse nature of the family local authorities are likely to remain wedded to traditional family values.

From status to contract?

One of the major themes in family law today is the move from status to contract. Family law used to be based around status, particularly that conferred by marriage. Although certain rights and remedies with respect to property and maintenance are still attributable to marriage and in that sense it still confers a legal status that does not extend to unmarried cohabitants, it is beginning to lose this central significance. Even so, the law remains reluctant to allow a married couple to regulate the consequences of a breakdown in their relationship by contract. In relation to children, the notion of marriage as a status-conferring concept is giving way to the primacy of parenthood. John Dewar refers to this as the 'child-centredness' of the modern law, primarily because of the life-long nature of parenthood compared with the increasingly dissoluble nature of the married relationship.[68] The increasing diversity of family forms, and particularly the rise in cohabiting relationships, was a further prompt to the removal of overt discrimination against children whose parents were not married. The labelling language of illegitimacy was thus removed by the Family Law Act 1987 although, as Andrew Bainham explains, it is still a moot point as to whether the very status of legitimacy/illegitimacy has been removed.[69]

Nowhere is there a better example of language and apparent status not necessarily reflecting each other than in section 39 (1) of the Adoption Act 1976. The statutory words require that the child adopted by a married couple be treated in law 'as if he had been born as a child of the marriage' while the child adopted by a single person be treated 'as if he had been born to the adopter in wedlock (but not as a child of any actual marriage of the adopter).' On the one hand this directive is an accurate reflection of the legal reality. Adoptive parents acquire all the legal attributes they would have in relation to a child born to them during their marriage and the child acquires the permanency and security that this entails – the status of membership of a traditional family if you like. But on the other hand there could be no greater fiction. The majority of adoptions today are of older children from care. They have obviously not been born to their married adoptive parents but have parents of their own whom they may remember

---

[68] For an interesting analysis see Dewar, *Law and the Family* (1992, Butterworth) at p. 71–72.
[69] 'Changing families and changing concepts – reforming the language of family law' [1998] *Child and Family Law Quarterly* 1, at p. 8.

well and may still even see. The social, as opposed to legal, reality bears no relation to the fiction created by the statutory words. Only in the adoption of babies does the language of the statute match the apparent social status of the child and her adoptive parents. Here, the parents and baby can pass themselves off as if they were the family conjured up by the statute. Secrecy, for the most part, is able to shroud the truth.

The tension between social reality and the language of section 39 is addressed by Nigel Lowe in his gift/donation versus contract/services paradigm.[70] Lowe suggests that the traditional adoption of babies – particularly prevalent in the 1960s – be labelled the 'gift/donation' model because the natural mother is perceived as, in effect, giving her baby away to the adopters who are then left to bring her up as their own. This is his closed or 'exclusive' model, closely resembling the image constructed by the language of section 39; in other words, the child is both *'de jure* and *de facto* transplanted to the adoptive family, with no further contact with the birth family'.[71] Lowe's point is that the 'mind-set' behind this 'gift/donation' model sits uneasily with today's reality. Baby adoptions have virtually ceased whereas the adoption of older children has become the norm. The gap between the legal status created by s. 39 and the reality of adoption today has thus become even greater for the majority of adopted children and Lowe proposes the construction of a new 'contract/services' model.[72] Cretney too argues that adoption law is still heavily related to legal status, to its detriment, and that it defies the general move towards the regulation of family relationships by private agreement.[73]

The essence of Lowe's new way of seeing adoption lies in understanding it as an informal contract between natural family, adoptive family and child. The contract would create a pattern of reciprocal obligations, with ongoing state and agency support, adoption allowances, updated information and post-adoption contact. The adoptive parents would effectively enter a contract to bring up a child, possibly damaged by years in care, as if he were their own. Under the current law of course he would become legally their own child, with all the accompanying advantages, but if this were also coupled with the mind set of the Lowe 'contract/services' model the new parents would view the adoption more as a life-long fostering arrangement than a life-long pretence. The argument that the notion of contract more accurately reflects the reality of adoption today is highly persuasive yet it cannot sideline all elements of status. Older adopted children cherish the status of family membership, of belonging and of permanence. Conflict between their need for such status

---

[70] 'The Changing Face of Adoption – the gift/donation model versus the contract/services model' [1997] *Child and Family Law Quarterly* 371.

[71] *Ibid.* at p. 371.

[72] *Ibid.* at p. 383.

[73] Cretney, *Law, Law Reform and the Family* (1998, Clarendon Press) at p. 184.

and the more objective reality perceived by social scientists and lawyers must be reconciled. The Government's new proposal for 'special guardianship', for those children for whom adoption is not appropriate yet who still require permanence, is without detail but appears to be something like a beefed-up residence order – designed to provide permanence without severing the legal tie with the birth family.[74] As already observed, the policy objective in adoption today is to move children out of care and into permanent families, using the legal machinery of adoption but updating it to meet the new demands.

Balancing the interests of family members

The child's interests – welfare and race

More than any other area of family law, adoption requires a balancing of the interests of family members. Not only are there three parties, but, as already observed, the child's interests are not the paramount concern. This means that the child's welfare is not the sole or only consideration, outweighing all others.[75] Instead, the need to safeguard and promote the welfare of the child throughout his childhood, as set out in section 6, is the first consideration throughout all parts of the adoption process, including whether to make an adoption order.[76] This is supposedly a less all-encompassing test. Whilst the distinction between the child's welfare as the paramount concern as opposed to first consideration has variously been considered difficult to apply, the latter standard in the Adoption Act heightens the scope for giving weight to the competing interests of the other parties. In *Re C (Adoption: Legality)*[77] for example (where a woman who had previously been rejected as a prospective adopter brought a child into this country from Guatemala, in breach of provisions of the Adoption Act 1976,[78] and in defiance of the criminal law) section 6 enabled the court to consider other factors – such as lack of compliance with statutory procedures – alongside the child's welfare. However, the fact that the court recognised it had been presented with a *fait accompli*, yet proceeded, quite rightly, to make the adoption order is evidence that the child's welfare is certainly the *first* consideration in adoption law. Along with consideration of other factors which do not necessarily have a direct bearing on the child, welfare is placed first in the balancing act, whereas under section 1 of the Children Act 1989, the child's welfare is viewed without regard for the

---

[74] *Adoption – a new approach* (2000) paras. 5.9–5.10.
[75] Although note the later discussion of *Re A (Adoption: Mother's Objections)* [2000] 1 FLR 665 in this chapter.
[76] Adoption Act 1976, s. 6.
[77] [1999] 1 FLR 370.
[78] It is illegal to make and then pay for private arrangements to facilitate the adoption.

welfare of others. Article 21 of the United Nations Convention on the Rights of the Child requires that 'any system of adoption shall ensure that the best interests of the child shall be the paramount consideration',[79] the 1996 Government White Paper[80] provided that the agency and court must give paramount consideration to the child's welfare, and the 2000 White Paper has stated that the interests of the children involved in adoption will be paramount.[81] Under the Human Rights Act 1998 the rights of parents[82] can be interfered with if this is necessary in the interests of the child.[83] Article 8 (the right to respect for family life) is a key article of the European Convention with a primary objective of protecting individuals against arbitrary action by public authorities. The Convention, however, does not provide that the rights of children are paramount.[84] Rather, a fair balance has to be struck between the interests of the child and those of the parents with the welfare of the child becoming relevant when the court is considering whether interference can be justified as 'necessary'. In *Johansen* v. *Norway* the European Court held that 'in carrying out this balancing exercise, the court will attach particular importance to the best interests of the child, which depending upon their nature and seriousness may override those of the parent'.[85] Adoption here, where the child was in care, was considered to be inconsistent with the aim of rehabilitation unless there were exceptional circumstances. This should be contrasted with *Soderback* v. *Sweden*[86] where the European Court appears to regard a step-parent adoption as a less significant breach of Article 8 than adoption from care even though both have the effect of depriving the natural parent of family life with the child.[87]

Consistency with section 1 of the Children Act would seem to be sensible from a legislative as well as the child's point of view although, as

---

[79] This point is discussed in Barton and Douglas, *Law and Parenthood* (1995, Butterworth) at p. 81.

[80] *Adoption – a service for children* (1996, HMSO) which included a draft Adoption Bill.

[81] *Adoption – a new approach* (2000) para. 1.20. The focus of the White Paper is claimed to be 'firmly on the needs of the child' with new standards and new processes planned.

[82] Douglas, 'The Family and the State under the European Convention on Human Rights' [1988] *International Journal of Law and the Family* 76, comments that the convention was drawn up with the rights of adults rather than children in mind.

[83] For excellent discussions of the impact of the Human Rights Act 1998 on the welfare principle see Herring, 'The Human Rights Act and the Welfare Principle in Family Law – conflicting or complementary?' [1999] *Child and Family Law Quarterly* 223; Fortin, 'The HRA's Impact on Litigation Involving Children and their Families' [1999] *Child and Family Law Quarterly* 237; Fortin, *Children's Rights and the Developing Law* (1998, Butterworth).

[84] Swindells *et al*, *Family Law and the Human Rights Act 1998* (1999, Family Law) at p. 91.

[85] (1996) 23 EHRR 33.

[86] [1999] 1 FLR 250, ECHR.

[87] Note also *Scott* v. *UK* [2000] 1 FLR 958, ECHR, where the adoption of the child from care did not constitute a violation of Art. 8.

Herring suggests, implementation of the Human Rights Act may well force a re-conceptualisation of the welfare principle.[88] What is clear is that when the court is considering the alternative of a residence order in adoption proceedings, or is considering making a contact order concurrently with the adoption order, two different weightings are being given to the child's welfare. Reconciling the two and giving the child's welfare paramount consideration at every turn is a powerful argument and one not displaced by the Human Rights Act.

When determining what course of action will best promote the child's welfare, issues around the concept of 'matching' have played a vital role in adoption case law and practice. Particular tension has surrounded social work policy with respect to race and ethnicity.[89] Despite the fact that large numbers of white foster parents care for children of different racial origin, local authorities have traditionally taken the view that placing a child with prospective adopters of the same race is vital to the child's well-being – not doing so is simply storing up trouble.[90] These beliefs, described as 'virtually unchallenged orthodoxy,' have led some local authorities to place a black or mixed race child with white adopters only as a last resort.[91] Such policies are supported by the view that it is damaging for a child to be deprived of an upbringing within her own racial and cultural community.[92] It has been argued that 'black children and those of mixed parentage are over-represented amongst children in care' and that rigid policies on 'same race placements are leading to black children remaining in unplanned care'.[93] There is a severe shortage of foster carers from ethnic minority groups[94] so that, combined with 'same race policies', children can be left to languish in care, their need for psychological and emotional security being subordinated to a compatible racial background. However, the Government is clearly aware of these issues and in its 2000 White Paper stresses that 'no child should be denied loving adoptive parents solely on the grounds that the child and the parents do not share the same racial or cultural background'.[95]

---

[88] Herring *op. cit.* n. 83, at p. 235.

[89] Lowe and Murch *op. cit.*, n. 9 at p. 164 found these areas to be particularly contentious.

[90] Hayes and Williams, *Family Law: Principles, Policy and Practice* (1999, Butterworth) provides an excellent analysis of the background to these issues at pp. 291–295. The authors note that the concept of same race placements is regarded as 'self-evident' by local authorities yet research is equivocal.

[91] Hayes, 'The Ideological Attack on Transracial Adoption in the USA and Britain' (1995) 9 *International Journal of Law and the Family* 1.

[92] See *Re O (Transracial Adoption: Contact)* [1995] 2 FLR 597.

[93] J. Thoburn, *Inter-departmental Review of Adoption Law* (No. 2, 1990, HMSO) at p. 50.

[94] *The Organisation of Fostering Services: a study of the arrangements for delivery of fostering services in England* (1997, NFCA) at pp. 35–36 and 48.

[95] Para. 6.15.

The courts, too, have been embroiled in the contentious nature of the issues. Is an adoptive placement with parents of the same race as the child of such overriding significance to the child that it outweighs the bond of attachment that might have already developed between, for example, a child from an ethnic minority group and white foster parents?[96] The Court of Appeal in *Re A (A Minor) (Cultural Background)*[97] answered this question in the negative – but only after hearing powerful expert evidence that regardless of the length of time the West African child had been with white foster parents she must be placed back with a West African family. It has been suggested that such views are illustrative of the powerful hold which a particular ideological approach has over some local authority social workers[98] whereas the courts tend to be more balanced.[99] Nonetheless, in *Re M (Child's Upbringing)*[100] the Court of Appeal ordered the Zulu child's return to South Africa – with Neill LJ stating that he had 'the right to be reunited with his Zulu parents and with his extended family in South Africa'[101] – despite expert evidence that he would be deeply traumatised by leaving the foster mother to whom he had been attached since a baby. Hayes and Williams note that the outcome of the court's ruling proved disastrous and the child eventually returned to his foster mother in England.[102] In terms of reform those authors call for a checklist of factors along the lines of section 1(3) of the Children Act, in the hope that such a scheme would prevent intense focus on one consideration such as race, to the exclusion of other equally important factors. Consistent with the Children Act, the 1996 draft Adoption Bill contained such a list. The need for balance was also evident in the 1993 White Paper on adoption. There the Chief Social Services Inspector emphasised that ethnicity and culture should not be considered as more influential than any other issue.[103] This theme is not analysed in any detail in the 2000 White Paper but the implication is that while 'birth heritage' is important the child's welfare will become paramount and thus adoption by a non-racially compatible family may be justified on this account.[104] Finding the family best able to maximise the advantages of adoption for a child is, of course, a tough job. However, the long-term needs of children unable to be rehabilitated with

[96] This was the issue in *Re JK (Adoption: Transracial Placement)* [1991] 2 FLR 340 where the court decided to leave the Sikh child with her English foster parents (with whom she had been for three years) with a view to adoption.

[97] [1987] 2 FLR 429.

[98] Hayes and Williams *op. cit.* n. 90 at p. 293.

[99] See for example *Re N (A Minor) (Adoption)* [1990] 1 FLR 58 where Bush J described the emphasis on colour as 'dedication to dogma'.

[100] [1996] 2 FLR 441.

[101] *Ibid.* at p. 454.

[102] Hayes and Williams, *op. cit.* n. 90 at p. 295.

[103] *Adoption: The Future* Cm 2288, (1993, HMSO) at para. 4.32.

[104] *Adoption – a new approach* (2000) para. 6.15.

their birth families demand that agencies retain flexibility in the recruit-ment of adopters – in terms of race, culture, age, and marital status – so that the best possible chance of finding a suitable 'match' is met.

The paramountcy principle has greater implications for adoption than in other areas of child law. If consistency were introduced where would this leave the natural parent in the face of highly competent and mature adopters, for example? Would it be harder for the natural parent to oppose adoption? Alternatively, would children be placed for adoption more readily, thus minimising the emotional damage that delay can bring? The issues raised by adoption arguably sit less easily with paramountcy than do other matters of upbringing. The reasons for this are worth con-sidering.

Birth parents and agreement

Intense significance has always been attached to the right of parents to bring up their own child. The focus is very much on the actual rearing or upbringing of children. Barton and Douglas comment that 'people who accept the role of parenthood ... have a moral right to the child as an aspect of their freedom ... to take on a project of human development which society values and must therefore respect'.[105] (And of course, the same can be said for the 'project of human development' taken on by adoptive parents.) The rearing of and attachment to one's own children is accorded full legal recognition and protection. This is illustrated by the Children Act provisions which ensure that when a child is taken into care, or when the parents divorce, parental responsibility is ongoing, even when day-to-day care is undertaken by another. Proceedings under the Children Act effectively regulate the operation of parental responsibility and orders can be varied at any time, whereas adoption involves a final legal severance between the child and her birth parents and relatives.[106] Their rights are extinguished in a way that is unique to adoption. One consequence of this is the proliferation of social science research into the fate and feelings of birth parents after adoption. Findings confirm that parents do not forget the children to whom they gave birth and who were subsequently adopted.[107] Their feelings amount to a form of life-long bereavement, par-ticularly in the absence of some post-adoption contact. Ryburn describes this as being 'as severe in its effect as a bereavement by death, yet the sharp focus for grief that death affords is missing'.[108] The fact that adoption is clearly different from other forms of family proceedings is probably the

---

[105] *Law and Parenthood* (Butterworth, 1995) at p. 27.

[106] The contrast between the two types of proceedings was addressed in *Re B (Adoption: Child's Welfare)* [1995] 1 FLR 895.

[107] For a review of the relevant research see Ryburn, 'In Whose Best Interests?' [1998] *Child and Family Law Quarterly* 53, at p. 58.

[108] *Ibid.* at p. 59.

most potent argument yet that the interests of birth parents should remain part of the whole welfare equation – that the child's welfare should remain the 'first' as opposed to 'paramount' consideration.

Perhaps the most powerful weapon though in the natural parents' hands is the legal requirement that their agreement to the adoption be given – 'freely and with full understanding'.[109] Parental agreement is fundamental and without it neither an adoption nor freeing order[110] can be made, even if such an order would be in the child's interests. Any agreement given by a new mother within six weeks of the child's birth is ineffective[111] and even after it has been given, it may be withdrawn at any time before the adoption order is actually made. In these ways it is intended that the rights of birth parents be taken into account and protected as far as possible.[112] In contrast, agreement is not required for Children Act orders. However, while the rights of mothers are arguably protected by the agreement requirement, what about the father?

Only the father with parental responsibility – whether acquired through marriage to the mother, a parental responsibility agreement or order, or a residence order in his favour[113] – is regarded as a parent for the purposes of agreement to adoption. This means that the agreement of an unmarried father without parental responsibility is not required,[114] thus clearly indicating that the law places the nuclear, married family at the apex of the hierarchy of family forms. Nonetheless, the legal machinery in section 4 of the Children Act enables the situation to be remedied and a large body of jurisprudence has grown up around the issue of unmarried fathers seeking parental responsibility – very often to protect their own interests in the event of an adoption application, possibly by the mother and her new husband. The strength of feeling associated with losing the potential for a relationship with the child without even being able to register a protest is considerable. The fact that the courts are prepared to grant parental responsibility orders, sometimes referred to as 'rights in waiting,' to enable a father to give or withhold agreement to adoption or freeing is evidence of the importance placed on natural parenthood and its integral rights and the need to achieve a balance of interests between the parties. The rights of a natural father to be heard on an adoption

---

[109] Adoption Act 1976, s. 16(b)(i).

[110] Adoption Act 1976, s. 18(1).

[111] She must have time to get over the birth, Adoption Act 1976, ss. 16(4), 18(4).

[112] *Adoption – a new approach* (2000), para. 8.28 states that the consent form will be amended in 2001 'to better reflect the reality that birth parents have agreed to the adoption on the basis that it is in the best interests of the child'.

[113] Adoption Act 1976, s. 72(1).

[114] Although he is entitled to be heard on the merits of the application if he is contributing to the child's maintenance. See *Keegan* v. *Ireland* (1994) 18 EHRR 342 where the European Court made plain that a natural father has a right to be consulted before his child is placed for adoption where family life is in existence between the father and child.

application are a particular concern with the European Convention under-pinning a culture of greater involvement of natural families and knowledge of the natural father in adoption practice.[115] A series of recent cases[116] on the circumstances in which fathers without parental responsibility should be joined as respondents to adoption proceedings provides a clear indication of a climate change. In particular, Dame Elizabeth Butler-Sloss P has asserted that, as a matter of general practice, judges should inform natural fathers of adoption proceedings unless this is clearly inappropriate.[117]

Only after a court has decided that adoption will safeguard and promote the child's welfare might it go on to consider whether it should dispense with the parents' agreement (including that withheld by an unmarried father who acquired the right to participate via a parental responsibility order).[118] Viewed dispassionately, dispensing with a parent's consent to the adoption of a child, is a profound step and one, we should like to think, where the views of the parents have a central role and extreme circumstances – such as serious ill-treatment of the child, or the parent unable to be located or unable to give agreement[119] – have been found to exist. But it must be remembered that dispensing with agreement is the second stage in a two-stage process as the court will have already found that adoption will promote the child's interests. To follow this finding with a decision not to dispense with the agreement of a parent reluctant to sign would indicate that the child's welfare is simply on a par with other interests in the balancing process. But that is not the case, it is the 'first' consideration. Virtually all adoption applications, whether opposed or not eventually result in the order being granted.[120] The prolific case law, particularly on s. 16(2)(b) – that the parent or guardian 'is withholding his consent unreasonably' – provides further evidence of attempts to strike a balance between the welfare of the child and the rights of parents to maintain some relationship with him.[121] It also shows how even the most reluctant parents are loathe to 'sign' their children away.

---

[115]   See *B* v. *UK* [2000] 1 FLR 1; *K* v. *UK* [1986] 50 DR 199; *Keegan* v. *Ireland* [1994] 18 EHRR 342; *Kroon* v. *Netherlands* [1994] 19 EHRR 263.

[116]   In particular see *Re R (Adoption: Father's Involvement)* [2001] 1 FLR 302; *Re H; Re G (Adoption: Consultation of Unmarried Fathers)* [2001] 1 FLR 646; *Re B (Adoption by One Natural Parent to Exclusion of Other)* [2001] 1 FLR 589.

[117]   *Re H; Re G (Adoption: Consultation of Unmarried Fathers)* [2001] 1 FLR 646.

[118]   See *Re O (Adoption: Withholding Agreement)* [1999] 1 FLR 451, for example.

[119]   Adoption Act 1976, s. 16(2) sets out six grounds on which the court may dispense with agreement to adoption.

[120]   Lowe and Murch *Pathways to Adoption* (1991) p. 210. But note *Re R (A Minor) (Adoption: Dispensing with Agreement)* [1987] 2 FLR 89 CA, where it was held that the judge should not have dispensed with a mother's agreement since it was not unreasonable for her to hope to re-unite her family one day.

[121]   Article 8 of the European Convention contains a presumption of rehabilitation between parent and child but not where this would have the effect of harming the child.

The leading case on the meaning of withholding agreement unreasonably is the House of Lords decision in *Re W (An Infant)*.[122] The reasoning in this case has been extensively analysed in leading texts so it will suffice here to reiterate some of the relevant principles. Consistent with the theme of balancing the interests of family members *Re W* asserts that the child's welfare is not the only factor to be taken into account by the parent but that it is relevant to the issue of giving or withholding agreement to the extent that a reasonable parent would so regard it. The reasonable parent will put the child's welfare first. It must be remembered too that the test is one of the reasonableness of the parent's decision, whether or not that parent had been culpable in the first place, and that the court must not substitute its own view as to what is reasonable for that of the parent. In other words, a decision should only be held to be unreasonable if no reasonable parent could have taken it.[123] Three recent cases illustrate the tensions apparent in the 'unreasonably withholding' test and its implications for the balance of interests between all the parties.

First, in *Re A (Adoption: Mother's Objections)*[124] the one-year-old child was well settled and attached to highly suitable and mature prospective adopters who opposed the young mother's application for summary return of the child after changing her mind about adoption. The mother had initially avoided forming a bond with her new baby and, with the passage of time, the child's relationship with the adopters had strengthened even further. To remove him would risk lasting emotional and psychological damage. Whilst commenting that he always had difficulty in thinking of any *reasonable* mother *agreeing* that her child be adopted, Sumner J nonetheless held that the hypothetical reasonable mother in these circumstances would consent to adoption – she would want what was best for her baby. In this he followed *Re O (Adoption: Withholding Agreement)*[125] where, similarly, a small child was securely bonded with prospective adopters yet the impeccable natural parent (here an unmarried father, who had recently learned of the child's very existence, had been granted parental responsibility in order to participate in the adoption proceedings and had applied for a residence order) would not agree to adoption. In upholding the first instance decision that the father was withholding his agreement unreasonably, the Court of Appeal reiterated the question the court should pose – what would a reasonable parent have done in the circumstances, bearing in mind that such a parent will put the welfare of the child first? In both of these cases, particularly

---

[122] [1971] AC 682.
[123] Per Lord Hailsham in *Re W* at p. 700. For an excellent short analysis of the leading principles in *Re W* see S. Cretney *Family Law* (4th ed.) (2000, Sweet & Maxwell) at pp. 345–347.
[124] [2000] 1 FLR 665.
[125] [1999] 1 FLR 451.

Re O, the natural parent lacked any sort of culpability and was following a procedure which any reasonable person was likely to do in the circumstances – that is, seek the return of the child.

To conclude that parents such as those in *Re A* and *Re O* were unreasonable in not agreeing to adoption is almost absurd – they both wanted to care for and bring up their own child, had the ability to do so, and neither had been found wanting in this respect. Circumstances, particularly the passage of time, had effectively conspired against them. In what other situation would an impeccable natural parent, such as the father in *Re O*, be expected to place such a premium on the welfare of his own child that he would agree to adoption even though this was totally detrimental to his own interests? What is not absurd though, is the decision – as seen from the child's emotional and psychological perspective – to leave the child in a stable home with the only parents he has known and with whom he is securely bonded.[126] Few would dispute that the small child's welfare would, in each case, be promoted and safeguarded by remaining with the adopters, the psychological parents. With respect to the balancing of interests between natural parents and children placed with prospective adopters as babies the child's welfare is certainly the first and indeed, primary, consideration. When a contested adoption application arises by force of circumstance the natural parent has little chance when pitched against ideal approved adopters to whom the child is already attached and with whom his long-term stability looks assured.

In *Re R (Adoption: Protection from Offenders Regulations)*[127] the adopters were, theoretically, less than ideal but the child's needs were particularly great. Here, the natural parents of a Down's Syndrome baby who had given her up for adoption in infancy wanted her back four years later when the foster mother and her new husband (a man with two convictions for offences against children some twenty years previously, albeit he now had a favourable psychiatric prognosis) applied to adopt. Sir Stephen Brown P found that in light of the very strong emotional bond between the child and the foster carers (who had shown total commitment to the child), and remembering that the natural parents had effectively given the child up for adoption, it would be seriously deleterious to the child not to make the adoption order. The natural parents' agreement was thus being unreasonably withheld as they could not realistically expect the child to be removed from the only home she had known and returned to them as strangers. The longer the period of time the child has been settled with the prospective adopters the less reasonable will be the natural parents' refusal of agreement to adoption.

---

[126] See the discussion in Wall (ed.) *Rooted Sorrows – psychoanalytic perspectives on child protection, assessment, therapy and treatment* (1997, Family Law) at p. 9.
[127] [1999] 1 FLR 472.

From the welfare perspective in each of the above cases the only attribute the natural parent has over and above those of the adopters is the biological one. However this is of less weight in relation to a child placed with foster parents as a baby than it is in relation to the older child. The infant forms fundamental attachments with its first carers whereas the older child retains memories of and attachment to the natural parent when he is later placed for adoption. Nonetheless, the agreement of natural parents of older children is sometimes dispensed with. In *Re B (Adoption: Father's Objections)*,[128] for example, the Court of Appeal took the highly unusual step of dispensing with the natural father's agreement to the 12-year-old boy's adoption by the mother and step-father. In the balance of interests here the scales fell firmly on the side of the child's welfare. His need for a lifelong and final order settling his future with his mother and her new husband following abduction and 140 court applications by the natural father outweighed the interests of that father in maintaining links with his child. This was a child who knew his father – and therefore knew his roots and lineage – but who had rejected him. This case illustrates the extent to which it is accepted that the court's assessment of the child's welfare is determinative, even when that means severing family links for all time.

Adoptive parents and freeing

Less emphasis has traditionally been placed on the interests of adopters than on the interests of the other two parties to the adoption triangle. The recent Lowe and Murch research[129] has attempted to remedy that by teasing out the motivation, characteristics and needs of adopters of older children in the hope of assisting future policy and practice. They produced some striking findings. Firstly, but not unsurprisingly, they discovered that people's motivation to adopt is complex and not necessarily prompted by infertility. Rather, 46 per cent of their research sample in-volved adopters who already had children of their own and were therefore experienced parents and 34 per cent were already foster carers, seeking to adopt the children they knew and cared for. As the authors themselves comment, this reality, coupled with the numbers of step-parent adoptions, flies in the face of the assumption that adoption of children is, by and large, by childless strangers. However, many who decide to adopt an older child do so only after finding they are not able to adopt a baby. Whatever the real motivation in taking on a potentially disturbed child in a permanent and lifelong way, the whole process is clearly a challenge for adoptive parents as well as for the child.

---

[128] [1999] 2 FLR 215. See *Re EH and MH (Step-parent Adoption)* [1993] Fam Law 187 and *Re PJ (Adoption: Practice on Appeal)* [1998] 2 FLR 252 for other unusual cases of the court dispensing with the natural father's agreement to a step-parent adoption.

Given that adopters are submitted to a tortuous selection process coupled with lengthy professional assessment, anxiety, the stress of uncertainty and of the unknown, and finally the often alarming demands of a child 'whose capacity to trust adults may have been weakened by a history of unreliable or broken attachments',[130] where do they come in the balancing of interests? Are they simply recipients of the 'gift' in the Nigel Lowe model? Perhaps the only attempt by the law to ease the process for them has been the freeing order. The procedure for freeing a child for adoption was introduced by the Children Act 1975 and enabled a parent, in proceedings started by an agency, to agree generally and unconditionally to the making of an adoption order. It was intended to both counter the right of birth parents to withdraw an agreement once given and avoid some of the tension and anxiety surrounding court proceedings if the agency anticipated parental refusal yet believed that the child's welfare demanded adoption. Fear of a traumatic contest with the birth parents had resulted in agencies being reluctant to place some children for adoption. The overall objective of freeing was thus to ease the adoption process, eliminate some of the worst aspects of uncertainty for the adopters and provide greater security for children with respect to placements.

Freeing has not been successful and its abolition was proposed by the review of adoption law in 1991.[131] Its major failing stems from the requirement that the birth parents either give agreement or have their agreement dispensed with in the abstract – that is, without reference to specific adopters. When the child has not even been placed it is thus very difficult for a court to conclude that a birth parent is withholding agreement unreasonably.[132] Alternatively, the birth parents may be presented as comparing unfavourably with ideal but hypothetical adopters and their agreement dispensed with even more readily. Other legal difficulties surround the consequences of transfer of parental responsibility from the birth parent to the agency; the child may be left in a kind of legal limbo, the whole procedure can exacerbate delay, and the relationship between freeing and post-adoption contact difficult to reconcile.

It can be argued, however, that the major impact of freeing has been to effectively erode the need for parental agreement where children are in care, contact has not taken place, and adoption is perceived to be in their best interests.[133] As Steyn and Hoffman LJJ put it, the court might properly

---

[129] *Supporting Adoption – The Summary* (1999, BAFF), *op. cit.* at p. 9.

[130] Lowe and Murch *Supporting Adoption – Reframing the Approach* at p. 7.

[131] *Adoption Law Review Paper No 2* (1991), para. 180.

[132] In *Re E (Minors) (Adoption: Parental Agreement)* [1990] 2 FLR 397, the Court of Appeal found that the birth mother was not withholding agreement unreasonably even though the long term future of the children was likely to be served by adoption.

[133] *Re C (A Minor) (Adoption: Parental Agreement: Contact)* [1993] 2 FLR 260, Balcombe LJ at p. 270 considered that insufficient weight had been given to the parents' interests.

ask whether, having regard to the evidence and the current values of our society, the advantages of adoption for the welfare of the child appear sufficiently strong to justify overriding the views and interests of the objecting parent.[134] In the hierarchy of interests birth parents have arguably been relegated to third place while the child most definitely comes out on top.[135]

The natural parent presumption

A general philosophy underlying the Children Act 1989 is to assert the rights and responsibilities of natural parents and thus uphold the autonomy of the family in matters concerning the rearing of children. The values this reflects were articulated in *Re K (D) (A Minor) (Ward: Termination of Access)*[136] where Lord Templeman stated,

> The best person to bring up a child is the natural parent. It matters not whether the parent is wise or foolish, rich or poor, educated or illiterate, provided the child's moral and physical health are not endangered. Public authorities cannot improve on nature.

In the same case, his Lordship confirmed that there was no inconsistency between this principle of English law and Article 8 of the European Convention entitling everyone to the right to respect for private and family life, with interference from a public authority only for 'the protection of health or morals, or for the protection of the rights and freedoms or others'. In an article outlining the development of a legal presumption in favour of the natural parent, Jane Fortin[137] described Lord Templeman's statement as a 'stirring reminder of the 'naturalness' of the child–parent relationship', suggesting that it was part of the wave of jurisprudence that gave the biological link between parent and child increasingly greater significance during the 1980s and 1990s. The jurisprudence was also prompted, Fortin suggests, by two other factors: anxiety that comparisons between the homes of relatively well-off foster carers and disadvantaged birth parents would invariably favour the former and lead to decisions which might be criticised as amounting to

---

[134] *Ibid.* at p. 272. In *Re F (Children) (Adoption: Freeing Order)* [2000] 3 FCR 337, the Court of Appeal reaffirmed that the judge must ask whether, applying the current values of our society, the advantages of adoption for the welfare of the child appeared sufficiently strong to justify overriding the views and interests of the objecting parent.

[135] It should be noted that the 2000 White Paper does not address the issue of freeing for adoption at all, and so it can be assumed that there will be little change here apart from proposed amendments to the consent form (para. 8.28).

[136] [1988] AC 806, at p. 812.

[137] 'Re D (Care: Natural Parent Presumption) Is Blood Really Thicker Than Water?' [1999] *Child and Family Law Quarterly* 435, at p. 437.

'social engineering'; and secondly, that the emergence of children's rights embraced the notion that children had a 'right' to be brought up by their birth parents. Fortin's conclusion is that the blood tie began to assume such significance in the courts that evidence favouring a child remaining with foster carers, for example, became devalued in comparison with a return to the birth parents. In 1990, Butler-Sloss LJ went so far[138] as to suggest that the appropriate question to ask when foster carers were pitched against birth parents was, is the natural family so unsuitable that the child's welfare positively demands the displacement of their parental responsibility? This was in preference to the question of whether the child would have a better home with the foster parents. If the latter question were asked, said her Ladyship, the court faced the grave danger of slipping into social engineering. The trend was to avoid depriving a child of the chance to be brought up in her own family and included the notion that parents should not lose the opportunity to exercise their parental responsibility. The Children Act principles could thus be given effect. But where does this leave the natural parent in the classic adoption dilemma – those cases where highly eligible adopters are compared with the much less suitable natural parent?

In *Re O (A Minor) (Custody: Adoption)*[139] the Court of Appeal again asserted the primary position of the natural parent in caring for the child. Here, the natural father sought custody of the child who had been placed with an adoption society at birth by the mother and had subsequently blossomed with short-term foster carers. Butler-Sloss LJ said the best person to bring up the child was the natural parent whether or not he had parental responsibility. For her Ladyship, the question again was, is the sole remaining parent a fit and suitable parent to care for the child? Only where he was unfit should the alternative of adoption be considered. A further strand in the balancing of interests between the parties can be observed in this assertion of the dominance of the natural parent's claim – the natural parent's right to care for the child is construed as the child's right. There is no straightforward comparison between competing sets of carers, but rather, the superiority of 'naturalness' is endorsed and thus favours the birth parent. *Re M (Child's Upbringing)*[140] is a classic example. In that case, a 10-year-old Zulu boy had come to England with the family (his foster family) for whom his mother had worked in South Africa. He had lived with them since he was 18 months old while his mother lived in separate quarters in their household. Once in England, the foster mother applied to adopt him. After lengthy proceedings the Court of Appeal ordered that the boy be returned to South Africa to his parents, with Ward

---

[138] In *Re K (A Minor) (Wardship: Adoption)* [1991] 1 FLR 57, for example.
[139] [1992] 1 FLR 77.
[140] [1996] 2 FLR 441.

LJ stating that, other things being equal, it was in the child's interests to be brought up by his natural parents. This presumption was, his Lordship said, subservient to the child's welfare being the court's paramount consideration (what had started out as an adoption application had become a residence issue and so the paramountcy principle was applicable). Comparison with the famous House of Lords decision in *J* v. *C*[141] is inevitable. There, of course, the 10-year-old boy was similarly living in England in a different cultural environment from his own with the consent of the natural parents, although he had been separated from his parents longer than the South African boy. The House of Lords upheld the decision that the boy should stay in England with his foster parents – on the basis that his welfare was the paramount consideration. Analysis of the two cases highlights the tensions inherent in consideration of the competing claims (including those of race and culture) of natural parents and prospective adopters. The variable responses of the courts show how the values of the time as well as values of individual judges impact upon precedent and established principle.

Fortin's analysis of the natural parent presumption also points to its possible diminution, if not demise. In her view the concept of the *psychological parent* with its focus on the child's psychological attachments as opposed to its biological links[142] may well underlie a notable change in judicial attitudes that 'is greatly to be welcomed'.[143] *Re P (Section 91(4) Guidelines) (Residence and Religious Heritage)*,[144] where Jewish birth parents sought the return of their Down's Syndrome child who had been placed with Roman Catholic foster parents as a small child, is highly relevant here. At first instance the critical issues were, first, the child's capacity to understand and appreciate her Jewish heritage and secondly, the degree of attachment she had to the foster parents and subsequent risk of harm if she were removed. The foster parents were granted a residence order in spite of the parents' opposition and the Court of Appeal concluded that there was no presumptive right (on the parents' variation application) that natural parents should be preferred to foster parents. Even contact with the natural parents, which was considered de-stabilising for the child given that her permanent home was elsewhere, was reduced and a restriction order under s 91(14) made in order to assure the child's stability with the adopters for the remainder of her minority.[145] The Court of

---

[141] [1970] AC 668.

[142] In *Re K (Adoption and Wardship)* [1997] 2 FLR 230, for example.

[143] Fortin, *op. cit.* n. 83 at p. 441.

[144] [1999] 2 FLR 573.

[145] A s. 91(14) restriction order was also made by the Court of Appeal in *Re B (Adoption by One Natural Parent to Exclusion of Other)* [2001] 1 FLR 589 to prohibit the mother from interfering with the child's stability and security under a residence order in favour of her father.

Appeal's focus was very much on psychological attachment and the harm its interruption could cause rather than the supposed advantages to the child in being brought up by her natural parents. It must be questioned whether this means that the importance of psychological attachment has simply been elevated in the judicial mind or whether the benefits of rearing within the natural family have been found wanting. The answer hinges primarily on whether the breaking of a psychological attachment with prospective adopters is the crucial factor from the child welfare point of view. While natural parents have rights under the European Convention those rights cannot be given effect if they would harm the child's health or development.[146]

In *Re A (Adoption: Mother's Objections)*[147] Sumner J was faced with a classic dilemma – would the harm that would flow from breaking the one-year-old's attachment to highly suitable prospective adopters be out-weighed by the benefits he would derive from being brought up with his natural family? Here the student mother had placed her baby for adoption at birth, although she later changed her mind, and the baby became well settled with the prospective adopters. The natural grandmother, a powerful and influential woman, was persuasive in the young mother seeking the return of her child. Sumner J opted for the psychological attachment argument in preference to the blood tie. If the child were removed from the prospective adopters, he said, there was a real risk of disturbance and lasting psychological damage and this overrode the significant right he had to be brought up by his natural mother.

Analysis of *Re A* leaves one with the overwhelming impression that the child's welfare is not just the first, but is possibly the paramount, consideration. Consistency with the tenor of reasoning in Children Act proceedings is apparent. Counsel for the child in *Re A* invited use of the welfare checklist in s 1(3) of the Children Act and, in responding that he 'had independently done so', Sumner J stated that it had reinforced the conclusions he had already reached. His Lordship even used the language of best interests, commenting that the harm that might befall the child were he to be moved 'must, in his best interests, override those other rights of his and those other rights of his mother'.[148] Welfare is thus seen as resting with psychological attachment rather than blood tie albeit the latter is still important. Here the loss occasioned by rebuttal of the natural parent presumption was mitigated by a range of factors including the 'open and honest approach' of the adopters who had met the mother, had a great deal of information about her and who would seek expert help and counselling

---

[146] See for example the point made in *Olson* v. *Sweden (No 2) (Reunion with Children in Care)* (1992) 17 EHRR 134.

[147] [2000] 1 FLR 665.

[148] *Ibid.* at p. 694D.

if difficulties arose. The calibre of adoptive or foster parents and their value in relation to the child's future security was thus seen as countering the loss of the less than perfect natural parent.

Adoption and contact

Perhaps the most tangible way of mitigating any sense of loss the child might have with respect to the natural parent is by post-adoption contact. Judith Masson describes contact as the 'practical demonstration of a continuing relationship'. It carries a sense of continuity and the enduring nature of relationships with it and is a conditional 'right' of a natural parent under the provisions of Article 8 of the European Convention. Whether contact is direct and face to face or indirect by way of the mailbox or an annual report and photograph, post-adoption contact (sometimes described as open adoption) is seen as potentially important for the child's sense of identity and knowledge of family background. It is strongly agreed that even though children, particularly older children adopted from care, will benefit from a permanent and stable home with approved adopters the maintenance of links with the birth family will assist the development of personal identity and sense of family continuity. This link is perceived as important to the long-term welfare of adopted children in that they will know their parents still love them, that they need not be anxious about the well-being of their birth family, and that they have their parents' 'seal of approval' to become emotionally attached to the adopters.[149]

The benefits of maintaining links for reasons of racial identity are also significant. These were explored in *Re O (Transracial Adoption: Contact)*[150] where contact between a Nigerian mother and her child after adoption was intended to give the child 'immediate exposure to Nigerianness' which wasn't otherwise available with the adoptive parents. Contact in this case was also ordered as a means of countering the fantasies the child harboured about her mother. According to Ryburn, one of the key advantages of any contact is that facts are able to replace speculation and fantasy about the birth family.[151]

All of these reasons for maintaining contact with the birth parents or some member of the birth family after adoption are advanced as a justification for the practice from the child's welfare perspective. If the court makes an order for contact under s. 8 of the Children Act the welfare

---

[149] Lowe and Murch *et al, op. cit.* n. 9 chapter 15 generally, and particularly p. 324. See also *Re E (A Minor) (Care Order: Contact)* [1994] 1 FLR 146, per Simon Brown LJ at pp.154–155.

[150] [1995] 2 FLR 597 where Thorpe J made a contact order although left the timing of its implementation to the local authority.

[151] 'In Whose Best Interests? – post adoption contact with the birth family' [1998] *Child and Family Law Quarterly* 53, at p. 60.

of the child is clearly the paramount consideration, but even where, as is most likely, contact is agreed between the birth family and adopters, it is the child's interests that are put forward as the determining factor. However, as Lowe and Murch found, contact between older children and their birth families was not only the most contentious practice issue their study explored but it sometimes led to confusion with respect to just whose interests were being addressed. The authors concluded that the child's needs must always be the priority when contact is being planned but in practice they are sometimes confused with the needs of the birth parents.[152]

Ryburn addresses the tension between the various interests being met by post-adoption contact in an article which reviewed much of the relevant research.[153] It is interesting now to revisit this article in light of the more recent Lowe and Murch research on older adopted children. Ryburn is an advocate of post-adoption contact and concludes that the messages from research, at least as at 1997, were sufficiently clear to support a general presumption in its favour. He discusses the advantages contact can bring to all three parties – ranging from the sense of reassurance the child gains from direct contact with birth parents (it sends a clear message that the placement is supported by the original family and in return shows the child that the adopters feel positively about that family) to the consequent strengthening of his or her attachment to the adopters. In a major 1991 survey of adoption and permanent foster care placements cited by Ryburn,[154] birth family contact was identified as the single factor able to enhance the stability of placements: direct contact gave adopters a sense of security and permanence in the parenting role, and contact generally made a significant difference to birth parents. Even indirect contact met these needs although, citing a significant finding from all the studies, Ryburn concludes that birth parents are nonetheless concerned that contact should not be a source of distress or disruption in the child's life.[155]

In the Lowe and Murch 1999 study, 77 per cent of the families questioned had some form of ongoing contact with the birth family. Contact was generally 'seen as helping children settle in their new family' but the overwhelming finding was that there were disagreements between agencies and adopters about the principles underlying contact, the appropriateness of the type and degree of contact and the timing and management of it.[156] It is clear that the tensions apparent in legal doctrine (the value of the presumption in favour of natural parents, for example)

---

[152] Lowe and Murch, *op. cit.* n. 9 at p. 326.

[153] *Op. cit.* at n. 134.

[154] Rowe and Thoburn, in Fratter *et al*, *Permanent Family Placement: A Decade of Experience* (BAAF, 1991), chapters 1–3.

[155] Ryburn *op. cit.* at n. 151 at p. 59.

[156] Lowe and Murch *op. cit.* n. 9 at p. 278.

are mirrored in social work practice. While the authors discovered benefits in contact for older children they also uncovered disadvantages. For example, while contact enabled birth families to feel more positive about adoption, it could also undermine the placement by providing a vehicle for communicating disapproval of the adoption. Similarly, while contact may enhance the adopters' relationship with the child and their feelings of security as parents, it might, alternatively, hinder the child's attachment to the adoptive family (a break with the past being necessary before beginning to identify with the adoptive family).[157] And while contact is said to help lessen the anxiety children feel about their birth parents, it can also make matters worse by confronting them with the reality of birth parents' illnesses and possible inadequacies. Some adopters (and agencies) believe that children have a right to a childhood free from that worry.[158] However, it is apparent that agencies in general have developed the professional view that direct contact should be agreed unless there is actual evidence to the contrary.

Quite what that evidence is, and whether contact is likely to be pursued despite its existence, was one of the tensions uncovered by Lowe and Murch. The evidence purportedly required before pursuing direct contact was, first, that the birth parents were fully in support of the adoption plan and, secondly, that they were of sufficient maturity to accept a different role in the child's life.[159] The difficulty is that the presence of these criteria effectively amounts to a very good reason why there should not be an adoption placement at all. If the birth parents are so understanding and the child's need for direct contact with them so great, long-term fostering may well be better than the total and irrevocable severance of adoption. Given Lowe and Murch's findings which suggest that contact is arranged for birth families who often do not meet these criteria, why is adoption with direct contact given such importance by social workers? The answer supplied by the study is that adoption probably is the right form of care for the particular child but contact, which in legal terms ought to be determined on the basis of the child's best interests, is being pursued in the interests of birth parents.

At first glance, these findings appear to highlight a further area of philosophical tension – that the value of contact with birth parents, in the interests of the child's sense of identity and knowledge of family origins,

---

[157] *Ibid.* at p. 281 where the authors also state that there is a fine line between birth parents showing they care for the child and usurping the parental status of adopters through contact.

[158] In one case in the research study, a child reacted very badly to seeing his father in prison. He was unwilling to continue visiting, but the social worker insisted. Ultimately, the adoptive mother had 'to fight social services to get the contact visits stopped'. The authors concluded here that while a one-off visit was constructive, ongoing face-to-face contact was extremely distressing.

[159] Lowe and Murch *op. cit.*, n. 9 at p. 297.

runs counter to the move away from the overriding importance of the blood tie as discussed earlier. In other words while the presumption that the child's best interests will be served by being brought up by the natural parent has possibly diminished, this trend is less obvious when it comes to contact. But when the reasons for direct post-adoption contact are examined more deeply it can be seen that birth parents' rather than child's interests are, arguably, being privileged. As Lowe and Murch make clear, social workers will often go to some lengths to get a 'good deal' for the birth parents regarding contact and adopters apparently view contact as a means of alleviating the birth parents' loss. In some cases within the research sample, contact was likely to be detrimental to the child yet an agreement was still sought by social workers whose sympathies rested with the birth parents. Lowe and Murch reach the overall conclusion that inflexible rules based in doctrinaire policies must be avoided and that contact is not always beneficial. The authors were clear in not committing themselves to the view that some form of contact between the child and birth family was always in the child's interests. Rather, the issue had to be governed by the welfare of the particular child plus that child's own wishes and feelings – both of which may change from time to time. The Lowe and Murch findings confirm the conclusions of Quinton *et al*[160] that it is not yet possible to make confident assertions about the benefits of contact regardless of family circumstances and relationships. Nonetheless, in its 2000 White Paper, the Government refers to its draft 'National Standards' as insisting that a child's need to maintain contact with the birth family 'should always be considered'.[161]

Post-adoption contact is very much a creature of social work practice and is a key element of professional activity in adoption work. However the process of negotiating a contact agreement can raise certain tensions between agencies and prospective adopters at the outset. Section 34 of the Children Act contains a presumption that natural parents will have contact with their children in care and so local authorities are required to plan for such contact.[162] At the same time, some adopters feel pressured to agree to contact claiming that it is used as a bargaining tool to get birth parents to agree to adoption. It is suggested that in practice contact is used to 'facilitate adoption', making birth parents accept what would otherwise be 'unacceptable in order to achieve the best possible outcome for the child'. Where agreement has not been successfully negotiated, or one of the parties cannot be trusted to keep it, the Children Act machinery enables the court to make an order for direct or indirect contact

---

[160] Quinton *et al*, 'Contact with Birth Parents in Adoption – a response to Ryburn' [1998] *Child and Family Law Quarterly* 349 at p. 350.

[161] *Adoption – the new approach* (2000) para. 6.43.

[162] This is consistent with Article 8 of the European Convention.

concurrently with an adoption or freeing order,[163] and enables a 'former' parent to apply for leave to apply for contact after adoption.[164] Prior to the Children Act the House of Lords held that there was power to impose conditions on an adoption order under s. 12 (6) of the Adoption Act 1976.[165] Through the little case law that has emerged[166] the primary message is that adopters must be agreeable to contact and should not be ordered to do what they do not wish to do.[167] The child's interests require that the adopters remain in control and that a situation of friction with the birth parents be avoided. Judicial reasoning highlights the philosophical tensions inherent in the notion of contact coexisting with the current secret legal transplant concept of adoption. The culture of permanence, stability and security created by adoption is arguably threatened when contact is legally imposed rather than agreed.[168] Equally, if contact is so desirable for the child that a contact order is required (and a s. 8 order can only be made in the child's best interests) the circumstances that also require an adoption order for such a child are bound to be exceptional.

Rather than interpret the judicial reluctance to order contact as simply a failure to keep up with current practice,[169] Masson views it as evidence that law is not needed in dealing with the human and social factors inherent in post-adoption contact.[170] In her view, an absence of regulation and the viewing of contact as a social problem best managed by social workers rather than as a legal problem to be handled by the courts, has created a climate in which all parties benefit and is an approach that should be more widely adopted in handling contact with children in care. However, while Masson argues that adoption agencies are better placed than courts to facilitate and manage post-adoption contact, Ryburn argues the reverse, urging that courts should 'ensure that more rigorous investigations are routinely made', that there be 'a more exacting examination by the courts' (of care plans which include adoption), and that although efforts should be made to achieve negotiated solutions 'there is still a great deal more that the courts could do to secure the welfare of children through sensible, negotiated, post-adoption contact arrangements'.[171]

---

[163] A natural parent can apply for a s. 8 contact order as of right.

[164] Children Act 1989, s. 10(9).

[165] See *Re C (A Minor) (Adoption Order: Conditions)* [1989] AC 1.

[166] Note the analysis and cases cited by Lindley in 'Open Adoption – Is the Door Ajar?' [1997] *Child and Family Law Quarterly* 115 at pp. 126–127.

[167] This view was expressed by the House of Lords in *Re C* (above) and following the Children Act, in *Re T (Adoption: Contact)* [1995] 2 FLR 792.

[168] And s. 1(5) of the Children Act requires that an order be better for the child than no order.

[169] A view expressed in Lindley (1997) *op. cit.* n. 166.

[170] Masson, 'Thinking About Contact – a social or a legal problem?' [2000] *Child and Family Law Quarterly* 15 at p. 28.

[171] Ryburn, 'In Whose Best Interests? Post-adoption contact with the birth family' [1998] *Child and Family Law Quarterly* 53 at pp. 67–70.

Whereas Masson argues for maintaining a reduction in regulation and court involvement, Ryburn urges that the 'robust stand' taken by the courts in private law contact be applied to contact after adoption.

These opinions from two leading scholars are more than simply contrary views on how post-adoption contact should be handled. They illustrate a fundamental dilemma in family and child law generally – can and should the law attempt to offer answers to problems which are primarily human and social rather than legal? Are not administrative systems better than the process of law at promoting individual interests? Perhaps a logical extension of the Lowe and Murch findings in relation to contact lies with the Masson approach but tempered by the development of less doctrinaire, more objective and workable guidelines for social workers. These might include the conditions which Lowe and Murch's research discovered to be most likely to lead to beneficial arrangements, notwithstanding the authors' view that contact will not always be in the child's interest.

Towards the future: reform of adoption law

Although reform of adoption law has been on the political agenda for some years now, no legislation has been introduced. The 1996 draft Bill lapsed but the Waterhouse Report *Lost in Care* inspired a rethink of adoption and the Prime Minister has put his weight behind the drive for reform. Now, despite the political difficulties inherent in any family law reform,[172] a Cabinet Office Review of Adoption was hastily produced,[173] a White Paper – *Adoption – the new approach* – was published in December 2000 and new legislation designed to 'overhaul and modernise the legal framework for adoption'[174] is planned for 2001.[175] What is needed is a conceptual overhaul of policy and practice bringing adoption law in line with modern thinking on child law.

The Prime Minister is in favour of adoption. He says 'it works', that it is 'hard to overstate the importance of a stable and loving family life for children', that the Government needs to ensure that 'children's needs come first', and that 'we need to better meet the aspirations of the many prospective parents who want to adopt'.[176] 'Adoption', he says, 'can work well … but we have to have a new approach'.[177] These statements are bald

---

172 Cretney *Family Law* (2000, Sweet & Maxwell) at p. 357.
173 Policy and Innovation Unit Report, July 2000.
174 *Adoption – a new approach* (2000) para. 9.1.
175 For an analysis of this report see Barton, 'Adoption – The Prime Minister's Review' [2000] *Family Law* 731.
176 Foreword to The Prime Minister's Review of Adoption.
177 Foreword to the White Paper (2000) by the Prime Minister.

in their simplicity but the promises contained within them are complex and not necessarily compatible. Before any legislation can be sensibly drawn up the issues and tensions inherent in adoption law and practice must be resolved. As promised in the 2000 White Paper, adoption must become firmly child- rather than adult-centred with, arguably, the child's welfare the paramount concern in both agency and court decisions. This would rid adoption of one of its major inconsistencies with other areas of child law, recognise its changing nature and purpose and help local authorities formulate their strategies for the future.

The current issues surrounding transracial adoption and the value of contact[178] are amongst the most pressing concerns, with both areas requiring policies based on sound research and common sense rather than ideology and pragmatism. And if the needs of the child are to become the paramount concern do not the needs of adopters also require greater consideration? Meeting their needs in whatever way it takes to assist them in becoming better parents must be in the child's best interests. Consistent with this would be the placing of greater weight on the psychological and emotional rather than biological welfare of the child. This would go some way towards reconciling the tension between the presumption in favour of being brought up by the natural parent and the need for the child to be permanently placed before even more damage occurs. The American experience is instructive here with the Adoption and Safe Families Act 1997 aiming to move 'abused and neglected kids into adoption or other permanent homes and to do it quickly and more safely than ever before'.[179] A greater readiness to place damaged children away from birth parents[180] may flow from giving the child's welfare paramount consideration but it nonetheless places birth parents in a more disadvantageous position. This may be the price to pay. Whilst their rights must be given the 'respect' the Prime Minister's Review intends, and they will be protected by the Human Rights Act, the right of the unmarried father to be heard on the adoption application needs further consideration. And if the child's welfare is to become paramount, more adoption will take place and more permanent homes will need to become available. This means removing many of the ideologically based constraints on the selection of adopters. To achieve the Prime Minister's ideal of a 'stable and loving family life' for many of the children now in care the concept of the 'family' needs to be broadened. Acknowledgement of the diversity of family forms – to which legal recognition is already being extended – demands a rethink. Enabling unmarried couples to adopt a child jointly,

---

[178] In her 2000 address to the SFLA, Dame Elizabeth Butler-Sloss, President of the Family Division, called for more research on post-adoption contact.

[179] In Bainham (ed.) *International Survey of Family Law* (2000, Family Law) at p. 380.

[180] Dame Elizabeth Butler-Sloss P, *op. cit.* n. 178 claimed that reform of adoption law – and especially of delays – was well overdue.

and to more readily consider gay couples and single people as suitable adopters is not only in line with current policy in family law but would enable more children to be rescued from care. Children are the priority.

Further reading

Adoption – a service for children (1996, HMSO).

Cretney, 'Adoption – from Contract to Status?' in Cretney, *Law, Law Reform and the Family* (1988, Clarendon).

Department of Health, *Adoption – a new approach* (29 December 2000, Department of Health).

Hayes, 'The Ideological Attack on Transracial Adoption in the USA and Britain' (1995) 9 *International Journal of Law and the Family* 1.

Lindley, 'Open Adoption – Is the Door Ajar?' [1997] *Child and Family Law Quarterly* 115.

Lowe and Murch *et al*, *Supporting Adoption – reframing the approach* (BAFF) (1999, DOH).

Lowe, 'The Changing Face of Adoption – the gift/donation model versus the contract/services model' [1997] *Child and Family Law Quarterly* 371.

Lowe, 'English Adoption Law: Past, Present and Future' in Katz, Eekelaar and Maclean (eds), *Cross Currents* (2000, OUP).

Murphy, 'Child Welfare in Transracial Adoptions: Colour-blind Children and Colour-blind Law' in Murphy (ed.), *Ethnic Minorities, their Families and the Law* (2000, Hart).

Quinton *et al*, 'Contact with Birth Parents in Adoption – a response to Ryburn' [1998] *Child and Family Law Quarterly* 349.

Ryburn, 'In Whose Best Interests? Post-adoption contact with the birth family' [1998] *Child and Family Law Quarterly* 53.

Thomas and Beckford, *Adopted Children Speaking* (1999, BAFF).

Index